NAVIGATING THE ZEITGEIST

NAVIGATING
the ZEITGEIST

A Story of the Cold War, the New Left,
Irish Republicanism, and International Communism

by HELENA SHEEHAN

MONTHLY REVIEW PRESS
New York

Library of Congress Cataloging-in-Publication Data
available from the publisher

ISBN (pbk): 978-1-58367-727-8
ISBN (cloth): 978-1-58367-728-5

Typeset in Minion Pro

MONTHLY REVIEW PRESS, NEW YORK
monthlyreview.org

5 4 3 2 1

Contents

DEDICATION

*To all who walked along the way with me and did their best
to come to terms with the times*

ACKNOWLEDGMENTS

I thank all those who contributed to the life I have led and encouraged me to write my way through it. I thank Monthly Review Press for thinking this book was worth publishing and working with me in a collegial and comradely way to bring it to fruition. I thank Sam Nolan for enduring everyday life with me and my obsessive ways.

Introduction

> Sometimes I feel as if I have lived through eons in a matter of decades. The waves of historical change, such as swept over centuries in the past, seem to have swept through my world several times over already. And who knows what I have yet to see? I am perhaps only halfway through the time I may expect my life to be.

I wrote these words in 1988, when I was forty-four. The waves kept coming, and no less convulsively or consequentially. I set out here to write the story of these decades as they flowed through me, as I navigated the tides of history, whether on sunny days or in raging storms. I am striving for something more than memoir—for a work of intellectual, social, and political history within the narrative frame of autobiography. I recognize the hazards of first-person writing. I have read many memoirs and autobiographies and found many lacking in critical self-reflection, proportion, sociohistorical consciousness. Few represent the relation between self and world satisfactorily. I believe that a person is neither a mere stimulus-response mechanism nor a mystical inner essence. I see a person as inherently relational, a nodal point in a field of forces, forged in a dialectic between self and world.

My story is also the story of others, not only those I knew directly, but also those whose stories came flowing into mine. Consciously or not, a person is formed within a torrent of processes and events. I decided from a young age to do so consciously, to bring the widest range of forces to the sharpest focus I could. I set out to navigate the zeitgeist, whether to go with the prevailing winds or to set a course against them. In writing my way through this, I have sought a form of writing that is experiential without being egotistical, expressing the epochal in the immediate, bringing into focus the characteristic conflicts and choices of the age amid concrete circumstances.

I have tried to tell my own story in a way that opens to the stories of others, especially those who have walked the same terrain as I have: that of the Cold War, of Catholicism, of academe, of the New Left, of the communist movement, of the new world order. I do so assuming that it is not only those who lived through these times who may be interested in reliving and reflecting on them, but that those who did not might want to know of times and places they escaped by being born later or by making other choices. I do so as coherently as I can. I do not regard myself as a de-centered postmodern subject. I have struggled to integrate the flow of experience, despite the fragmenting forces of my time and the positivist acquiescence in them and the postmodernist glorification of them. I have always actively assumed that experience could be unified both as biography and as history.

This is therefore not only a narrative, but a defense of grand narrative. I am seeking to tell the story of my times in world-historical terms. It is, of course, only *a* story, which might contribute to *the* story, which will be forever in the making, open to addition, correction, reconstitution. It is inevitably and unapologetically perspectival. It is both limited and enhanced by such experiences as were open to me. It is partial and uneven, varying in focal length, depending not only on my experiences, but on my memories, sources and emphases. I have relied on recollection augmented by research, both in public records and my own papers. I kept sporadic diaries, wrote and received many letters, took notes at many conferences, documented the flow of ideas and events more thoroughly than most, but not as thoroughly as I wished when I came to write this. My stress on certain events was determined not only by availability of sources, but by my assessments of significance.

I am bearing witness to lost worlds here. It is no longer possible to step into a pre-Vatican II convent or to travel to the USSR. These were strong and seemingly stable worlds that vanished stunningly and suddenly. They seemed destined to last forever until they were gone. I want to testify to the power of their existence and absence.

The story begins in the United States, capturing, I hope, both the cohesion and contradictions of Cold War America and pre-Vatican II Catholicism. It portrays the last days of the old order, first in the wider society and then within the walls of a convent. It explores the relativizing effect of Vatican II and the Kennedy years. It conveys the social turmoil of the 1960s in universities, in homes, and in the streets. All this ferment came at the time of my life where it was natural to question my received worldview and to lay the foundations for my mature outlook.

The stable world of my youth was shattered. Once the web unraveled, every thread had to be taken up again and either discarded or rewoven. My whole worldview came into crisis. Of course, not everyone lived through these tempestuous tides in the same way. Indeed, many of my contemporaries pursued their daily rounds and private pleasures, living lives remarkably like those of their parents—selling insurance, pushing prams, mowing lawns, watching soap operas, and securing pensions, untouched by epochal engagement. They felt no need to hurl themselves at history in the making, no obsession with being at the cutting edge of their era. Others of my contemporaries, however, had other priorities. With them, I felt the pulsations of powerful forces converging.

Later the story comes to Ireland, with forays into the rest of Europe, East and West, dealing with experiences of republican, social-democratic and communist parties and social movements, and exploring the patterns of social change in Irish society from the perspective of a political activist. In Europe, especially in my times in the East, I witnessed the dying days of the socialist experiments that had shaped the twentieth century. I felt the ground shifting under my feet again. As the world turned upside down, I traced the ideas, debates, events, and life stories that played out as it transpired.

I earned my living doing various jobs, but primarily as an academic, eventually a professor. Across decades and continents, I have tracked many transformations, for better and worse, in the *modus operandi* of universities. Here again I looked for the patterns and underlying forces shaping these developments, even while participating in them and sometimes resisting them.

In writing my way through this, I relived and reassessed my life, my times, my relationships. I think that we resynthesize our life experience all the time, sometimes in small and nearly imperceptible ways, but other times more overtly and dramatically, as new experiences bring old ones up for consideration again. I have been conscious of a dynamic between me then as a character in my story and me now as its author. I have tried to be scrupulously honest about this and not attribute my mature views to my younger self, while still bringing to bear my mature perspective in interpreting events in a way that I might not have done then. The writing of any story is itself a story. I remembered things I had forgotten. I discovered things about the past that I did not know at the time.

However, the biggest story of writing the story for me was finding people I had lost along the way and coming to terms with questions about those whose lives intersected with mine before taking another path. It was easier with some than others. A person I particularly wanted to find was most difficult to locate, but after employing my best detective skills and persisting long after a less obsessive person would have abandoned the search, I finally found him again. I resumed contact with him and others, but discovered that others were dead. I grieved for them, not only because they were gone, but because I was too careless of their continuing presence in the world before they left it. Many of these were long-distance relationships, which were harder to maintain in pre-Internet days. Still, I could have done better than I did and regret that I didn't. I found the Internet invaluable for pursuing the trail of the past. I only wish it had come sooner.

On a whim, I started naming chapters after songs and wondered if I could sustain it. It turned out that there were enough songs from the soundtrack of my life to capture the themes I wanted to express. I initially intended to write my story in a single volume, but arrived at a book-length manuscript when I was only up to 1988. I decided to make this project a two-volume work, as my later life was no less eventful than my earlier one, and I still had a lot to say. In fact, the world turned upside down with the end of the Cold War, which had so shaped my life and times until then. My next book will open with those dramatic events as I experienced them, often in Eastern Europe, as socialist regimes were falling and the transition to capitalism was beginning, and will proceed from there through several decades of life in the new world order.

1

Born in the USA

Born in the USA, I was a child of war, first a hot one and then a cold one. This is the first of many ironies to unfold in my story, as I have spent so much of my life protesting against wars, particularly those conducted by the nation where I was born. I was conceived on a US Army base in Georgia during the Second World War. By the time I was born in July 1944, my father was on the front lines in Europe and his letters to my mother were from Somewhere in England, Somewhere in France, Somewhere in Germany. After the war, he did not return immediately, as he was assigned to duty in the American sector in Berlin as the hot war turned cold. We finally met when I was eighteen months old. My parents, Eugene Sheehan and Helen Kernan, were typical of their time, place, and generation. Their lives were circumscribed by many forces, including depression and war. They were unquestioningly compliant within the system structuring their fates. They were particularly loyal to the United States of America and to the Roman Catholic Church. They did not live in an atmosphere of philosophical or political debate and saw no reason to question the prevailing orthodoxies of their time.

Going back generations, as far as I can tell, most of my ancestors lived in such a way, buffeted by forces they neither comprehended nor questioned, subjected to famine, war, and depression, then lifted by rising standards of living, all underpinned by stifling dogmas they embraced as self-evident truths. Perhaps somewhere in those generations there was some questioning, but I can find no signs of it, except for my great-grandmother's cousin, who was an early critic of banks and railroads and the power they already wielded.

My father's father, Thomas Sheehan, found work of one sort or another, even amid high unemployment, before settling into a job as office manager of a Teamsters Union local. He married Elizabeth Thomas and they lived in a row house in Upper Darby, Pennsylvania, inhabited by a large extended family. Their oldest child was severely disabled after a nurse pushed his head back into the birth canal to delay childbirth until the doctor arrived. There were no lawsuits or social services to ameliorate this burden. My grandmother's life was dominated by this tragedy. She went on to have other children, including my father. When her brother's wife died in childbirth, she took her nephew and raised him as her son. She also looked after her own brothers and her sister, who never married. Despite all this, she had a sunny manner, and I remember times with her as full of fun. My mother's father, Clarence Kernan, worked as carpenter, door-to-door salesman, and summer stock opera singer, but was often out of work. Despite their poverty, my grandmother, Margaret Moore, born in Virginia, had the air of a grand southern lady. You would think that she had been the mistress of a large plantation. She grew up on a small farm. Her father, Dr. John Moore, was a country doctor, who was murdered in 1895, when she was only a year old. Her mother was a cousin of William Jennings Bryan, populist politician, congressman, three times the Democratic Party candidate for US president, Secretary of State under Woodrow Wilson and prosecutor in the infamous Scopes trial. He was in the history books we studied in school. He was famous for saying "You shall not crucify mankind upon a cross of gold," lambasting East Coast wealthy-class forces that advocated the gold standard against the interests of working people.

This branch of the family, that of my mother's mother, left more traces than any other. More photos and other records have survived. When cousins on both sides went about constructing family trees, this line was the one that could be traced furthest back. They acquired property and education beyond that of my other ancestors. My grandmother's ancestors were all Protestants until John Moore converted to Catholicism and then converted his wife, mother, siblings, and children as well. The rest of my relations were Catholic. They were peasants turned proletarians. They did not go to university, and they left few photos, records, or writings. They came mostly from Ireland as victims of famine. My great-great-grandfather, Richard Sheehan, left Kill, County Waterford, with his two brothers, and arrived in Philadelphia in 1848. The Kernans too came from Ireland to Philadelphia, via Canada.

Census records from 1880, 1910, and 1920 list the occupations of my male relations as laborer, cooper, smith, printer, clerk, box maker, brewer, electrician, wagon builder, gager, soldier, mailman, packer, druggist, tester, watchman, lineman, milkman, bookkeeper, salesman, office manager. The occupation fields for my female ancestors list saleslady, shoe paster, paper bag maker, and dressmaker. The others registered as widows or housewives. The causes of death specified on death certificates are myocarditis, nephrosclerosois, intestinal nephritis, circhios hepatio, carcinoma, apoplexy. Looking at these documents, it is striking how many of the children died soon after birth. In one case, both the first and last child of James Kernan and Catherine Furey were named Leo. The names of dead children were often passed to their siblings.

The lives of these dead generations are shadowy to me. Aside from William Jennings Bryan, they left no texts. They left so few traces. As were the majority of those who lived for centuries, they were silent on the stage of history. The few traces extant have been gathered by cousins, who have dug out census records and death certificates and street directories, have only deepened their obscurity to me. I find it hard to reconstruct their lives and imagine them as individuals. Yet in a wider sense, I have a strong sense of emerging from this silence to a time and place where I can write, even a duty to those who did not write, even though I believe that they would not approve of what I write.

I went to Kill in County Waterford with my son to see where our ancestors struggled to survive famine before emigrating to

America, never to return. The parish priest came to speak to us as
we searched the graveyard. He said the locals didn't like to speak
about those who died or emigrated, because they themselves were
descended from those who survived. Some even prospered and
accumulated property from the abandoned farms. My sense of this
time comes from works of academic history or historical novels
more than anything passed directly to me through my own ancestors. Liam O'Flaherty's *Famine* and Joseph O'Connor's *Star of the
Sea* are haunting accounts. One of the saddest fragments revealed
to me from my direct line is that my great-grandfather Richard
Sheehan joined the US Army and fought the Apaches in Arizona.
Why did he feel justified in fighting the Apaches? It was the
story of all wars: the oppressed are the foot soldiers against other
oppressed people. Buffy Sainte Marie's song "Universal Soldier"
evokes the lives of those who fought from below at the behest of
those who ruled from above.

Like many others, my ancestors eventually came up in the
world, but not exactly according to the rags-to-riches storyline.
By the 1930s, they owned the modest roofs over their heads.
However, both Sheehans and Kernans lost their houses during the
Depression—not because they were not paying their mortgages,
but because the banks had called in the entire value of their mortgages as single balloon payments. As home prices plummeted,
the houses became negative equity and worth far less than the
mortgages. After the New Deal, the banks were prohibited from
changing the terms of mortgages and repossessing homes in this
way, but back then they could do so with impunity. The Sheehans
then bought another house at a lower price. As my grandfather's
credit rating was destroyed, he bought the new house in the name
of his wife's sister, who lived with them. The Kernans could not
afford to buy another house, even at depressed prices. The family
then moved to my grandmother's family farm in Virginia. My
mother, going to school in both North and South, learned about
the Civil War from both sides. She was told in the North that it was
about slavery and in the South that it was about states' rights. She

spoke of the Civil War as if there were equal merit on both sides. After they moved back to Pennsylvania, my mother and her sisters attended public school rather than Catholic school, because they could not afford the uniforms. Nevertheless, my parents and all my aunts and uncles graduated from high school, except for my disabled uncle, who never attended school at all. None of them went to university. Both families lived frugally during the years of my parents' youth, but they were little different from everyone else they knew. Many endured even harder times.

When I look at photos of my parents in their teens and twenties, they do not look poor. Quite the opposite: some show them promenading on the Atlantic City boardwalk in their Easter outfits, the men in suits and fedoras, the women in tailored suits or dresses, elaborate hats, and high heels. Except for the shoes, my mother made everything herself. Another striking feature is the formality of their dress, making them look not only much more prosperous, but also much older than they were.

The Depression was ended by the war, but these were even harder times. In their world, that of the working class, almost all men went into the armed forces and women went to work in industries supporting the war effort, such as munitions factories. Like most of their contemporaries, my parents spent most of the time during the early years of their marriage apart from each other. When babies were born, our fathers were absent and there was always the possibility that they would not return home at all. My mother sent a constant stream of photos of their newborn daughter to the battlefields of Europe, to be shown proudly to the other young fathers with their own similar photographs. If they ever got mixed up, it would have been hard to tell the difference.

My mother and I lived with her parents in Upper Darby until my father returned. For a time, he too lived in this tiny house, along with my mother's parents, sisters, brother, and aunt, until he found it intolerable and we went to live in Atlantic City in a small summer house a mile from the ocean, owned by his parents. He commuted every day between there and Philadelphia to his job as

a draughtsman at Philadelphia Electric Company. Later we moved
to rented accommodations in Philadelphia.

Eventually they saved enough to buy a house with the help of the
GI Bill, and we moved to Roslyn, Pennsylvania, in 1949. By this time,
there were five of us, as two brothers had arrived in the intervening
years. (In all, my parents had nine children, although the youngest died as a baby. I had six brothers and two sisters.) For a while,
my father worked as a construction detailer by day and a real estate
agent by night. Since before I was born, my mother never worked
outside the home. I didn't know any mothers who did otherwise in
those years.

We began a suburban life. There were many places like Roslyn
and many families like us. The fathers had fought in the war and
went to work every day, primarily in Philadelphia. The mothers
stayed home and kept their dream houses with their new labor-
saving gadgets and looked after their ever-expanding broods of
children. The neighborhood kids bonded by playing games in
the yards and in the woods. Our strongest relationships were
with those who were Catholic. Everyone was either Catholic or
Protestant. Suburban routines became established. Every day there
were deliveries by the paperboy, the breadman, the milkman, and
the mailman. There were periodic visits from the Avon Lady, the
insurance man, and many door-to-door salesmen. A photographer came to the door with a pony and left a photo of me sitting
on it dressed as a cowgirl, incongruously in front of the suburban
picture window. Every year we had our pictures taken with the
department store Santa Claus. The mothers read magazines such as
Life and *Better Homes and Gardens* and read books by Emily Post,
Benjamin Spock, and Norman Vincent Peale to learn the correct
ways to live in this new setting. This was all part of a consolidating
national culture that was overriding various subcultures based on
class, ethnicity, locality, religion. There was much popular psychology in the air, with concepts such as "inferiority complexes" and
being "well adjusted" entering everyday speech. It seemed to many
that this was the best of all possible worlds, and that there must

be something seriously wrong with anyone who was ill-adjusted or malcontent in it. After years of depression and war, my parents and their generation did have a sense of moving with a rising tide of increasing prosperity. As a child, I accepted their version of the world and was blissfully happy in it—for a while.

Life was full of nursery rhymes and fairy tales and toys delivered by Santa Claus and baskets of jelly beans and chocolate eggs left by the Easter Bunny. There was always something new and fun to fill our play: hula hoops, comic books, trading cards, coonskin caps, Mouseketeer ears. There were swings and sliding boards in the playgrounds and merry-go-rounds and Ferris wheels and bumping-cars in amusement parks. There were circuses and carnivals. Every story ended with everyone good living "happily ever after." We ate sugary cereals, peanut butter and jelly sandwiches, potato chips, pretzels, hot dogs, hamburgers, cookies, and popsicles. Occasionally, we had more nutritious food, especially when we stopped to buy fresh tomatoes, corn-on-the-cob and watermelons sold along the road in New Jersey on our way home from the shore. My mother bottle-fed us all, thinking it both more modern and more modest. I saw my aunt, her sister, breastfeeding once and sensed my mother's disapproval.

I spent summers in Atlantic City with my grandparents, aunt, and uncles. We spent all day at the beach and most evenings on the boardwalk. I was spoiled there and ate far more candy than my parents would have allowed. I got caught up in the Miss America pageants and my aunt's movie magazines. Hollywood was a source of many wonders. The spectacle of Grace Kelly, a native of our hometown, marrying a prince from a faraway land was a modern-day fairy tale. I accepted it all at face value. My aunt, the one who introduced me to movie magazines and often took me shopping, seemed as glamorous as Grace Kelly to me. She married a medical student and made me a flower girl at their wedding and I saw it as our own fairy tale. He may have been a poor Italian immigrant, whose mother scrubbed floors, who worked his way through medical school, but he was soon a doctor. They bought a beautiful split-level house with a swimming pool in Rose Tree. I baby-sat for them, as the babies arrived one after another. One night I overheard my uncle speak about a baby he had just delivered, who was neither male nor female. I couldn't really understand that, but couldn't ask, because I wasn't supposed to know.

Going to the movies was a great thrill. The smell of the popcorn, the darkened social space, the grainy newsreels, the trailers for forthcoming films—all built up anticipation for the feature films. Many of these were set in the past. Hollywood possibly did more to form our sense of history than any other medium. We understood the ancient world in terms of *Land of the Pharaohs, Quo Vadis,* and *The Robe,* the Middle Ages in *Knights of the Round Table* and *Ivanhoe,* the nineteenth-century West through *Broken Arrow* and *High Noon.* When drive-ins arrived, we piled into the station wagon, already in our pajamas, supplied with drinks and snacks, ready for a new adventure. In time, we were allowed to go on the trolley with our friends to the matinees. We thrilled to every technical innovation, especially 3-D and Cinerama. Across all genres—westerns, musicals, mysteries, romances, comedies— we entered with utter credulity into fictional worlds as they formed our sense of our real world, not only in the past, but in the present.

Another medium, however, was on the rise. In the early 1950s, television came to everyday America in a big way. Suddenly, the small-screen box seemed to dominate every house, and our eyes were glued to the wonders of *Howdy Doody, Frontier Playhouse.* TV dinners were piled into supermarket shopping baskets. Daily and weekly routines were reorganized around television schedules. New rituals clustered around the new presence. We excitedly returned greetings from presenters and breathlessly shouted warnings to characters in trouble. We identified with cowboys—Roy Rogers, Matt Dillon, the Lone Ranger—as they brought law and order to the frontiers of the American way as it expanded westward, and we gloried in their victories over bandits, cattle rustlers, and Indians. The crime series brought the same motifs into a more contemporary and urban setting. How secure we felt in a world in which Joe Friday, Mike Barnett, and Perry Mason were standard bearers in the inevitable triumph of good over evil. The adventure series chronicled the same struggle in mountain and sea rescues, exotic jungles, and military maneuvers. All was set to rights by Sky King, Ramar of the Jungle, Superman, Fury, Lassie, and Rin Tin Tin. Women usually came into the picture more as the rescued than the rescuers. The spy series in their turn showed good versus evil in terms of the forces of religion and democracy locked in deadly combat with those of atheism and tyranny. Capitalism was the "free world," as a bulwark against communism, the dark, sinister world behind the "Iron Curtain." Agents of foreign powers constituted the enemy within. What cold, alien, menacing creatures they were in *I Led Three Lives*, the story of Herbert Philbrick, who infiltrated the Communist Party for the FBI. Across these genres, there prevailed an iron confidence that good would be rewarded and evil punished. Whatever terrors came into play, we could be sure that by the end of each episode, all loose ends would be tied up in a comforting happy ending. We knew, too, that the resolution would come through acts of individual heroism. Whether embodied by the Lone Ranger, Joe Friday, or Superman, perfect righteousness unfailingly foiled the demonic designs of the villain of the week. We knew the formulae of every show, yet we thrilled again and again to the ritual.

Another prominent prime-time television genre was family drama for family viewing. All of these, whether serious or sitcom, unfolded in a world in which the nuclear family was the secure and stable base of all human interaction. The ups and downs of domestic life were all tidily sorted out in the virtuous glow of the world of *I Remember Mama* and *Father Knows Best*. There were other dramatic genres not meant for children. These were the daytime soap operas scheduled during school hours and the anthology plays scheduled for when we were supposedly in bed. However, many of us saw as many of these as school holidays and parental indulgence would allow. These dealt with more problematic areas, although within clearly defined and very restricted boundaries. Whatever the problems and pitfalls encountered by these characters in their pursuit of the American dream, they never ceased to believe in it. It was later at night in the anthology drama series that the outer limits of what television could do in this period were explored. These dealt with the lives of people very much like their audience: people who didn't look like Hollywood stars, people who didn't carry guns, people like Marty, a simple Bronx grocer trying to cope with loneliness and a need for love in Paddy Chayevsky's "marvelous world of the ordinary." They registered social change in their own way. The pull of tradition against the push of modernity was a recurrent source of dramatic tension. These plays were among the brighter sparks that emerged from the darkness that severely circumscribed the creativity of those who managed to work in the industry at this time, that is, the whole Cold War atmosphere surrounding them and the specific pressures of the witch-hunting and blacklisting focused on film and television. The ideological parameters surrounding television production were carefully policed.

Life was not altogether unlike what appeared on the television screen, especially in the dramas of domestic life. Most American citizens really were patriotic and law-abiding, almost childishly trusting of the powers that be, unquestioningly loyal to "the land of the free and the home of the brave." Both on television and off, there was a striking lack of psychological probing. Class consciousness and sociological awareness were equally absent. Popular media portrayed most of America as middle class, defined by white collars and white picket fences rather than relationship to the means of production. The working class was confined to blue-collar manual workers in the image of Ralph Kramden, Chester Riley, or Ernie Bilko, dreamers and schemers in the grip of get-rich-quick fantasies and rags-to-riches myths. Like many others, my family saw itself as middle class, because my father wore a white collar and tie to work and we lived in a mortgaged suburban house, though we depended no less on wage labor than did the families of bus drivers and plumbers. No one questioned the prevailing division of labor, patterns of exchange, or distribution of wealth. There was no sense of how it was all structured or how it could be structured differently. People were rich or poor, that was it. It was an inherent right to be born rich—but at the same time, with a bit of luck and effort, anyone might strike it rich. There was no querying the right of those who produced nothing to consume lavishly, while those who did produce bowed and scraped before them. Any disaffection seething beneath the surface tended to be of the inarticulate rebel-without-a-cause type or the campy, anarchist beatnik. There was high culture, too, of course, but it was not part of our world. In Philadelphia, as in most US cities, it was possible to attend theater, ballet, opera, and art exhibitions, and to read challenging books and journals, but no one I knew growing up did so. Even in universities, life revolved more around sororities and fraternities, football scores and grade-point averages, upwardly mobile careers, and suburban dream homes than around any sort of critical thought or alternative visions.

School might have been expected to open a wider cultural and intellectual perspective, but it did not go very far in that direction. I began school in 1949 at Saint Luke's in Glenside. I couldn't wait to start. From my first day in kindergarten, I saw the nun standing in front of the class and wanted to become her. All my teachers, from kindergarten to eighth grade, were Sisters of Saint Joseph. One Halloween, my mother made me a costume that was a small but exact replica of the SSJ habit. I not only donned it that night to collect candy bars, but also wore for years afterward on the porches of Rosewood Avenue "playing school," with me as the teacher and my playmates as the pupils. I showed them no mercy, bossing them around and working them hard. It is a wonder that anyone would play with me. One of their fathers named me Sister Mary Impatient of the Outrageous Order. (Unlike those who dreamed of becoming baseball stars only to become insurance agents, I later lived out my childhood fantasy.) There were Catholic schools from primary and secondary schools on to university level staffed by various religious orders. Primary schools were mostly coeducational, but high schools and colleges were not. Catholic boys who aspired to attend university could choose between Villanova, La Salle, or St. Joe's, while girls could go to Rosemont, Immaculata, or Chestnut Hill. No one spoke of Harvard or Princeton or even Penn or Penn State. It was unimaginable.

Every morning we gathered in the schoolyard. When the bell rang, we lined up and marched into our classrooms in our blue and white uniforms. We pointed our hands to heaven and said our prayers, followed by the pledge of allegiance, which was recited, hands on our hearts, in the same voice and with the same solemnity as our prayers. I had already started to read, but the process stepped up in school, starting with the primers of the day that featured the bland adventures of Dick, Jane, and Sally with their pets Spot and Puff. From there, we moved to stories of saints and crusaders and missionaries and statesmen. I frequented the public libraries and was especially keen on biographies. They were hagiographical accounts of the lives of Martha Washington, Abigail Adams, Harriet Beecher Stowe, but I knew no better at the time. Lessons were organized around rote learning. We memorized prayers, hymns, poems, multiplication tables, answers to catechism questions, lists of presidents and dates of battles and state capitals. We competed in spelling bees. We spent much time practicing penmanship. None of these activities encouraged critique or creativity. We heard constant slurs against what was called "progressive education," which purportedly allowed children to do whatever they wanted, turning them into spoiled brats. Strict discipline, we were told, was an essential factor making our schools superior. The core component of our superiority was that we had the truth. Other school systems were full of laxity and error.

I did well in school, but my parents did not put much emphasis on academic success—motivated more, I think, by a desire to pump up my brothers than to put me down. The notion prevailed that you were either smart at school or good at sports and mechanical things. I accepted the caricature more than I should have, making myself less adept at sports or mechanics than I might have been, but I preferred to be smart. I valued learning and I became less tied to their values or dependent on their approval. Church and school and library became more important to me than home.

Religion permeated the whole curriculum. We didn't always adequately digest what we were taught. We were told that the Trinity and transubstantiation were mysteries we couldn't possibly understand. We memorized the Ten Commandments without grasping much of their meaning. I was particularly intrigued by the wording of the Sixth Commandment. I came home one day and shouted at my mother through the letter box, "Thou shalt not commit adultery." She was in the living room talking with the insurance man and was mortified. Eventually in school we were told that the word meant "impurity in thought, word or deed." (I confessed to it once. When the priest inquired further, I had to explain that I had urinated in the woods, which was extremely embarrassing.) We prepared for first communion, first confession, confirmation, and liturgical rituals during school time. Every year a girl in eighth grade was chosen to be May Queen and to dress as a bride and crown the statue of the Virgin Mary in the May procession. We were asked to contribute our allowances to the "ransom of pagan babies." Every $5 made it possible for one more child in Africa to be baptized, we were told—and we could even choose the child's new name.

Everything was precisely codified: ten commandments, six precepts of the church, seven sacraments, eight beatitudes, seven capital sins, twelve apostles, fourteen stations of the cross, nine first Fridays, forty hours' devotion to the blessed sacrament, five joyful mysteries, five sorrowful mysteries, five glorious mysteries. All over the world, mass was celebrated in the same way and in the same language, so that we could go anywhere and be at home wherever there was a Catholic church. It was all prescribed down to the smallest detail. We worried about inadvertently doing something wrong. We were required to attend children's mass on Sundays and to sit with our class, boys on one side of the aisle and girls on the other. The nuns would click for us to stand, sit, kneel, genuflect, file in or out in unison. Every movement, every gesture was predetermined.

Growing up in this world got me into the habit of thinking cosmologically, for which I have always been grateful—even if the cosmology of a three-storied world, composed of heaven, earth, and hell, eventually came to seem utterly implausible. But at the time, this all-encompassing worldview seemed self-evidently true and beyond question. It was as if all historical change belonged in the past and history had come to a kind of final resting point. All important issues were presented as basically settled; the answers only had to be looked up somewhere. Eisenhower was president of the greatest country in the world and Pius XII was pope of the one holy Catholic and Apostolic Church, together personifying the stability and complacency of the world over which they jointly presided. Our church and our country embodied truth and goodness. The other, the adversary, was communism. It was falsity and evil. At the end of every mass, we prayed for the conversion of Russia. Likewise, during the presidential contests of 1952 and 1956, between Dwight Eisenhower versus Adlai Stevenson, I saw "I like Ike" buttons and bumper stickers everywhere. Our house was for Ike, because he was a soldier and the other guy was an "egghead."

I was affected by death for the first time in the early 1950s. A boy in my class died, then another boy on our street, and then two of my grandparents. I found their sudden absence from the world shocking and haunting, but was comforted by the belief that they were in heaven looking down on me. My mother said she heard her father being released from purgatory. She believed that God, saints, angels, and devils intervened in her life daily. We lived in constant expectation of miracles. If it could happen to peasant children in Lourdes or Fatima, why not to us? Indeed, some children in Philadelphia in 1954 claimed that Mary appeared to them. We went to the roped-off spot where people left rosaries and money and cards with special intentions. We prayed to Our Lady of Fairmount Park. I wondered why no one from heaven appeared to me.

In 1952, we moved to Springfield, Pennsylvania, in Delaware County, where my extended family lived. I attended Saint Francis of Assisi School from third to eighth grade. There was no difference in curriculum or custom, as all was standardized in the Philadelphia archdiocesan schools. The family grew, and the house was extended. In addition to the babies arriving, my disabled uncle moved in with us. It was a noisy and busy household, but never chaotic. My parents were highly organized. My father was particularly meticulous and laid out domestic projects much as he drafted plans for manholes and substations at work. My mother started doing the Christmas shopping during the post-Christmas sales nearly a year in advance.

Holidays took a lot of logistical skill, as huge numbers of diapers, pajamas, bottles, peanut butter sandwiches, and much more were piled into the station wagon along with kids who started scrapping before the car even pulled out of the driveway with cries of "He touched me" and "He's breathing my air!" We always went within driving distance, mostly to New Jersey or Virginia. We stayed at a Sheehan bungalow in Atlantic City or the Moore Farm in Virginia. Occasionally we stayed in motels and all piled into one room. Once my father took the three oldest of us on a train to New York and we stayed in a hotel. We went to the top of the Empire State Building, walked around the crown of the Statue of Liberty, took a boat trip around Manhattan. It was so exciting. I was keen to go to Greenwich Village to see beatniks. Although I didn't have a very good grasp of what they were at the time, I could feel the lure of forbidden fruit. We never traveled anywhere by air, but we did make excursions to Philadelphia airport to watch the planes take off and land. Other trips were organized through the Brownies and then the Girl Scouts. We went camping in the woods, toured Independence Hall in Philadelphia and the United Nations in New York. We earned merit badges for sewing, cooking, and camping. My parents aspired to military precision in running our home. Our dining room was called the "mess hall." My father was deeply marked by his time in the army and acutely proud of his military service. He showed us the insignia of the 7th Armored Division in which he served, the Purple Heart he had been awarded, the Luger he had taken from a German soldier. When we misbehaved, my mother took out a horsewhip that my father had reportedly taken off a Nazi officer he had killed. She told us how many strokes we would be getting, made us lie down on the bed and expose our bare flesh, and on she went. She sometimes said that it hurt her more than it hurt us, but we never believed it. One day, after many years of this, my brother, by then stronger than my mother was, broke the whip in her face. Corporal punishment was common in those days, both at home and in school. The military ethos was powerful. We marched around the house singing the anthems of each branch of the armed forces. It all seemed like good fun at the time. Little did we realize that, when the wars of our generation would come, we would find ourselves on opposite sides of the barricades.

The idea of masculinity was inextricably tied up with military combat. Any man who had not done military service was a dubious character, and even those who had been in the military but not engaged in combat seemed vaguely suspect. Each of my brothers would come to terms with this in his own way, but they were all shaped by it. Whatever his other children's achievements, I believe that the military service of my two brothers meant most to my father, certainly more than my degrees and publications. He also felt a special bond with his cousin Jim Thomas, who had been a prisoner of war. Jim was one of the quietest men I ever met. I sensed that he was inarticulately damaged by the experience, and he later had what was mysteriously called a "nervous breakdown." But men did not talk much about such matters. It was only decades later that a public discourse began about the devastating mental impact of military service and post-traumatic stress disorder.

The idea of femininity was similarly constricted. The only women in the world of my youth were housewife-mothers and teacher-nuns and shop assistant-maiden aunts. The one thing I knew for sure was that I was not going to be a housewife-mother, not least because, as the oldest in a large family, I was under constant pressure to be just that, even while still a child myself. Any book I wanted to read was preempted by a seemingly never-ending list of domestic tasks. It was assumed that no one chose to be a shop-assistant-maiden-aunt, but it happened because some unlucky women were "left on the shelf." I thus intended to be a teacher-nun, aiming toward something larger and higher than the small domesticated lives of other women. When my mother advised me never to let a man think I was more intelligent than he was, I dismissed her words with disdain. As the years went on, I had less and less respect for women like my mother, particularly housewives. I had more and more respect for men and actively sought their company and respect.

There was a tension for me between being intellectual and being feminine. It caused me to develop in a one-sided way. I grew confident intellectually, but not sexually. Many girls of my time developed in the opposite direction, but it was still one-sided. That most girls no longer face such caricatures and choices represents one of the great advances in human history. Although even as a child I increasingly felt the existing sexual division of labor was problematic, I could not yet articulate a critique. There was no trace of feminism in my life-world at that time. The male of the species was perceived as rational, the female emotional. I found it hard to think of rationality as opposed to emotion, since they seemed to flow through me as one. The male was destined to inhabit the world of the political, the scientific, the economic, while the female was confined to the domestic realm. I could not accept it, but without a critique of it, all I could do was to feel increasingly uneasy with being female and sometimes wish that I had been born male. At the same time, I was a heterosexual female attracted to the male of the species in the conventional way. Not that I understood much about sexuality of any kind. I'd heard vague suggestions that some men were a bit effeminate and some women a bit butch, but the idea that people of the same gender had sex with each other was not a part of the picture.

Sometime, starting in second grade, I became uneasy, no longer so blissfully happy, no longer so at one with it all around me. I can't pin it to any one thing. It was a gentle dawning of critical consciousness, I suppose, although I didn't yet have much of a critique. I no longer took my parents and teachers to be founts of wisdom. My pre-feminist fretfulness about gender was part of it, but it was more than that. As the fifties progressed, I felt like a "rebel without a cause." Like others of my generation, I saw James Dean as an icon of something struggling for expression. We went mad for *Mad* magazine and rallied to the rhythms of rock and roll. My parents had 78 rpm records of Tommy Dorsey, Bing Crosby, and Frank Sinatra. That was their idea of music. My first record was a 45 rpm of Elvis Presley singing "Hound Dog" on one side and "Don't Be Cruel" on the other. In my home, as in homes all over the country, my parents denounced that "jungle music." The generation gap had opened.

I found adolescence excruciating. I don't guess it was easy for anyone, but it seemed that some were sailing through it by comparison. Along with my peers, I developed an attraction to the opposite sex, but it ran according to script only for those at the top of the cruel and crude pubescent hierarchy of the popular and cute. At parish dances, where girls were grouped on one side and boys on the other, many of us on both sides watched and languished as the popular ones took the floor. How painful it was standing there in our carefully crafted curls and crinoline skirts and high heels before anyone asked us to dance. It was even worse at unchaperoned dances that turned into "make-out parties." The popular kids kissed and the rest of us pretended that we preferred to talk and to dance. Games like Spin the Bottle and Post Office were agonizingly awkward. My first crush came at the age of ten, when a new boy arrived in school. I was constantly aware of his presence, blushed when his name was mentioned, and recalled every scrap of casual conversation between us. When our mothers happened to meet at church, it turned out they knew each other and were second cousins, making us third cousins. Thereafter he addressed me as "Cuz," which killed our one-sided romance.

Sexuality was a mysterious force and I did not come to terms with it easily. For multiple reasons—from my early sense of religious vocation to my adolescent physical insecurity—I felt excluded from full participation in it. As I watched the high school kids on *American Bandstand*, dancing to the rhythms of rock and roll, I longed to fit into the world as seamlessly as they did, but felt I never would. There was an added dimension to my unease, beyond the usual awkwardness of adolescence. It was the incipient philosopher in me struggling to be. I hardly knew the word. I knew no professor of philosophy or professor of anything. I began to feel that people were so busy going somewhere that they didn't think about where they were going. I wanted to see the big picture. By the time I was in high school, this became very intense and I started reading works of philosophy. My education began to diverge from the curriculum more and more.

All this unfolded amid a distinct historical atmosphere. Throughout the 1950s, even when innocence and credulity and fun outweighed my emerging unease, a sense of apocalyptic fear hung over all that I did. From my earliest years, I knew the deadliest weapons the world had ever known were being developed. The problem wasn't that our country had them, but that our enemies had them too. An "Iron Curtain" divided the world between freedom on one side and tyranny on the other. The other side sought nothing less than world domination. The third world war, we were warned, would be a nuclear war. We held regular air raid drills in school and saw frightening films depicting a nuclear attack. We crouched under our desks, as if that would somehow save us from nuclear annihilation. There were debates about fallout shelters, specifically about whether you would be justified in killing someone who tried to get into your fallout shelter. I thought a lot about this, although no one I knew even had a fallout shelter. My mother did have the cellar well stocked with enough tinned food to last for many months. Aside from worries about an attack, I became so concerned about the levels of strontium 90 in the atmosphere as a result of nuclear testing that I wrote letters to US senators about it.

We were taught that communism was the enemy. It was not just a fallacious political ideology, but a cosmological evil. It was hostile not only to our country, but to our religion—the work of the devil. I imagined communists entering my bedroom and demanding that I renounce my nation and religion, even my own parents. I believed that I would be brave and be a martyr if necessary. The whole apocalyptic scenario was heightened by the "third secret of Fatima" in a letter which couldn't be opened until 1960. I got the impression that it somehow had to do with communism and the end of the world. I had a terrible foreboding about the year 1960 and a sense that I could not count on any future after that. I didn't actually know any communists, yet Senator Joseph McCarthy said they were everywhere, even in the government, the army, and the film and television industry. I watched the Army-McCarthy hearings and was on the side of McCarthy. He was not only patriotic but Catholic, so he had to be right. I even read his biography, *Tail Gunner Joe*. I wanted all these evil subversives rooted out. Nothing seemed more inconceivable than that I would one day become one. *Sputnik* sent us into a spin, because it felt as if they were getting ahead of us, not only in the space race, but perhaps in other ways as well.

By the late 1950s, observing mainstream debates between liberals and conservatives, I decided I was liberal. I didn't think it was right that some people were rich while others were poor, and that a disproportionate number of poor people were black. I was stirred by events in the South, especially when Rosa Parks refused to go to the back of the bus in Montgomery, Alabama, and when the army had to be brought in to defend pupils entering high school in Little Rock, Arkansas. My mother insisted that communist agitators were behind it. I doubted it, but also began to wonder if they were in fact behind it, whether communists were really so bad after all.

The 1960s arrived, and the world didn't end. Things were changing, both in the wider world and in my perspective. The stability
and smugness of the system I took for granted was starting to show
cracks, revealing its vulnerabilities and delusions and hinting at
other possibilities. There were new faces at the top, symbolizing
the stirring from below. The election of John Kennedy as president
and John XXIII as pope put faces on a new mood, a new energy, a
new path forward. The faces of the other side changed, too. When
we watched Khrushchev debating Nixon in a kitchen and bang-
ing his shoe at the United Nations, we didn't fear him as we had
Stalin. The Iron Curtain didn't seem so iron any more. When revolution reshaped Cuba and Fidel Castro came to the United States,
we regarded him as a folk hero. When he became a communist,
it was more a push to question our attitude toward communism
than toward him and the revolution.

We entered a new phase of the Cold War and of Catholicism
as well. Vatican II was a kind of Protestantization of Catholicism,
which had a powerful questioning and relativizing effect. At first it
was just a new sense of freshness and dynamism, but eventually it
set me on a course that led far beyond anything reformers intended.
I took to the new vocabulary of dialogue and renewal, along with the
exotic imported words such as *kerygma* and *aggiornamento*. In the
political realm, the rhetoric of the "New Frontier" created a sudden
sense of history in the making, of an energy breaking through the
malaise of the Eisenhower era. It was not at all clear to me then what
the Kennedy era meant in ideological terms, clouded as it was by the
whole Camelot mystique as well as by my own political naïveté. It
became clear that Kennedy stood for a more social democratic, technocratic, neo-colonial form of developed capitalism. Nevertheless, I
responded to the atmosphere of vigor and vitality, to a more liberal,
sophisticated approach to many things.

In the world of television, corporate sponsors loosened their
grip on scripts, and the whole machinery of blacklisting was
gradually dismantled. The first signs of change came in news
broadcasts. For the first time, global events appeared on the screen

in close to real time: the debates during the 1960 presidential election, the Kennedy inauguration, Khrushchev at the UN, Castro in Harlem, the Bay of Pigs, the Cuban missile crisis, the Kennedy assassination and funeral. At the same time, TV dramas continued in much the same manner as before, with the same programs, the same formats, the same standardized settings, plots, and patterns, the same stereotypical characters. It began to jar. Newton Minow, the Kennedy-appointed chairman of the Federal Communications Commission, declared television to be "a vast wasteland," and many agreed with him. In response, the networks introduced more substantive programming in series like *East Side West Side, Mr. Novak, The Defenders,* and *Dr. Kildare,* showing social workers, teachers, lawyers, and doctors dealing with the urgent problems of American society—racial tension, inequality, unjust laws, generational conflict—without pretending they could always be resolved neatly by the end of each episode.

The western, crime, spy, and space genres saw a shift from the drama of righteous individual heroism to a more technocratic team professionalism. It corresponded to a consolidation of a shift from the values of a laissez-faire market economy to those of a more managerial corporate system. The lone lawman gave way to the tough teams of *The Untouchables* and *77 Sunset Strip.* More attention came to be focused on the macho world of international intrigue, with *Mission Impossible* and *The Man from UNCLE* emerging as prototypical productions of the period. The cowboy code of honor no longer applied in this arena. Conflict centered less on principle and more on technique. The end justified the means, with less and less emphasis on the end and more and more on the means. The picture of the enemy likewise changed in the transition from the spy stories of the 1950s to the peaceful coexistence, cultural exchange-cum-espionage tales of the 1960s. Agents on both sides became less ideological in orientation and began to look and sound more alike. Agents of foreign powers had less of a furtive, sinister, scruffy look and began to resemble our own, so much so that it was possible for plots to revolve around the chic macho men and glamorous miniskirted women of the one side passing for the other. The spy spoof *Get Smart*, sending up all sides in ludicrous scenarios, reflected in its own campy way the easing of Cold War tensions. In the New Frontier mood, more eyes turned to space as well, in the mood articulated in the opening sequence of *Star Trek*, as the starship *Enterprise* set off on its mythic odyssey into the dark unknown of space, "the final frontier."

The more liberal values of the Kennedy-Johnson years did not go unchallenged. Companies threatened to cancel their sponsorships and southern stations refused to carry certain episodes of network programs that transgressed traditional norms. This happened with increasing regularity as black actors began to appear more often and in more serious roles, and as the civil rights movement put more and more pressure on the deeply rooted racism of American society. But such ideological tensions as came to the surface in the early 1960s remained within the liberal-conservative spectrum, defined roughly by the ideological distance between Kennedy and Nixon. Despite real differences and acute tensions over civil rights and welfare legislation, there was still considerable consensus. Any discordant notes outside this consensus were still few and far between and somewhat muted.

I attended high school from 1958 to 1962. My grandfather thought I should go to Holy Child Academy in Sharon Hill rather than Archbishop Prendergast in Drexel Hill. I think he believed that posher was somehow better. Not many granddaughters of teamsters or daughters of draughtsmen went there, but daughters of doctors and lawyers and bank managers did. That seemed to be the point. He insisted on paying my fees, and my parents carried on doing so after he died, which was not easy considering they had so many other children by this time. I did not want to seem ungrateful, but there was much that I didn't like about the school. I thought the nuns who staffed it were sheltered, neurotically fixated on Christ as a child and ridiculously preoccupied with the beatification of their foundress, Cornelia Connelly. One nun cautioned us to be modest about our bodies and advised us to wear cardboard under our undershirts (as if we wore undershirts) and to avoid patent leather shoes or strapless dresses, so as not to be occasions of sin to the opposite sex. As we were segregated by gender for schooling, we had all too few occasions of sin. The yearbooks from that time show a vanished world. It is not only that the school no longer exists, but the images in *Althean* provide a window into a pious, conformist, Pollyanna life nearly impossible to imagine now. Girls in blue blazers and plaid skirts are shown at prayer, at play, and at work, all in the care of solicitous nuns. There were numerous campus groups: glee club, mission club, secretarial club, forensic club, dancing club, dramatic club, and more. The school newspaper carried such news as golden jubilees and feast days of nuns, rehearsals for the spring festival, and inter-varsity basketball and hockey scores. Graduation photos show rows of young women carrying red roses and wearing long white dresses rather than caps and gowns, making us look more like debutantes than graduates.

Our classes involved memorizing Latin and French vocabulary, grappling with conjugations and declensions, mastering algebraic equations and geometric theorems, and cutting up helpless frogs. Biology classes were premised on a blend of creationism and evolutionism. We were told that God created all that existed, including the process whereby the ape evolved into man. It was necessary to believe, Mother Jeanne d'Arc emphasized, that at some point God intervened and created a soul. This accorded with the overall idea that God not only created the universe and set the laws of nature in motion, but constantly interceded in the process, so that, if we prayed, it might not rain on the day of the school picnic. Civics classes revolved around papal encyclicals, particularly *Rerum Novarum* and *Quadragesimo Anno*.

I did try to make a go of it for the first two years. I was happy to be out of primary school, but I was not happy to be in an all-female institution. Still, I made many friends, took part in extracurricular activities, and received high marks. I was especially active with the forensics club, and I represented the school in inter-varsity debating tournaments. On a trip to New York to compete in a debating tournament, I was in my glory. Researching the assigned topic of debate—right-to-work laws and union shops—I took a new interest in my grandfather's job as a union official and started asking him questions about the labor movement. Several news stories had recently appeared on Jimmy Hoffa and corruption in the Teamsters Union. He did not welcome my probing into these areas. My high school was supposed to be a world away from all these things.

I was happiest at debating tournaments, which opened to me my first serious steps beyond home, church, and school. My best friends were debaters from other schools, especially from male schools. I developed a particularly strong relationship with Ken James, who was intelligent, articulate, and handsome. He was also black. My parents were not too pleased. They could find no fault with him; it was just that they subscribed to "separate but equal," especially my mother, with her roots in the South, while my father was uneasy about his daughter with anyone of the opposite sex. Although I was attracted to him in that way, it remained a platonic relationship, albeit a deeply serious one. We talked for hours and could express our intellectual yearnings with each other. We also confided to each other our intentions to enter religious orders.

My most serious relationship in those days was with a teacher. Gregory Strickland was a Jesuit who taught high school and coached the debating team at St. Joseph's Prep. He judged me in a debating tournament and saw potential. He spoke to me in a way that no one ever had. We spent many hours talking throughout my high school years. He inspired me to reach out to life in a higher, wider, and deeper way. Greg was the most exciting person I had ever met. There was something so fresh, so bold, about the ideas he introduced and the way he pursued them. He recommended books and then discussed them with me at length and in depth. One was *Great Dialogues of Plato,* which I carried everywhere for a while, imagining Socrates roaming the streets of ancient Athens and probing the world from unexpected angles. I not only saw him at debating tournaments, but went to visit him at the Jesuit community in North Philadelphia where he lived, and we talked for hours on the phone. When he came to my house and met my family, my parents were uneasy. Why, they wondered, would a man of thirty spend so much time with a girl of fifteen? I veered between thinking myself quite grown up and wondering if I was just a mixed-up kid with a schoolgirl crush. Although I saw it as "purely spiritual" and he never touched me during my high school years, it was still quite physical in the sense that he was quite alert to physicality—his own, mine, and that of other people and the natural world. It wasn't so much about sex—though he did stir me in that way—as about his sensitivity to eye contact and directness of speech. I felt a fierce sense of loss when he was transferred from Philadelphia to Washington, but we still kept up an intense correspondence, supplemented by long phone conversations. After he left, I latched on to the next debating coach at St. Joe's, William Watters, who was quite different from Greg, more traditionally pedagogical and pastoral, but similarly generous with his time and attention, nurturing my development.

The places where I went to meet Ken, Greg, and Bill were inner-city neighborhoods considered dangerous, particularly for a white teenage girl on her own. My family and classmates never ventured into these places. I was determined to do so, even though my heart was pounding as I walked the streets. I became ever bolder in my steps away from the well-worn paths. I spent several summers frequenting City Hall. Every day I took the trolley and subway from Springfield into Philadelphia with a copybook to take notes of the trials, conversations, and city council meetings that took up my day. I got to know politicians, judges, and lawyers, all of whom were amazingly indulgent of my presence and took a surprising amount of time to talk to me. I became particularly attached to Judge Raymond Pace Alexander, grandson of slaves and son of a poor working-class family, who had become a distinguished civil rights lawyer, politician, and judge. I spent quite a lot of time in the criminal courts, which were windows on a world quite unknown to me. (I recorded words I didn't know, such as "sodomy." I guessed it had something to do with Sodom and Gomorrah. I looked it up in a dictionary, which defined it as "unnatural sex acts," but I still didn't really know what it meant.) I was fascinated by politics. I corresponded with various senators, including John Kennedy, asking questions, requesting reports, and commenting on the world situation. I wrote letters to newspapers on political matters. I took the train down to Washington and sat in on sessions of Congress and talked to political staffers, who got me the passes to go where I wanted. One summer I got a job working for a city councilman in Philadelphia, who was later at the center of a municipal corruption scandal. I was very disturbed by this, but convinced myself he was somehow innocent. During the 1960 elections, I was "All the way with JFK." I became active in Democratic politics and volunteered for the campaign. JFK shook my hand one day when he met with election workers before a rally in Upper Darby. I spent hours talking with men about politics and big ideas. I was into all the razzmatazz: the hats, bumper stickers, buttons, slogans, songs. I went around singing "High Hopes." I couldn't get enough, and I couldn't bear the thought of missing anything while at school, so I got into the habit of truancy. I left in the morning wearing my uniform before ducking into a public lavatory to change clothes. This involved a lot of lying, which makes me cringe even now. My parents opposed my activities, which took me ever further out of any world they could map. My mother was constantly searching my pockets, bags, and drawers. She was a persistent detective, and one day she called election headquarters and I answered the phone. I was caught. As punishment, I was barred from electoral activities (including victory parties), from inter-varsity debating, from my junior prom, from trips to City Hall or Congress, from writing letters to the paper, from doing almost everything I really wanted to do. The deceit continued, as I tried to find ways to free myself from these constraints, but this only tormented me further, as every lie violated the integrity I so sincerely sought. Finally, I decided never to lie again—a vow I've kept ever since.

I felt increasingly alienated from home and school. Sometimes I wanted nothing more than to get away from my parents and teachers, but I was trapped. I wanted to fly free. I sent for many college catalogues, the farther from home the better. I would need a scholarship, so I worked hard at my studies, earning a place on the honor roll and winning academic prizes. I was ill at ease with my peers. I dated throughout high school, often with other debaters, but they seemed so young and shallow compared to the older men whose company I persistently sought. I felt torn in my aspirations. As each university catalogue arrived, I imagined going there, enjoying brilliant lectures and intense conversations with professors and students. I fantasized further about going on to be a professor or politician. I toyed with the idea of joining the Peace Corps. I filled out many applications for scholarships, but mailed none. I was destined to do otherwise, I somehow sensed.

I moved far beyond the curriculum in my reading: books on philosophy, theology, history, literature. I burned for knowledge. One summer my mother enrolled me in a typing course, but I went to the park and read an enormous book on world history instead. While grounded, I still had books, though my many domestic duties made even reading difficult. At the time there were three babies in diapers in my house, and my disabled uncle was dying a protracted death in our house. Toward the end, he could do nothing for himself. I recoiled before the caring tasks assigned to me. My mother bore the brunt of it and she struggled to cope. The house was noisy and tense. My mother, whom her grandchildren remember as sweet, generous, and accepting, was bad-tempered, demanding, and repressive. I got up very early in the morning to have some quiet for reading and reflection, and left for school early to get to the library before classes. The dark morning hours brought some degree of peace and much-sought silence.

I still did not question the basic tenets of church or state, but I sought a more intellectually sophisticated version of them. I did wonder about the Church's warnings about the dangers of venturing outside its limits, asking why I should believe in the religion into which I happened to have been born, when others were equally convinced that the religions into which they had been born were true. Was I brainwashed? I latched on to apologetics textbooks to answer my questions and address my doubts. I pored over the *Summa Theologica* of Thomas Aquinas. I enthused over *Orthodoxy* and *The Everlasting Man*, not only because they expressed the ontological position I was seeking to justify, but also because I took to G. K. Chesterton's clever and paradoxical style.

I savored novels with political or religious themes, such as *The Last Hurrah* and *The Edge of Sadness* by Edwin O'Connor, *The Power and the Glory* by Graham Greene, *Advise and Consent* by Alan Drury. I took to Frank O'Connor's stories and nearly split my sides laughing at "First Confession." I sought sociological analysis in *The Lonely Crowd* by David Riesman and *The Hidden Persuaders* by Vance Packard. I took early morning walks in dark streets pondering words I memorized from my reading, such as lines from *We Hold These Truths* by John Courtney Murray: "The barbarian need not appear in bearskins with a club in hand. He may wear a Brooks Brothers suit and carry a ball-point pen. . . . The real enemy within the gates of the city is not the communist but the idiot." One day in downtown Philadelphia, I bought a Communist newspaper. It would be hard for anyone who didn't grow up as I did to realize how daring this felt. However, lightning did not strike me dead, and I felt improved by exposing myself to the other side. I didn't find its contents so implausible either. At times, I seethed with contempt for the conformism and mediocrity of the older generation in general, and of my own parents in particular. What enraged me was that they held up this complacency, which they called normality, as the peak of wisdom, the goal to which I should aspire.

After I graduated from high school, I got a job in a detective agency in Philadelphia. I was only a clerk, but I thrived on the office banter with the investigators and on reading reports before filing them. They were mostly cases of suspected adultery or insurance fraud—no murders—but I found it a quirkily enlightening experience. I also liked the independence and the salary. My parents had laid down the law that at eighteen we were on our own financially. If we wanted to continue to live at home, we had to pay our own board. My earnings allowed me to explore further the joys of Philadelphia's city center, to meet friends in restaurants, movies, and concerts. As I worked full-time and stayed out most evenings and weekends, my mother needed more helping hands at home. Rather than make the demands on my brothers that she had made on me, she hired a "cleaning lady." It was Ken's mother. My mother couldn't understand why I thought this inappropriate, as she needed the help, and Mrs. James needed the money. I saw Ken often at the time, and we both found this embarrassing.

I was also still involved in politics. Dick Doran, with whom I worked during the Kennedy campaign, contacted me and said it wasn't enough to get our man elected, that we had to go out and garner support for the whole "New Frontier" program. I did so enthusiastically. I was back in City Hall again, too, chatting with politicians, judges, assistant district attorneys, and public defenders.

I felt a burning desire to touch life at all possible points, to live as fully as a person could live. I wanted to push my knowledge and passion to their limits. I was fluttering my wings and wanted to fly free. Nevertheless, I did the opposite.

2

Faith of Our Fathers

Why would I renounce all my aspirations and ambitions to explore the wider world in order to enter a cloister? To understand it, it is necessary to grasp the grip that Catholicism had in those days, not only in its institutional hegemony, but in its psychological power. More than anything else, the all-encompassing presence of the Roman Catholic Church had dominated my life. My family was Catholic. My friends were Catholic. My schools were Catholic. My books were Catholic. Most of my mentors were Catholic. *Imprimatur* and *nihil obstat* were as natural and essential as title and author in the opening pages of books, at least those dealing with higher matters. Above all else, it was the rituals of the Church that gave rhythm and order to the days and months and years of the first two decades of my life. Its rites of passage marked most decisively the stages through which I moved through my life world. Each year revolved in the grooves of Advent, Christmas, Lent, Easter, May procession, Pentecost. Its theology provided answers to every philosophical question. Philosophy, I was told, existed to take human reason as far as it could go, but could only be completed by divine revelation. Theology stood at the summit of the hierarchy of knowledge.

In time, I discerned different streams within this overall flow. It was this gradual realization that brought me into the realms of philosophy and theology. Despite being female, I developed an aversion to the trappings of female spirituality: rosaries, scapulars, apparitions, sugary sentimental prayers. I had little respect for women, including nuns. All my role models were men, and I gravitated toward traditions of male spirituality, Jesuit ones in particular, which I found stronger, more rational, more active. I believed in the harmony of faith and reason, with the emphasis on reason. When we graduated from eighth grade, we were presented with a book called *The Question Box*, which gave answers to every anticipated question and objection to Catholic doctrine. I read it avidly and felt even more confident of the Church's omniscience.

I wanted to give myself without reserve, even though it meant enclosing myself in a world of women, leaving behind my notions of a career in academe or politics, sublimating my sexuality, sacrificing my freedom. I prayed in the spirit of Ignatius of Loyola: "Teach me to be generous, to give without counting the cost, to fight without heeding the wounds." It was inevitable that I enter the convent, because I yearned to have a comprehensive worldview and to live in harmony with it. I thought that the people around me were so busy going somewhere that they forgot to find out where they were going. This became axiomatic for me. What I saw most people doing was what I was most resolved not to do. Catholicism addressed the big picture and demanded that its chosen commit totally to contemplating and communicating it.

I felt called. I believed that this thrust toward totality, which I felt so strongly and which kept me so preoccupied with questions of origin and destiny, was God's way of pulling me toward the religious life. The Church's constant emphasis on "vocation" had conditioned me to believe that this restless searching was a sign of having been chosen to play a special role in understanding and teaching. When I decided to enter the convent, I believed I had resolved my struggles, although that was far further from being the case than I could possibly have imagined. I had my worldview worked out, so I thought, and I had only to advance in higher knowledge of it and give myself in total commitment to it.

I applied and was accepted to the Sisters of Saint Joseph in Chestnut Hill. We had to supply academic transcripts, SAT scores, baptismal and confirmation certificates, and letters of reference from our teachers and pastors. We underwent psychological and physical examinations—the latter testing for virginity. Not everyone who applied was accepted, although I don't think that those who were rejected necessarily failed the virginity test. The fact that the Sisters of Saint Joseph had a Jesuit founder—Jean-Pierre Medaille, who established the congregation in Le Puy, France, in 1650—was significant for me. In fact, I would have preferred to join the Jesuits, but this seemed the next best thing. I wanted to be a teacher, and this was a teaching order. I also had two cousins, both on the Sheehan side, who were SSJs.

The day I entered the convent in September 1962 was one of the most drastic rituals of closing one chapter of a life and beginning another that I have ever known. I shut my huge trunk, full of the required number of undershirts, slips, stockings, nightdresses, slippers, pencils, bars of soap, and bottles of shampoo, and placed on the top an envelope with the "dowry" I had worked all summer to earn. It was not only that we had to bring exactly what was on the list, but we were also strictly prohibited from bringing anything not on the list. I had to let go of my most treasured possessions: books, letters, photos. I donned the black serge dress and cape of a postulant. I said goodbye to friends and neighbors and siblings, looked around the house for what I believed to be the last time and got in the car. My parents and my cousin-sponsor chattered away about what a beautiful autumn day it was, how it was better to be early than late, how long it would take to get to Chestnut Hill, how I would never again worry about having a roof over my head. I let it all pass over me, impressing on myself the enormity of what I was doing and anticipating the contemplative silence that lay ahead. When we arrived at the postulate, a new building about a mile away from the mother house and college, I was taken away, given my number in the order, shown to my cell in the dormitory, and brought to a hall to say my goodbyes. When the bell rang, we formed ranks in the order of our numbers and processed into chapel. One by one, we approached the altar and received the postulant's veil. There were ninety of us who entered that day.

From that day on, we followed the strictest regime: mass, meditation, meals, manual labor, spiritual reading. We were given precise instructions down to the smallest detail: how to walk (noiselessly, eyes down, hands inside cape, close to the wall, measured steps), how often to wash our hair (once a week), how often to change our underwear (every three days), how to undress without looking at our bodies (slip the nightdress over the head before taking underwear off), how to make our beds (square corners), how to eat a banana (with a fork) and an orange (with a spoon). Between night prayers and morning mass, we were to observe a grand silence, which could only be broken by a major emergency, and an ordinary silence at all other times, punctuated only by speech necessary to the execution of tasks. When the bell rang, it was the voice of God, and we were to stop sewing in mid-stitch, stop conversation in mid-word, stop anything we were doing that very second. We were assigned fixed places in refectory, chapel, and recreation. Recreation was the one hour a day when we were allowed to speak. There were rigid guidelines about topics that could and could not be discussed. We were not to speak of our past lives or to speak critically of our present ones. We were not to criticize our superiors or even comment on the food. We were forbidden to use the adjective "my." It was *our* book, *our* veil, *our* slip, and so on. If told to put my name in something, I was to write "For the use of Sister Helena Sheehan."

Communication with the outside world was severely limited and subjected to tight surveillance. There were no letters, except to and from our parents (but not during Lent or retreat), and even these were censored. Any letters we wrote that were judged insufficiently edifying or marred by sub-par grammar or handwriting were handed back to be rewritten. Some sisters smuggled letters out on visiting day. I didn't, although I wanted to do so. I composed letters in my head to Ken and Greg, but I didn't want to violate either the letter or spirit of the rules by writing or sending them. Many sisters were homesick, but I wasn't. I didn't miss my home, but I did miss the wider world. Postulants were breathless with excitement when visiting day came and they could sit in a circle in an auditorium and talk—of elevated subjects, of course—with their families. I was glad for the break in routine and interested to see how my brothers and sisters were growing up, but the people I most wanted to see were not allowed to visit me.

There were no newspapers. There was no reading of anything not assigned. There was no radio or television. Sometimes we laid newspapers (which could be read by superiors) over newly scrubbed floors, and it was hard not to peek at the articles. When parents came to visit, it was difficult not to ask about current events. Occasionally we were told about news. The inauguration of Vatican II was announced, although the spirit of renewal surrounding the council made little impact on our congregation during my time there. I was attuned to such trends before I entered, and it was deeply disillusioning that this new thinking had almost no discernable effect on our religious "formation." The winds of change did not blow through our postulate or novitiate. It seemed so solid, even though it was about to be blown to bits. Just as Vatican II began in October 1962, the Cuban Missile Crisis rocked the world, even our cloister. The mistress of postulants announced it in a most apocalyptic way. We fell to our knees with a strong sense that the end of the world might be near. I trembled with world-historical fear. The Cold War was threatening to become a hot one, the ultimate one, and peaceful coexistence seemed in shreds. Then, after some days, she announced that it was all over. Naturally I wanted to know far more—how? why?—but that was forbidden.

Our mistress of postulants terrified us at times. We met with her regularly, primarily as a group, but also one-on-one. She told us God would decide who would stay and who would go. Not everyone who was a postulant would become a novice. All the doors opened out, she reminded us. Observing some behavior not to her satisfaction, she solemnly pronounced, "God will not be mocked." As the months went on, postulants disappeared one by one. They were not allowed to tell anyone they were leaving or even to say goodbye, and their departure was never announced. There was only the empty space in chapel and at the breakfast table. Later that day, numbers would be reassigned. We were never to mention them again, but we could not help wondering who went willingly and who was asked to leave. For a time, things regularly went missing, and we gossiped about "the klepto." When one postulant disappeared and the thefts stopped, we assumed that she was the one, though we would never have suspected her.

During these months, we received instruction in the Holy Rule and in the vows of poverty, chastity, and obedience. The chapter of the Holy Rule on chastity was remarkable in that it dealt with virtually everything except sex. It began: "The sisters shall live in the congregation as the angels live in heaven, that is, their life is to be altogether interior and spiritual and detached from everything sensual." We were never to look anyone in the eyes. We were never to touch another person. We were never to converse with one person alone, instead always gathering in groups of three or more. We were to have no "particular friendships." We were to have no unnecessary conversations with men "whether lay or ecclesiastical." For conversations necessary to our daily tasks, another sister was to be present and report to the superior. All the while, something in me rebelled against this monastic ethos, against the whole negative vocabulary of death and renunciation. We were to be "dead to the self," "dead to the flesh," "dead to the world." The habit we were sewing and would soon be wearing for the rest of our lives was to be our shroud. Yet wasn't it God, I wondered, who had created the world, the flesh, ourselves, our feelings for others? But according to Thomas à Kempis, "I go into the world of men and I return less a man."

I couldn't accept it. The attitude of blind, unquestioning obedience was alien to me. I often thought of a line from the film *The Nun's Story*, spoken to the protagonist, Gabrielle, by her father on the day of her entrance into the convent: "I can see you poor, I can see you chaste, but obedient—never." I believed in discipline. I wanted to purge myself of all indulgence and give myself to something greater, but I could not renounce my standards of intellectual and emotional integrity, which, however immature, were nevertheless very strong. But this, of course, was intellectual pride. I was constantly reprimanded for this particular sin, even when I said nothing. They knew the signs. They could read it on my face, which had not yet gone blank the way it was supposed to do. We were to do our best in the tasks we were given, yet when we did them well, we were accused of pride. When others came to me for help with their studies or sewing, at which I excelled, I was caught in a contradiction: I felt confident in my abilities and wished to be gracious and generous toward others who were not so confident or able, but feared that to help them was to be proud and arrogant.

For feast days, we had celebrations with songs and pageants performed by the postulants. My role was writing and delivering a script about the meaning of the feast. My work was very well received, as I found fresh language to articulate what they believed, delivered in a way that moved them. This too was treacherous territory, as any resulting self-affirmation and acclaim posed a danger to my soul. To keep me in check, I was never assigned to read in the refectory. Every time our weekly assignments were read out, I hoped for it, whereas most dreaded it. I was told I had to conquer my pride, and though I tried to be humble, no sooner did I make some progress than I took pride in my humility. Such a spirituality built around constant self-scrutiny and striving for perfection was torment to me, taking my already extreme self-scrutinizing and perfectionist tendencies and turning them from constructive into destructive forces. The problem was less the self-monitoring and drive for perfection in themselves, as much as their basis in a dualism of body and spirit, of reason and faith, which undercut my quest for wholeness. The anti-physicalism, and even more the anti-intellectualism, felt like a constant assault on my character. Yet others seemed simply to accept these impossible contradictions without torturing themselves the way I did.

We were divided into two groups. It was never said, but clearly understood, that one was considered to be of a higher academic standard than the other. Except for one sister who had graduated from college before entering, we all took courses at Chestnut Hill College that would count toward our degrees. There was no consultation or differentiation in what we would study. We would all pursue a B.S. in education, to prepare us to teach primary school. After several years, some might be selected for higher studies and teaching at high school or college level. I hoped I would be chosen. Our college classes were a series of introductory courses in literature, art, and music, as well as religion. Unlike some orders, we did not take classes with ordinary college students. Our nun instructors came to the postulate and gave special classes for us alone. I also suspected that marks were not given strictly on academic merit. If it was thought that a sister needed to be humbled or boosted, her marks might be adjusted accordingly. The ban on "particular friendships" was a constant source of tension. We were not to be more friendly with one person than any other, but it was of course impossible to like everyone equally, and we naturally preferred the company of some sisters to others. Lesbian tendencies were evident, though in a deeply sublimated mode. Some sisters had a crush on a high school teacher-nun, who had inspired them to join the convent, and soon developed new crushes in the postulate and novitiate as well. Even those who would not have been so inclined in the outside world developed infatuations toward other women that in another environment would have been channeled toward men.

Meanwhile, my family's status in their local parish was enormously enhanced by my entrance into the convent. They had always been regarded as a good Catholic family, and my mother was admired as a daily communicant, even with her squirming toddlers in tow. But they never put themselves forward to be leaders of the Catholic organizations to which they belonged: Sodality, Holy Name Society, or Knights of Columbus. They had not been among those on the most favored terms with the priests and nuns. All this changed suddenly. My brothers reported being singled out to take messages from one classroom to another. My father was

given the privilege of driving nuns attending Saturday classes to
and from Chestnut Hill. Yet there was no question of his seeing me
while he was there waiting for them. Week after week, they made
the most minimal small talk, and otherwise recited the rosary all
the way to school and back. After a while, my father had enough.
He found the sisters' behavior inconsiderate and rude. He was a
working man with a house full of young children and lots to do
on a Saturday.

As the months went by, we were gradually introduced to a series
of secret practices: things never to be discussed outside the order,
or even inside it, except to our superiors: Examen, penances, acts
of humility, chapter of faults, and what was called "the discipline."
We knew nothing of the discipline until Holy Week. We had moved
from the postulate up to the mother house to begin our novitiate.
We were in deep retreat, preparing for the ceremony on Easter
Monday when we would be formally received into the order. We
had been immersed in the Good Friday liturgy, full of the vivid
imagery of scourging at the pillar, bleeding from the wounds, carrying the cross, crucifixion, death for our sins. We then met with
the mistress of novices; she produced an instrument, a chain that
branched out into a number of sub-chains, each with a hook at
the end, and instructed us in precise techniques of self-flagella-
tion. Every Saturday night from then on, the bell would ring, the
lights would go out, and the shades would be drawn. We would
pull our veils over our faces, our sleeves over our hands, our skirts
up over our backs, and expose our bare flesh. We would then use
our instrument to inflict as much pain as possible without drawing blood, while reciting prayers in unison. We were shocked, but
we had come this far, and had accepted so many things leading
up to this, that we accepted it and moved on to the excitement
of Easter and Easter Monday, which, in total contrast, brought
the most absurd fussing over our physical appearance, as we set
our hair in rollers, practiced walking in high heels, and broke the
solemnity and self-abnegation of the novitiate with girlish giggles
and the silliest ceremonial preparations. Of the original ninety,

seventy-nine of us were left, all to be dressed as brides the next day. I was uncomfortable with the bridal imagery, but others gushed with sublimated eroticism and embraced it.

On Easter Monday, clad in long white dresses and wedding veils and new hairdos, we solemnly filed into the chapel of the mother house to the strains of the novitiate choir singing "Veni Sponsa Christi": "Come, bride of Christ, receive the crown that has been prepared for you." At the appointed time, we prostrated ourselves in the aisles and gave the prescribed answers to the prescribed questions asked by the bishop: "What do you ask, my children?" "I ask for the grace of God and to be admitted into this congregation." It went on in this vein. We promised to live by the rules of the congregation. We declared ourselves dead to the world, dead to the flesh, dead to our old selves. Then, one by one, we approached the bishop, who placed in our hands the habit of the order. Out we processed in white, carrying the black habits reverently. Outside, in a designated room, we were undressed down to our slips by our sponsors. Then much of our hair was chopped off (the next day our heads were shaved). We were then clothed in the habit: the long black serge dress, the cincture around the waist with a heavy rosary attached, the stiff white guimpe covering the chest, the white linen cornet framing the face, the band across the skull, and then, crowning it all, the flowing black veil. We processed back into the chapel, where the bishop then read out our names: "Helena Sheehan will be known as Sister Helen Eugenie." These, we were told, were the names by which we would be known in heaven. We had been asked to submit three names in order of preference, but the name given might not be any of these. In my case, it was not. Many sisters wanted to take the names of their parents. I did not, but my superiors decided otherwise. After the ceremony, we were allowed in the grounds to visit with our invited guests. My relations fussed over me. What meant the most to me was that Ken was there. He was a Dominican seminarian now and I was so happy to see him. It was also a measure of the disparity in freedom between male and female religious orders, as

I would never have been allowed to attend a comparable ceremony for him. It was the only time I saw him during my convent years. I was deeply disappointed that Greg could not come. He had been transferred to Weston, Massachusetts, and I missed him terribly.

Our mistress of novices seemed ancient. She had been in the position for decades, presiding over the formation of several generations of nuns. She saw no reason to do anything differently from the way it had always been done. She was the type of old nun who had lived in that world for so long that she had no idea what went on outside it, no idea even of what certain words meant in the wider world. She warned us to avoid unnecessary "intercourse" with seculars and to encourage those in our care to "ejaculate" often. In her world, short prayers were called ejaculations. Life in the novitiate, especially during what was called the canonical year, was even stricter than life in the postulate. We went into deeper cloister. We had even less contact with the outside world, and no more university studies other than theology. We endured more meditation, more penance, more severe scrutiny, more merciless admonition. The occasional letters we were forced to write home were bland beyond belief. Any mention of what went on behind our cloistered walls was out, as was any reference to our personal feelings. Most letters were lyrical descriptions of nature and the change of seasons, with dutiful and clichéd praise of the glory of God. Even in such passages, any real literary flair would result in the letter being handed back for rewriting, with a strong rebuke for vanity and another exhortation to empty the self.

Meals were full of tension. Except on Sundays and first-class feasts, they were taken in silence, while a sister read aloud the assigned book of spiritual reading. Several factors contributed to stress in the refectory: the difficulty of keeping custody of the eyes when a senile older sister started acting up, the challenge of not laughing when something struck us as funny. Every morning the lives of the saints on their feast days were read at breakfast. One day it was the story of a saint who was so chaste even from infancy that he refused even his mother's breast. It set off a giddiness in me that I could not repress, no matter how hard I tried. In fact, amid such solemnity and tension, the harder one tries not to laugh, the harder it becomes to stop. Needless to say, I was made to do penance. Even for lesser offenses, such as dropping a knife at dinner, it was necessary to get up from the table, pull down our sleeves and veil, walk to the top table, kneel before the superior, kiss the floor, and ask for a penance for making an unnecessary noise. We would then kiss the floor again, rise, go to our place, kneel down, kiss the floor, say the prayers, kiss the floor once more, rise, pin up our sleeves and veil, sit down, and try to finish eating at the same time as everyone else. Trying to do all this promptly and correctly often caused such nervousness as to make it almost impossible not to then drop a fork or make some other "unnecessary noise," and be forced start the whole cycle over again.

Another regular ritual was chapter of faults. Every Friday night after recreation, lights would go out, shades would be drawn, veils pulled over faces and sleeves over hands, and one by one, we would approach the superior, kiss the floor, prostrate ourselves, and confess our infractions of the holy rule. If any sister knew of an infraction another had committed but not declared, she was obliged, in charity, to accuse her. The superior would then admonish her and give her a penance to perform. It was often a farce, because sisters consistently confessed routine infractions, such as breaking ordinary silence or failing to keep custody of the eyes, while concealing those that would bring down serious opprobrium, such as smuggling out mail or pursuing particular friendships.

We rarely ventured outside the novitiate grounds. We were not to speak to college girls if we encountered them on the campus that the mother house shared with the college. Medical appointments were a way to go out and one day I was taken to a dentist. For many reasons, it was the most memorable trip to a dentist in my life. The dentist drilled my teeth without anesthetic, using an old-fashioned, heavy drill. While he was drilling inside my mouth, workmen were drilling the pavement just outside the window. I had to take the pain without complaining or even remarking upon it. We were returning to the novitiate on a public bus when a black woman got on and, in tears, announced to everyone on board that the president had been shot. Everyone started talking and expressing their shock and sorrow. People spoke to us too, although we were not supposed to engage in any unnecessary conversation in such situations. I think that I spoke when spoken to, but I was so stunned that it is hard to remember what I did. I know I cried, which was definitely considered out of order in public. When we got back to the novitiate, the president had been pronounced dead. We prayed through our shock and tears. The Kennedy funeral was the only time we were allowed to watch television during the novitiate, and I cried all the way through. As he was not only president, but the first Catholic president, most sisters were sad and prayed for the repose of his soul, whatever they thought of his politics. In fact, most had few thoughts of politics. For me it was different, given my history campaigning for his election and for the New Frontier program. I was not to speak or think of such things during my novitiate, but I couldn't help it. I cherished the moment when I met him. They could not take it away from me. John XXIII also died that year and we mourned him, too, even as the congregation evaded the call for renewal that he issued. Together these two Johns had presided over the transformations of Church and state that inspired us so strongly in these years of transition.

While it was possible to leave the novitiate for brief medical appointments, we could not go into the hospital or stay anywhere overnight. For a time, I woke up each morning in excruciating abdominal pain. The superiors decided I needed exploratory surgery, but to avoid breaking my canonical year, I was operated on in the mother house infirmary. They opened my abdomen, but never told me what they found or did. We were forbidden to demand to know anything other than what we were told. Ever since, whenever asked about my medical history, I have had to say I had a mysterious abdominal operation when I was nineteen. I healed from the surgery, but the pains continued. To this day I don't know what was wrong, but the stress of my situation must have been at least a major contributory cause.

I persevered through the novitiate, although it was a severe struggle. I was totally alone in my battle with its contradictions and with my own irrepressible urge to rebel. I couldn't control my rebellion, either of my mind or my body. The questions wouldn't go away, nor the floods of tears at night, nor the crippling pains in the morning. I could not reconcile myself to the constant negation of what I felt so deeply should be affirmed. I could not bow to the persistent pressure to separate my soul from my mind or body. Nevertheless, there were moments of exhilaration. I remember singing the Requiem Mass in the novitiate choir after a nun in the order had died. It seemed as if the world came together and everything was in its place. There were many simple pleasures, too. My companions in the postulate and novitiate, even if they often irked me, were decent, earnest young women, who could even occasionally be fun. Despite all the privations of convent life, the food was better and more varied than what I had grown up eating.

At the end of the canonical year, we were sent down to Cape May to clean the retreat house for the sisters who would be staying in the summer. It was invigorating to leave the mother house and meditate with a view of the ocean. Nature was rarely so inspiring. We then moved back to the postulate for education studies and preparation for our first mission. During this time, Greg came to visit me. I hadn't seen him for four years. He had recently been ordained, although there was no question of my being allowed to attend his ordination or first mass. However, to receive a visit and the blessing of a newly ordained priest was considered to be a special and sacred thing. I was overjoyed to see him. I spoke to him more honestly and intimately than I had ever spoken to anyone. He listened. He prayed with me in a fresh and relevant way. He looked into my eyes. He touched my face and held my hands. He told me what was going on in the Church and in other religious orders that were not resisting change and renewal. He conveyed the searching, the liberation, the joy of it. He summarized the latest books and debates. He told me of new experiments among other orders: consultation about what studies and work to pursue, freedom to form relationships of all sorts, even intimacies between priests and nuns. My mind was soaring. My heart was thumping. It went on for hours. After he left, I was chastised by my superior for spending so much time with him, even if he was a priest. She threatened me with dismissal, saying I was critical and disobedient, that I had no idea what religious life meant. The rebuke stung, but I was not sorry. If she had known what actually transpired, she would have hit the roof. I told no one, not all of it, anyway. I did discuss some of the ideas and debates with other sisters; some were sympathetic and excited, while others were shocked and afraid.

Most religious orders were then caught between an old guard clinging to traditions and a new, questioning breed seeking change and renewal. Most priests and nuns could be placed along a spectrum between these two extremes. In my circle, I was at the one extreme, while the order as a whole was dominated by those closer to the other side. The new thought emerging in the Church affirmed my loneliest thoughts, which fed my growing confidence that I was not wrong—and that I was not alone. It was a healthier, more positive attitude, not as preoccupied with crippling negation. It supported the questioning mind and responsible commitment over unquestioning faith and blind obedience. That kept me going.

After two years, the time had come for us to leave Chestnut Hill and embark on our first missions. The mistress of novices read out our assignments. Except for the college graduate Joanne, who was assigned to high school, we would all be sent to teach grades one through five. I was hoping for fifth grade in an inner-city school. Finally, I heard: "Sister Helen Eugenie, Corpus Christi, 5G." I got fifth grade in an inner-city school, but it was a disappointment in that it was one of the few schools that divided classes into boys and girls, and I had the girls.

I arrived at Corpus Christi with two other sisters. The convent at 27th and Allegheny in North Philadelphia consisted of three ordinary row houses merged into one. Most sisters had rooms of their own, except for the youngest four of us, who shared one room. Much about a mission, especially the atmosphere in the convent, was determined by the superior. I hoped for someone open to renewal, not resisting it. My superior was neither. She was of the old guard, though she was not resisting renewal, because she had no clue about it. I turned this into an advantage. The first thing I did was acquire the book I most wanted to read: *The Nun in the World* by Cardinal Suenens. I had to ask my superior's permission to accept and to read any book. Suenens's text was hugely controversial and causing a major stir in religious orders, but she had no idea. It was by a cardinal, so why should she object? I went on in this way and received and read books by Hans Kung, Andrew Greeley, Karl Rahner, and Pierre Teilhard de Chardin. My superior's laxity allowed me to send uncensored letters to Greg and others, where I spoke of my feelings and problems with a directness I could never express in letters submitted to a superior-censor.

I threw myself into my teaching. I made tasteful and progressive decorations for my classroom. I prepared my lessons with great care. I liked being out of the cloister and mixing with people in the wider world again: the pupils, their parents, the parishioners. I volunteered for a job supervising the putting out and putting away of folding chairs for weekend functions with the eighth-grade boys. I liked the banter with the boys. During the week, I stayed after class, so the girls could come talk to me if they wanted. Soon the eighth-grade boys started coming, too, along with stray kids from other classes. This brought resentment from other sisters, particularly the one who taught the eighth-grade boys. A few accused me of courting popularity and trying to show up other teachers. The superior admonished me to stop singling myself out and doing whatever stirred up such resentment. I remembered the instruction given to Sister Luke in *The Nun's Story* to fail her examinations because another nun felt humiliated by her academic achievement. My situation wasn't as drastic, but it came from a similar place.

Further problems arose from the racial tension then wracking the parish. Riots had broken out in North Philadelphia in August

1964. It was difficult to deal with the racism of the white working-class parishioners, who feared that their livelihoods and modest properties were threatened by the arrival of black families in the area. It was even more painful to discover the racism of the pastor and principal, who wanted to impose a "legitimacy rule" to keep black kids out of the school. More than a righteous support for civil rights, it was a strong attachment to the school's black students that fired me. Sometimes they would come crying to my classroom and everything in me wanted to pull their faces toward me and caress them reassuringly. The pastor was as backward as the superior. He conducted the liturgy tediously, and saw no reason to change anything from the way it had always been done. Vatican II might as well have happened on another planet. I felt that I had to do everything in my power to bring renewal to the parish, starting with my own classroom. I was critical of the syllabus. I followed the basic structure, but tried to infuse it with vitality and meaning, moving away from rote learning and toward active engagement.

By then the election of 1964 was underway, and I was passionately for Johnson and against Goldwater. (Nuns were discouraged from politics, but allowed to vote. I could not vote, as I was only twenty, whereas most others in the convent could vote, but showed little interest in doing so, not least because both candidates were Protestant.) The civil rights movement was on the move, too. Watching news broadcasts on the march from Selma to Montgomery in spring 1965, I saw nuns walking with all the rest. Why couldn't I be doing that, I thought. I went around singing "We Shall Overcome" in my head and taught it to the kids in my class.

Nuns were treated like goddesses, not only in the parish, but on the streets. I found it especially awkward when old women would get up to give me, a healthy twenty-year-old, their seats on buses. I was happy to volunteer for any errand that would take me on public transport and into the streets—always, of course, in the company of another sister. One day I went into City Hall and looked up some of my old mentors. I had a particularly fine visit with Judge Alexander. My companion was quite charmed by him too, astonished by an encounter with such an elegant and educated black man. It was a bit beyond the bounds, especially as he was not a Catholic. From then on he regularly sent me books and letters and called when I was at Corpus Christi. One day, walking around the parish, I spotted a girl, the older sister of one of my pupils, playing guitar and singing in an alley. As I listened to the lyrics, I was mesmerized. It was as if the world was speaking to me with utmost urgency. Every word was weighty and expressed exactly what needed to be said about the world as I saw it. It was "The Times They Are A-Changin'." I stopped and asked her about the song and told her how moved I was. This, of course, was yet another instance of "unnecessary intercourse with seculars," which I had been doing a lot lately.

Eventually I reached the conclusion that virtually everything in me that was natural and human and healthy violated some convent rule, and my relation to the whole monastic ethos came to a point of crisis. The times they were a-changing, and I wanted to change, too. Around this time, Greg came to see me at Corpus Christi. He celebrated mass for the sisters in the convent chapel. It was the first time I had seen him say mass, and he did it in a manner that was more expressive, more meaningful, than any mass I had ever attended. He said my name and looked me in the eyes when he gave me communion. He came to my class and taught the kids to sing "Kumbaya." Then we talked for hours and I let loose all my stress, my questioning, my frustrations, my crushed aspirations. He listened. He sympathized. He affirmed me in my refusal to repress my thoughts or my passions. He held me. After he left, I stayed up all night crying, praying, pushing myself to the point of decision. By dawn, I had achieved some sort of clarity, and I decided to leave. The next day was one of the most difficult days of my life. I had a day's work to do as a teacher, but everything was different. I was still wearing a nun's habit and being addressed as Sister Helen Eugenie, only I didn't feel it was me anymore. I still had to arrange my departure and finish the school year, but I no longer abided so strictly by the rules. I made phone calls and mailed letters without permission. I couldn't live this way for long. I couldn't bear the feeling of not being at one with myself.

My superior was bewildered by the reasons I gave for leaving. She told me not to mention it to any of the other sisters or parishioners and sent me up to the mother house to explain myself. She was only one of many who were oblivious of the change about to sweep through the Church like a tidal wave. There were not many leaving then, but just a few years later nuns and priests would be leaving in droves. It was arranged for me to leave on the last day of the school year. I would not come to class that day, which was hard, as I couldn't say goodbye to my pupils. The other sisters were to leave for school as usual without noticing my absence, When my mother arrived with clothes, the superior brought them to me and sent me into the nearest lavatory. To be asked to remove this habit, which had been given to me in such splendor, in such a desultory fashion, infuriated me. I took it off, remembering what each part of it symbolized and how carefully I had always handled it, and left it in a heap on the lavatory floor.

I believed I was leaving for all the same reasons that I entered. I still felt called. I even considered joining another order more in tune with the whole spirit of *aggiornamento*. I did not anticipate that the questioning that had brought me this far would ultimately lead me not only away from the convent, but out of the Church altogether. People later told me that I had been "ahead of my time," that I had come too soon, that if I had waited, the institutions around me would have changed, and everything would have been all right. But by then, I too had moved on. I may have been moved by history, but I was tossed and torn at the crest of each wave and not dragged onward at the tail end of each unavoidable advance. For the time being, I still burned with the faith of our fathers (and mothers). When I sang "We shall be true to thee to death", I meant it. I felt that I would stand up for it "in spite of dungeon, fire and sword." However, not all promises, no matter how sincerely made, can be kept.

P.S. ON SSJS: ALTHOUGH I PARTED WAYS with the Sisters of Saint Joseph, whose way of life has dominated this chapter and I had little to do with them after 1965, these years decisively marked my life. Various episodes throughout subsequent years brought these years and those who shared them with me back to my attention. I saw the film *The Nun's Story* many times and I could never see it without tears. No other film has ever captured an aspect of my life experience so accurately. The convent eventually become more like what I had wanted it to be back when I was in it. Nuns could read newspapers and watch television. They could receive and read books without permission, write and receive uncensored letters, articulate their own preferences regarding their studies and their mission. They began to aim for self-actualization rather than self-abnegation. They could form healthy relationships without secrecy or suspicion. They modified the habit several times and then abandoned it, although sisters could choose to keep it. They could go back to their original names, although they were free to retain their religious names. Gone were chapter of faults and acts of humility. Summer schools became dating and mating fairs for priests and nuns. In my post-exit encounters, they told me that I was ahead of my time, that I should have stayed and all would have gone my way. However, I had moved on and it wasn't my way anymore. One of my group became mistress of novices and then left. In the 1990s, my text *Portrait of a Marxist as a Young Nun*, which had been published in various versions in a journal and an anthology, became available on the World Wide Web, generating a steady stream of email about convent life in the past, even from some SSJs. One forwarded me a list of the thirty-three of the ninety who entered with me who remained. In 1999, I visited Chestnut Hill and met sisters I knew from the past. Some were wearing shorts and sneakers. The congregational photo directory of 1998 showed page after page of pleasant-looking older women with short gray hair, glasses, and normal clothes. Among them were my former teachers, my contemporaries, and our mistress of postulants. A sprinkling of them were wearing short veils, some of them in a later modified habit. Numbers had declined drastically, as in most other orders. In 1998, they had no novices. According to their projections forward to 2007, they expected to have no sisters under forty and more than half of their membership over seventy. The days of the congregation are numbered.

This chapter bears witness to that lost world.

3

Bridge over Troubled Water

The day that I left the convent was another one of those days when the sharpest line was drawn between one way of life and another. Unlike the day I entered, when my mind was more on what was beginning than on what was ending, this day I was overwhelmed by what was ending and had no idea of what was beginning. As my mother drove us away, I could not talk to her about how I felt, but confined conversation to practical matters. We stopped and got an application for a learner's permit, so I could drive, and an application to summer school, so I could continue to work toward a degree. We talked about jobs. I was considering VISTA, a domestic equivalent of the Peace Corps. I liked working in the inner city. I arrived home, a place I had thought I would never see again. It was still a hectic and difficult household and I once again felt trapped in it. Sometimes I heard my mother talking on the phone about why I left. She would say I didn't have a vocation after all, or that I decided it wasn't for me. Once I shouted at her that I had decided it wasn't right for anybody. My parents had been proud of their daughter who was a nun and assumed their problems with me were over. Little did they know that worse was ahead. I got all sorts of reactions from others: *What a shame. What a waste. Aren't you glad it's all over? Do you regret it? Come on and tell me all the gory details.* Did I regret it? This was a question I asked myself. As I caught up with events and trends in the world, I did regret that I missed the early days of SDS, that I had not been marching for civil rights down south, that I was not further along toward a university degree. However, I knew things had to play out in the way they did, given who I was and the world into which I was born. Moreover, there was a sense in which I felt that I turned negative to positive. I had survived a years-long, near-total assault on my intellectual, emotional, moral, and bodily integrity, and was stronger for it. Not that I knew yet how to bring such strength to bear upon my life. All I knew was that I wanted to continue my education and be socially and politically involved.

The year 1965 was the most difficult year of my life. I turned twenty-one in turbulence. I struggled not to drown in the tides threatening to engulf me and to find a bridge across troubled water. On so many levels, I felt like a misfit in the world to which I returned. It was not just the Rip van Winkle effect of discovering how things had changed while I was gone. It was a feeling of being neither here nor there, of being thoroughly out of joint with my surroundings, of belonging to no clear place. Even on the most superficial level, life was strange. I struggled to adapt to wearing ordinary clothes again. I kept feeling the lack of the long flowing veil and the swish of the long heavy skirts. I was a frightful sight. I had less than a half an inch of hair on my head, having been shaved so recently. My mother bought me a wig just the right shade of red as to look like my own hair. When I went down the shore one weekend with some of my classmates from high school, I was miserable. I had found them irritating and frivolous in high school, but I had even less in common with them now. On a deeper level, I plunged into darkness. The questioning that had unsettled the foundations of convent life for me was now unleashed full force, tearing relentlessly through my whole Catholic worldview. I grew obsessed with the question of the existence of God. I went over and over all the answers in the apologetics textbooks. I struggled with logic. I prayed for faith. I managed to continue to believe, but only by a thread and through the new theology. I responded most fully to the work of Teilhard de Chardin. I loved his passionate affirmation of matter, his respect for science and reason, his world-historical and teleological grandeur.

I got a summer job in Operation Discovery, a project of the Johnson administration's "War on Poverty," intended to offer enriching experiences for inner-city kids. I was teamed up with a handsome seminarian with whom I got on well, and we took the students, all of them black, on excursions all over the city and state. We went to concerts, museums, and art galleries. The banter with co-workers and kids was so freewheeling, so easy, without all the rules and regulations and stress that stifled my interactions with pupils, parishioners, and sisters at Corpus Christi. My new freedom was heady. I could decide how to spend my time, what to read, whom to see, what to wear. I delighted in things that others took for granted.

I started summer school. I had enough college credits from my three years at Chestnut Hill to count for one year at St. Joe's. I was, unsurprisingly, exempt from all theology requirements. To qualify for any degree in a Jesuit university at that time, students were to take courses on theology and even more in philosophy. A total of twenty-four credits in philosophy was required, which suited me just fine. I started as required with logic and then proceeded to epistemology, metaphysics, ethics, and aesthetics. I also registered for classes in biology, psychology, sociology, and literature.

My first philosophy teacher was the witty and clever David Marshall, who used the classroom as a platform to talk about what-ever was on his mind. As well as entertaining us with his views on everything under the sun, he managed to make logic seem fun and fascinating, and I mastered the principles and procedures of both syllogistic and symbolic logic. I also had him for philosophy of science, ethics and aesthetics. In all these courses, he ranged through the whole history of philosophy in sweeping strokes. My next philosophy teacher was John Caputo, an ex–Christian Brother and still a postgraduate himself, who taught epistemology, metaphysics, philosophy of man, and philosophy of religion with far more rigor, demanding tighter analysis of the arguments of each thinker and less of the broad sweep. With exacting clarity, he guided me through the prime texts of modern philosophy, a fateful experience for me. He later became an academic star and advocate of post-modernist theology, a position that held no appeal for me, but he was an excellent teacher for me at this stage of my development. My literature teacher was John Mullen, well-organized, sardonic, and demanding a high level of critical reasoning and clear writing. He believed that philosophical questions were often dealt with more meaningfully in literature. He also thought that some works of science or philosophy were themselves fine literature. He introduced me to the work of physical anthropologist Loren Eiseley, through his book *The Immense Journey*. It formed my sense that factual writing could and should be as creative and as literary as fiction. Outside class, I read Maslow, Frankl, and Fromm for an alternative view to that offered by Pavlov, Watson, and Skinner in my psychology classes. The former thinkers' emphasis on the whole person, on the flow of lived experience and the search for meaning, were urgently important to me as my life world was undergoing a total transformation.

A battle of ideas was raging in most Catholic universities at this time, as the relativizing effect of Vatican II was unraveling so many accepted principles. The divide was especially sharp in philosophy, where the hegemony of scholastic philosophy was cracking. The old guard, mostly priests, considered the philosophy of Thomas Aquinas to be the last word in the discipline, and all subsequent philosophy merely a series of approximations and errors. They used textbooks written by some priest who taught modern philosophy according to the formula "Descartes was wrong because . . . ," "Kant was wrong because . . . ," and so on. The new breed—mostly laymen, but including priests and ex-priests—sought to incorporate alternative philosophies. Existentialism and phenomenology were particularly strong currents in the philosophy departments of Catholic universities. For a time, this made St. Joe's a congenial environment for my studies, and existentialist voices at first spoke most directly to my condition.

I studied philosophy with extraordinary intensity, which was a source of affectionate amusement to my teachers. When one of

them heard I was heading for the beach for the weekend, he specu-
lated that my beach towel was emblazoned with "The unexamined
life is not worth living." Such moments brought light relief from
my fierce existential angst, which nevertheless continued to weigh
heavily. Another teacher predicted a prolonged virginity for me,
because: "After all, who wants to talk about Hegel at the breakfast
table?" He must have felt it was safe to assume nobody had yet
been subjected to such discomfort, since I had only recently left
the convent and as yet had only got as far as turning into a secular
equivalent, a Heideggerian variant of "being-toward-death" after
taking off the veil. I reeked of *Sturm und Drang*. I brooded with
neantization. I ached for authenticity. One of my teachers did not
see it that way, and we bonded, to the point where I was on the
verge of losing my virginity, but he stopped and decided it was
a line we should not cross. My virginity was one thing, but my
integrity was another. Another teacher offered to pay me to write
a postgraduate paper for him. Desperate as I was financially and
flattered that he thought an undergraduate able to do his postgraduate work, my integrity was really all I had left, and I had given up
much already to keep it. He was not happy at having exposed himself without getting what he wanted. Though he believed I could
ace an A for him on his postgraduate course, he gave me a B in my
undergraduate class.

Philosophy preoccupied nearly my every waking moment. I
pondered the great questions of the ages: between idealism and
materialism, monism and pluralism, realism and conventionalism, structure and process. Above all, I weighed the arguments
for and against the existence of God, as if deciding were a matter
of life or death. Thomas Aquinas's Five Ways didn't really work for
me anymore. There was also the problem of evil. Where was God
during the Holocaust? Where was he now, as some lived in luxury
while others lived in rat-infested ghettos in Philadelphia or bomb-
devastated hamlets in Vietnam? I struggled to believe. Much of
what I read spoke of the eclipse of God, the absence of God, the
death of God. I felt the full force of these phrases. I prayed for faith.

I prayed to this hidden God, while asking myself how a hidden God was different from no God at all.

I turned every assignment into something meaningful and important for me to explore. I read texts that had enormous impact on me, such as Dostoevsky's *The Legend of the Grand Inquisitor,* Nietzsche's *Thus Spoke Zarathustra,* and Camus's *The Myth of Sisyphus.* I memorized the most arresting passages:

> Sisyphus teaches the higher fidelity that negates the gods and raises rocks. He too concludes that all is well. This universe henceforth without a master seems to him neither sterile nor futile. Each atom of that stone, each mineral flake of that night-filled mountain, in itself forms a world. The struggle itself toward the heights is enough to fill a man's heart.

Although I was still at a Catholic institution, many of these readings were on the Church's index of forbidden books, which would have filled me with foreboding in high school. By then, we hardly noticed or cared which books were on the index. It was formally abolished by Paul VI in June 1966, which was just as well, because some of the titles were already required reading for my philosophy courses.

I met new people. I liked many of my classmates, but preferred the company of my teachers. The ones I liked best were as indulgent with me as the mentors of my teenage years. I wanted to be around people who pushed me, challenged me. We formed a philosophy club comprising both faculty and students. I saw a lot of Greg during this period. I went down to Baltimore, where he was stationed, as soon as I could. Another time we met in New York, walking the streets of Manhattan all night long. We talked and laughed and even danced. There was still no one to whom I could speak with such freedom and openness. I also saw Ken again. He had left the Dominican order and entered the psychiatric ward of Philadelphia General Hospital. The story was that he had a "nervous breakdown," a term used widely and loosely then. To this day, I don't know what happened to him. We were no longer on the same wavelength. The last time I saw him he had joined the Marines. I dated quite a lot, despite the *Sturm und Drang*. I "played the field." I enjoyed male company after being so starved of it in my convent years. There was a high school teacher, a scientist, an ex-seminarian (who then became a priest after all), even a businessman. I didn't fall in love with any of them. They didn't touch me at my core. I did know what it meant to love someone, even if I had never expressed it sexually. I was seething with erotic desire, but my strongest attractions were to men who were unavailable in that way, even when we became quite close in other ways.

Through it all, I was still a Catholic. I went to mass. I attended joyfully the first masses of seminarians I knew. Around my own parish, I ran into my former classmates from primary school, whose Catholicism seemed untroubled and unchanged since eighth grade. Meanwhile, my doubts were multiplying and intensifying. In this aspect of my life, which was starting to swamp me, I felt utterly alone, no matter how many great people I had around me. I still did not know a single person who was not a religious believer. No one I knew was going through such a crisis of faith.

In the fall, I went to work as a sixth-grade teacher at Our Lady of Charity School in Brookhaven. I would have preferred to be in the city and not the suburbs, but this was what the archdiocese offered. At that time, it was unheard of for an ex-nun to continue to teach in the same school system. I won that battle, against the wishes of the order I had left, and got a job teaching in a different school staffed by a different order. I also fought for and won my appointment to teach religion as a layperson, arguing that if I had been qualified to teach it the year before, I was still qualified. I threw myself into teaching, unaware of the controversy it would provoke or of the forces moving against me. I was only a mild liberal: I taught religion in the spirit of Vatican II theology. I taught the kids to sing "We Shall Overcome" and talked about the civil rights movement down south. That was all, but in 1965, it was considered too much. I became an early casualty in the post-Vatican II struggle between the advocates of *aggiornamento* and defenders of orthodoxy.

One day in late November, I was called out of my classroom, stopping my history lesson in mid-sentence, and told by the principal-superior to go immediately downtown to the office of the superintendent of education. When I arrived, the assistant superintendent, who knew me from the previous controversy, assured me that I was an excellent teacher—and then fired me in nearly the same breath. I was right, he said, and he was on my side, but I was too controversial. Parents, priests, nuns, and fellow teachers were complaining (to everyone except to me), and I had to go. He reminded me of the grand inquisitor.

I was shocked. I tried to pray. For the first time in my life, I felt that there was no one there to hear. By the time I left his office, it was already dark, with thunder and lightning and pouring rain. I felt as if the ground had vanished from under my feet. That day, all the questions of centuries came to a crescendo in my mind. I could no longer cling to the beliefs that had sustained me in my life so far. I felt the full force of all my accumulating doubts, sending me into free fall through a void, bereft of all my bearings, deprived of all my traditions. I lost my faith, my job, my home that day. I lost the very meaning of my life, all within twenty-four hours. That morning, I had proclaimed the gospel, teaching others what, by nightfall, I would no longer believe myself. The shock jolted me toward a break that was already inevitable. When I arrived home, I told my parents, who were horrified. They sided with the school, saying I had rocked the boat once too often and that I had set a bad example for the younger children. I stormed out in anger, stuffed everything I owned that I could carry into a suitcase and left. For weeks, I walked the streets and lived out of bus terminals and railway stations. I was as alone and desperate as it was possible to be. My world was in ruins. In time, I would rebuild on new foundations. But between the collapse of one worldview and the construction of another, there was only an abyss. I often wonder where I found the strength to endure that emptiness. Maybe it was simple curiosity, a need to know: If the world was not as I had thought it was, what was it? Or perhaps it was sheer animal survival, the sort of natural evolutionary striving that brought our species up from the primal mud and the dark. Whatever it was that got me to the turning point, I did begin to find my way through a long dark tunnel, into a most intricate labyrinth. Eventually I discerned a shaft of light, which I followed to the point where I could stop stumbling in the darkness and see some kind of road ahead.

Philosophy, purged of theology, became the driving force of my life. In a way I lived through the history of philosophy in my own mind, emerging from the Middle Ages into the modern era and coming in a rush to the conflicting voices of my own time. It was exhilarating, but rigorously demanding and sometimes frightening. There were no shortcuts between the dissolution of a complete worldview and the emergence of a well-grounded alternative. A long and winding road stretched between what was lost and what was yet to be found. I was living a life of unexpected risk, of heightened responsibility, but also of new freedom. Prometheus defying the gods and seizing fire, Sisyphus negating the gods and raising rocks, Zarathustra proclaiming the death of God and the transcendence of man, Atlas, proud and unyielding, sustaining alone the world he had fashioned—these were the most powerful images illuminating the darkness and pointing beyond it. The rebellion, the higher fidelity, the transvaluation of values, the free man's worship—these were some of the crucial concepts in adjusting to a universe without a master and affirming it as neither sterile nor futile. But learning to say yes to life by searching for the meaning of life in life itself was only a beginning, an orientation. It was not enough.

Existentialism carried me through the transition to the point of taking up the challenges of my own times once again, this time more rooted in concrete experience and aware of the open-ended and precarious character of human existence. However, it had too many lacunae for me to build anything more solid on it. Its emphasis on the individual alone with his fate addressed my own isolation and alienation, but it did not do justice to the sociohistorical context of human existence (or even of the experience of isolation and alienation). Its tendency to undervalue the rational and to reject systematizing thought was a necessary counterbalance to past systems, but it could not form the basis of a new synthesis.

Nothing less than such a synthesis would do. I could not live without a comprehensive picture of the world in which I was living, without seeing my story within a larger story. Even as a child, I struggled to see things whole. I sought to grasp the totality, and could not settle for anything less. Catholicism, a ready-made totality, had nurtured this in me. The intellectual comprehensiveness and ritual grandeur of pre–Vatican II Catholicism had shaped my world. Even when the bottom fell out of it and I could no longer believe in it, leaving me raw, rootless, and roaming a world that felt like a wasteland, it nevertheless left a taste for totality I could not shake, no matter how well I subsequently learned to live without the whole supernatural dimension. Indeed, I believed that I should not shake it. It was an urge too basic to depend on the validity of one particular way of seeing the totality. I acknowledge this debt to Catholicism, however radical my rejection of nearly everything else about it. It inculcated a belief in having a comprehensive worldview and a demand for total commitment to the values flowing from it, which has stood me in good stead, even if it has been turned to purposes the Church never intended. I know all the arguments against this made by positivists, neo-positivists, existentialists, postmodernists, all the sneers about changing one religion for another, but I stand by it. It was not as if I simply took another totality off the shelf. I knew what I was leaving behind, but I did not yet know what I would find ahead.

On a practical level, I had to get a job and a place to live. At first, I found work in a downtown department store as a credit interviewer. I was to ask prospective customers a list of questions, and if certain boxes could be ticked, I could authorize credit. If the boxes could not be ticked, I had to deny it. For borderline cases, I had to consult the credit manager, who would glance out of his office to see who was standing at my hatch. I began to see a pattern. White customers were approved and black ones denied. Once I was sure of it, I confronted him, and was promptly fired. Then I had to get another job, although it was getting difficult now, having been fired twice in a matter of months. Next I worked for a market research company, doing telephone interviews about how certain advertising campaigns were received by the public. It was an intensely repressive environment. Everything was heavily monitored; even every trip to the lavatory was counted and timed. Meanwhile, I got a roof over my head. A classmate from St. Joe's, a Filipino, took me in, and I slept on her floor for a few weeks. She and her friends introduced me to the New York nightclub scene. It wasn't really for me, but I wanted to experience what I was rejecting as well as what I was embracing. As soon as I could afford it, I got an apartment of my own.

Life was hard. I completed three years of university in two years, while also working full-time at jobs I hated and traveling long distances on public transport. I studied every possible minute I could. My teachers saw how I was struggling and tried to help me. My literature teacher, John Mullen, suggested I quit my job at the market research firm and work for St. Joe's. He arranged a scheme whereby I would be paid to grade assignments and exams, starting with his own freshman composition papers. Then Dave Marshall took me on to grade his logic papers. Several others in philosophy, literature, and education did likewise, and I earned enough from this to scrape by under far better conditions than in my other jobs. I even made up with my parents, though our relationship was still strained, and moved back home for a while to make ends meet.

Above all else was the quest for a new worldview. It did not come easily. At the center was the challenge of learning to live without God, to explain the natural world without recourse to supernatural forces. Religion was not the only force in my life being called into question. It was everything. Not only in my life, but also in the world around it, everything was changing. Everything was undergoing a radical reassessment. Gender was high on the list. Finally, I found a means of understanding my extreme unease about gender in a way that allowed me to feel whole. Like many others, I was struck by Betty Friedan's *The Feminine Mystique*, and even wrote an article on the book for a college magazine. I questioned traditional definitions of masculinity and femininity. I objected to the life world of a woman confined to the beautification of the body, the seduction of men, the production of children, and the care of the home. I argued for psychological wholeness and social participation.

Situation ethics was creating a buzz at the time. Theology and moral philosophy were shifting from adherence to rules and laws toward consideration of the contingencies and exigencies of concrete situations. The idea was that it was love, not the pastor or judge, that determined whether sex was moral. It applied to matters other than sex, of course, but most of the discussion surrounding it was about sex. I broadly agreed, but needed a firmer grounding for morality. I was acutely aware of my need to build a new ethical position now that the moral precepts of religion had fallen out of the picture. I was less inclined toward case studies of isolated moral or immoral acts and more on an overall moral grounding. I focused on integrity of personality and responsibility to society. I was disposed (at least theoretically) to be flexible about sex, but believed strongly that ethics had to be about truth and justice, and I wasn't inclined to be all that flexible about deceit or injustice. So many questions. Were the answers really blowing in the wind? I wondered.

I attended my first philosophy conference, at Pennsylvania State University, in October 1966. It was on existentialism and phenomenology. In beautiful autumn weather I took the bus to the center of the state brimming with anticipation. I read the program on the way, which caught the attention of a man seated next to me, who was also going to the conference. It was the first of many conversations with philosophers during that weekend. They treated me with extraordinary seriousness and respect, given how young and new I was to such things. I attended every session and listened with awe. I was particularly impressed with Paul Ricoeur and Richard Rorty. The latter spoke of the two dominant trends in contemporary philosophy—analytic and phenomenological—and memorably articulated the insights and blind spots of both. As far as I can recall, I was the only young woman at these sessions. (There was a "ladies program" for wives.) I also met a philosopher from Duquesne, who asked if I knew a friend of his who was lecturing in theology at St. Joe's. When I told him I was avoiding the theology department, he made me promise I would get in touch with him.

Back in Philadelphia, true to my word, I went to the theology department and introduced myself to John Malinowski. We talked and talked. When I got up to leave, he offered to drive me home, although it was far out of his way. We stopped at a bar for happy hour and didn't leave for many more hours—all of them happy. After that, we were nearly inseparable. I guess it was love at first sight. It marked a change for me to feel attracted to someone who was not out of reach. Jack was good-looking, articulate, critical, conscientious—the sort of person who entered the seminary in those days, though he never did. He was in tune with all the new thinking in the Church. He was drawn more toward social activism than supernatural intervention. He grew up in Mahony City, a tiny mining town full of churches and surrounded by a devastated landscape of strip mines. He had studied history at Duquesne and theology at Notre Dame, and was earning his PhD in religion at Temple University while teaching at St. Joe's. We soon got an apartment near the college, where I lived while he came and went, fulfilling his duties as a proctor at a college dormitory.

In June 1967, I graduated from St. Joe's and married Jack. The wedding was a bit tricky to organize, as I was an agnostic, although still a very Catholic one, and Jack was still a Catholic, although a very agnostic one. Those gathered around us urged us to be married in the most liberal church in the city. There was also the fact that Jack was teaching theology at a Catholic college. I saw the need for compromise, but I was resolute in my rejection of inauthenticity.

The night before the wedding involved intense negotiations with the officiating priest, who was Jack's brother (which was already a compromise, as I would have preferred Greg). I refused to profess anything I did not believe or promise anything I would not do. I was adamant about not promising to obey. I also declined to be given away by my father. Jack and I walked up the aisle together. It was not a lavish affair. I made my own dress and he wore his best suit. We had a buffet for guests in the church basement. The bill from the caterer was far higher than we had expected, because it turned out that someone had sent an open invitation to radical Catholics all over the city, who flocked to it. It featured the latest in progressive church singing and participation. I met for the first time some of Jack's friends, such as Kevin and Dorothy Ranaghan, who were leaders of a new charismatic renewal movement in the Church who hoped to persuade Jack to join. He had shown me their letters, which kept getting stranger and stranger. I was curious to meet them. They were warm and friendly, but there was a huge gap between us. Jack and I both thought that this movement was seriously unsound. They were speaking and singing in tongues, becoming obsessed with ecstatic experiences and turning away from political engagement.

I had been intending to go away to pursue a PhD in philosophy. I applied and was accepted and offered fellowships to a number of graduate schools and planned to go to Purdue, but decided to stay in Philadelphia and do my postgraduate studies at Temple, because of Jack. It was a compromise, not only in city, but in milieu. I wanted to move away from Catholic circles and study in a more secular setting, focusing on philosophy, not theology. I was now in a secular institution, but still surrounded by a Catholic subculture, particularly the radical Catholic set. At the same time, my relation to religion still felt far from settled. I was an agnostic, but it was a deeply uncomfortable position. I still wrestled with basic cosmological questions. For my PhD, I took courses in religion, philosophy, and history, primarily at Temple, but also at the University of Pennsylvania and City University of New York.

Many of my fellow graduate students were Catholics, some of them ex-priests in the first days of their laicized lives. They were great company and we had much in common, but they were still within the Church in ways that I wasn't. They would react indignantly to the latest statement by Cardinal Krol, but I no longer cared what he said. They were organizing underground masses. They sang and played guitar beautifully, but I couldn't believe with them that bread and wine became the body and blood of Christ. They asked me to sign a petition supporting the ordination of women. I would have gladly done so a few years earlier, but since I no longer saw the point of having priests at all, the gesture felt pointless.

Another issue was that they were only discovering sex, as indeed was I, but they went on as if it made the world go round. When some of these ex-priests and ex-nuns married, they threw themselves into it with almost fanatical fervor. There was something positive in the commitment to celibacy, I thought. I rejected the denigration of the body and sexuality, but accepted the argument that celibacy helped free a person to serve others. I wanted to affirm sex and intimate relationships while prioritizing commitment to the wider world. We were all finding our way to new identities and ways of life. I arranged for one couple, an ex-priest and ex-nun, to be married by Judge Alexander in his chambers in City Hall, who even had champagne on hand. Another pair had a much-publicized wedding where the groom wore his Roman collar and the bride wore traditional white dress and veil, a stunt that bordered on street theater, which was then coming into vogue. I was surprised to find myself married at all. It hadn't been part of my plan. I didn't especially like the idea of marriage, though I lacked a coherent critique of it. The many married couples around me seemed too self-obsessed, too domestic, too coupled, too content. As Jack and I joined our lives together, we felt committed not only to look to each other, but to look together to the world. We were far more engaged in the politics of the era than some of those around us. However, I didn't want to be Mrs. Malinowski. At first I thought only movie stars had any choice in the matter of name change, but I soon went back to being Miss Sheehan and then Ms. Sheehan, while aspiring to be Dr. Sheehan. At St. Joe's I became a "faculty wife," though I refused to join the faculty wives' club. In our years together, Jack and I were visited by a stream of priests, and occasionally nuns, sharing with us their sexual crises. They had promised celibacy and made vows of chastity at a young age and in a different world than the one in which they were now living. They hardly knew what they were renouncing. They had given many more years to religious life than I had and struggled far more to come to terms with the transition. One of them was Greg. One night he came to our apartment for dinner and the three of us had a spirited and convivial conversation about the great issues of the times. Then Jack went to bed, leaving Greg and me to talk into the night. As a Joan Baez record played in the background, he revealed to me his realization of his homosexuality and his struggle about what to do about it. I held his hands and felt his concerns flow into me. I had not seen this coming. I worried about what it would mean for him. He left the Jesuits not long after that and began, at forty-one, a search for another path that would take him out of the Church as well.

In my studies, I was particularly fascinated by the history of ideas, by the way systems of thought were rooted in their socio-historical contexts. This marked a sharp break from my earlier quasi-Platonic conception of ideas. I made the history of philosophy my own during these years. Even if I would later question the canonical version of that history that I accepted then, it was important that I immersed myself in it as I did. I saw it as the story of our species struggling to conceptualize the universe. I was riveted by the ways that perennial questions found distinctive expression in each era, tied to the movements of history and the development of other social forces. It was a major revelation to look back in time to find that neither our bodies nor our minds, neither our ideas nor our institutions, had sprung fully formed from the hands of a creator, but emerged through a long and complex evolutionary history. Many of our courses took the form of delivering and defending papers and interacting with our professors and peers as they too did so. It was rigorous and challenging. The intellectual standard of both professors and peers was very high. If we disagreed, as we often did, each side had to mount a strong case. We were highly respected when we did so well. We were not only making our careers but seeking truth, even while utterly aware of all the problems and ambiguities in the concept of truth itself.

I was studying religion in a radically different way, focusing on the challenges of science, historicity, secularization. None of my fellow students were atheists, but they held on to their religious traditions in increasingly complex ways. Although I was an agnostic, I still needed to define my relationship to religion in general and Christianity in particular. There was much ferment around the reformulation of Christianity in light of the challenges posed by new developments in knowledge, from empirical discoveries in science to questioning of the theoretical foundations of the humanities, as well as the changing character of contemporary experience. Many of the leading thinkers in this movement were Protestants, often ordained ministers and professors of divinity. Books such as Harvey Cox's *The Secular City*, Paul van Buren's *The Secular Meaning of the Gospel*, and Van Harvey's *The Historian and the Believer* were creating quite a stir in the mid-1960s. We were also rediscovering older writers who had been going in this direction, such as Dietrich Bonhoeffer, the Lutheran pastor who had participated in a plot to assassinate Hitler and was executed in 1945. In his prison writings, he spoke of a world coming of age and compelled to live without the tutelage of God. In 1966, *Time* magazine ran a cover article on the "Death of God movement," which was much discussed in my circles. In this new environment, I wanted to understand the origins and evolution of religion and come to a clear position on its historical role and truth value. My emphasis was primarily on the philosophy of religion, but also on its history and psychology and sociology of religion within a broader sociohistorical context.

I explored alternative philosophical approaches, not only to religion, but to everything. I continued to study existentialism and phenomenology, while branching out to analytic philosophy and process philosophy. My outlook was becoming more and more empiricist. I insisted on the rigorous use of logic and evidence, but much analytic philosophy struck me as banal, arriving pretentiously at conclusions that were boringly obvious. Often its efforts to achieve conceptual clarity came at the cost of creativity, scope, and depth. Nevertheless, I had to master it and learn as much from it as I could, even as I found radical empiricism and pragmatism more productive than positivism or neo-positivism. Both saw the foundations of knowledge in sense experience, but the latter tended to a world of static and disconnected facts, whereas the former focused on the flow of experience and the interconnections and contexts of facts.

A lively debate was then unfolding in analytic philosophy over the analysis of religious language. Much of the literature arose in response to an article by Antony Flew, which began with a parable. Once upon a time, two explorers came upon a clearing in a jungle, full of flowers and weeds. One remarked that there must be a gardener tending the plot, but the other disagreed. They set a watch to find out, but no gardener was ever seen. The believer said it must be an invisible gardener. They then set up a barbed wire fence and patrolled it with bloodhounds, but still found no evidence of a gardener. The believer insisted there must be a gardener—invisible, intangible, and insensible to electric shocks, with no scent and making no sound. The skeptic then despaired, asking how an invisible, intangible, eternally elusive gardener differed from an imaginary gardener, or even from no gardener at all. Flew concluded that the original assertion had in effect suffered death by a thousand qualifications. Many theologians and philosophers of religion took up the challenge and sought various ways to redeem the believer's position, primarily by arguing that religious language was not a matter of factual assertion or metaphysical explanation, but a symbolic expression of hopes and values. A player in this debate was Paul van Buren, my PhD supervisor. He refused to choose between theism and atheism and instead refocused the issue in terms of a plurality of "language games," each with distinct and sometimes incommensurable criteria, as a way to defend religious expression from being judged by the standards of scientific or metaphysical language. He even proposed that we write a book together. I was flattered and considered the idea, but by then my thinking had veered ever further from his. I rejected the emphasis on the discontinuity of language games with radically different criteria appropriate to each. I felt it let the theologians off too easily. I wasn't reductionist, but I defended the continuity of criteria. Even if metaphorical or mythical language couldn't be judged by the same norms as literal, descriptive, or explanatory language, religious language did make factual claims and engage in metaphysical explanations, and so couldn't be exempt from the standards of logic and evidence applied elsewhere. Despite all the sophisticated skirting around this issue, I eventually had to face the fact that there either was or was not a supreme being who created the universe.

Our ethics seminars with John Raines were vigorous discussions of alternative philosophical foundations for morality as well as the specific moral dilemmas of our times. Raines insisted that morality was not just about what went on in bourgeois bedrooms, but what happened in the streets and in the corridors of power. We were very fond of him, but we all tried to sit as far from him as possible, as he puffed on a big cigar at the head of the seminar table. Before he arrived we opened every window in the classroom for the sake of those who would end up seated close to him. My course in biblical criticism was a fascinating contrast with a New Testament course that I had taken at Chestnut Hill. It was taught by Gerard Sloyan, a Catholic priest who initially looked and sounded very straightlaced, but brought a rigorously scholarly and radically honest approach to problems regarding the historicity of biblical texts. Although absolutes were generally out and relativity was in, one professor believed in an Absolute, however relative its forms. Bernard Phillips was chair of the department, and every first-year graduate student took his course on world religions. Some found him mesmerizing. He was certainly interesting. He himself had experience of every major world religion, having successively converted to each of them. Born into Judaism, he was in an Islamic phase at the time, fasting for Ramadan as he delivered his lectures. I did not see him as a guru, although others did. Grading my papers, he decried my relativist and empiricist "orthodoxies." I did try to give a clear and fair account of each of the religions we studied, even if I interpreted their supernatural claims from a naturalist perspective.

I had become convinced, through the arguments of Feuerbach, Durkheim, and Freud, that gods in the heavens were projections of men on earth, that varying ideas of god reflected changes in sociohistorical circumstances. The shift from polytheism to monotheism came with the increasingly complex organization of society. God was an idealized humanity, and the supernatural world was the glorified natural world. Theology was actually anthropology. My questions then became: Once we understand God as the imaginative projection of man, a symbol of our own values and desires, where do we go from there? Once we see our religious traditions as products of the development of human societies, how do we relate to them? More starkly: How do we understand our myths once we recognize them as myths? I argued for a symbolic interpretation of religious language, that still allowed for a way to engage with the stories that shaped us and our ancestors without violating the more advanced knowledge of our age.

I developed my position in terms of myth. Myths were paradigmatic stories, expressing universal themes of human existence: birth and death, initiation and estrangement, good and evil, war and peace, ignorance and enlightenment, quest and fulfillment, exile and promised land, golden age and apocalypse. Myths gave symbolic answers to basic questions. The story of Christianity was still my story, in a sense. I didn't have to renounce it any more than I had to renounce Greek or Celtic mythology. I saw Adam and Eve, David and Goliath, Moses, Job, and Jesus as mythical characters in the same sense as Odysseus, Prometheus, Sisyphus, Socrates, Buddha, Cuchulainn, and Robin Hood. That Buddha, Socrates, and Jesus were historical persons did not make them any less mythic. There was much talk then about "de-mythologizing" Christianity, as thinkers like Rudolf Bultmann and Jurgen Moltmann argued the need to strip religion of myth. I thought, on the contrary, that it made more sense to strip myth of religion. To me, the point was to re-mythologize, to see our myths as myths, and to reinterpret them in a way that was true to contemporary experience. This was far easier said than done. If religion was not what I thought it was, then I wanted to know what it was. I had invested so much thought, energy, creativity, and commitment in it, as had generations before me. I remember once leaving a philosophy of religion seminar and hearing Gregorian chant resounding from a chapel on campus. I felt the pull of both. Nevertheless, I had to choose contemporary knowledge and find a new relationship to the superseded beliefs of our species.

I was laying the foundations of a new worldview, taking elements from various periods in the history of philosophy, including contemporary trends. Analytic philosophy, then focusing on the study of language, was a strong presence at Temple, and I learned a lot from it. It sharpened my arguments, compelling me to anticipate challenges from this direction. Nevertheless, I rejected the narrowness of its horizons and its dismissive attitude toward the whole history of philosophy before it. I was much more enthusiastic about pragmatism, radical empiricism, and process philosophy. I thought it was in these areas that the United States had made a real contribution to the history of philosophy. I studied Peirce, James, Dewey, Whitehead. I was especially drawn to John Dewey. I agreed with the prevailing consensus that we had to renounce the quest for certainty, but also believed that we could find grounds for warranted assertability, which was no small thing. I sought out the works of contemporary philosophers working in this vein, such as John Herman Randall at Columbia and Eugene Fontinell at Queens College, and wrote my master's thesis on this current,

focusing on naturalistic interpretations of religious experience.
Although I was reading widely and learning from many sources,
I was not interested in an eclectic combination of elements from
various philosophies. I wanted to work out a synthesis, a philosophical position that would ground my thinking about everything. I
sought an alternative to either positivist objectivism or idealist
subjectivism. I developed a perspective that was processive, con-
textual, naturalistic, holistic. I believed that the natural world had
to be explained by natural forces, with no recourse to supernatural ones. I shifted from a metaphysics based on static categories
of substance and accident to a more dynamic one of process and
relation. I moved from a correspondence theory of truth to a par-
ticipational one. Knowledge lay neither in subject or object, but in
interaction between ourselves and the world. There was no subject
without object and no object without subject, and no knowledge
was untouched by sociohistorical forces. I was concerned to cut
through the dualisms that characterized many philosophical
debates: facts versus values, object versus subject, reason versus
emotion, mind versus body, analysis versus imagination, science
versus humanities. This all might sound rarefied or abstruse, but it
shaped my thinking in the most everyday way. It gave me a line of
approach, a clarity that cut through confusion. It gave me traction.
I began to feel as if I were no longer blowing in the wind.

From my first year at Temple, I worked as a teaching assistant. At first I taught an introductory course called "Religion and
Human Life," which was so popular that it was offered in nearly
every possible schedule slot and took a huge team to teach. It was
not organized around a professor lecturing while teaching assistants led seminars and graded exams. Each of us had complete
charge of our own class and did everything from lecturing to
assessing. We did follow a common syllabus. It began with *Waiting
for Godot* and progressed through philosophical, sociological, and
literary approaches to religion and then to an overview of major
world religions. Teaching assistants had a common office where
we discussed pedagogical approaches to our classes, exchanged

choice quotations from our students, explored possible topics for our seminar papers and doctoral theses, and had many good laughs. The collegiality was great. The atmosphere in university classrooms in those days has become the stuff of legend. Students clamored for material relevant to their own concerns and experiences, and I totally sympathized. We had intense, meaningful discussions. Many students in the late 1960s tended to romanticize Eastern religions, seeing in them a panacea for all that ailed the West, and I tried to lead them toward a more nuanced understanding. I took care not to let class discussions wander too much, and was sure to cover the material in the syllabus. I was also strict about grades, as I did believe in differential assessment, despite students' demands to abolish them. I valued logic, evidence, and reflection over unfounded opinion, and defended these principles to my students.

Next I taught a second-year course on religion and contemporary thought, which strongly emphasized philosophical critiques of religion and corresponding contemporary approaches to the reconstruction of religion. Eventually, I progressed to a course on nineteenth- and twentieth-century intellectual history that could be taken by undergraduates or postgraduates. When I arrived on the first day, I discovered that everyone taking the class was not only doing so for graduate credit, but they were all also substantially older than I was. There were several priests among them, and even one SSJ. One told me that I looked too young to be taking the course, being a particularly young-looking twenty-five-year-old wearing a miniskirt, before I went to the front of the class to teach it. I struggled to establish my credibility, but I think I succeeded. I loved university teaching. I felt born to do it.

My first academic publications appeared at this time in the *Journal of Ecumenical Studies*, based at Temple and edited by Leonard and Arlene Swidler. They regularly gave me philosophical books to review. Len had been Jack's teacher back in Duquesne, and we all lived in the same apartment building. We baby-sat for them, and they in turn extended many kindnesses to us. They were

radical Catholics who believed in fighting for what they thought
was right and good within the Church. Although I had abandoned
all that, I couldn't help admiring their persistence. They were also
far more *au fait* with high culture than we were and we imbibed a
lot from them. They bought us season tickets to a classical concert
series as a wedding present, and invited us to many other events we
might have missed otherwise. Their knowledge of European intellectual culture likewise impressed us.

I got on well with most of my professors and peers, though inevitably better with some than others. Some I saw only in class, while
others were integral to our social lives. There were many dinner
parties. While we all usually worked in relative harmony, there
were moments of discord. In one course, which I thought would
be a breeze since I had already read much of the literature on my
own, the relation between curricular and extracurricular dimensions went awry. The professor seemed all right at first, although
I immediately noticed his irritating tendency to quote his own
writing constantly. He asked me to dinner, and I went. It was not
unusual for me to have intellectual discussions with men over
lunch or dinner. When he groped me in the elevator at the faculty club, I didn't know what to do, so I carried on politely through
dinner as if nothing had happened. When he dropped me off at my
apartment and I had to force my way out of the car, it made all the
talk of "I-Thou" relationships seem ridiculous. Today it would be
called sexual harassment, but we didn't have that vocabulary then. I
was relatively inexperienced about these things, as I could never see
sexual advances coming, and thought that maybe I had missed cues
and given off wrong signals. Later, assigning a paper for the course,
he told me he wanted me to focus on his work, saying, "I want you
to encounter *me*." On this I was defiant, and wrote a paper without
a single reference to him or his books. I received a B, although I was
an A-student in all my other courses. His egotistical and bullying
behavior surrounding my paper bothered me even more than the
grotesque groping. I reported him. It was discussed by department
faculty, but as far as I knew, there were no consequences.

Of course, it was the 1960s, and norms of sexual morality were changing. We were rethinking all this. The following year, when another professor made advances, I did not resist. It was my first affair. I was excited by the fusion of the intellectual and sexual charge between us. I told no one, although I told no lies either. It was obvious to all that we got on exceptionally well. As it was ending, I told Jack. We were both finding our way to a new morality, and we talked it through in this way. I did not believe one person had exclusive rights over the intimacies of another. I thought that fidelity was something much deeper and much different than mere monogamy. It meant being honest, though this did not necessarily mean disclosing details of intimacies with others. It definitely meant telling no lies. It meant being emotionally present for a person in far more complex ways. Another aspect of this affair, of course, was the student-teacher dimension. I took a much more permissive view of these involvements as a student than I did as a teacher. While student-teacher dynamics between adults at times carry an undeniable erotic charge, they are nevertheless defined by relations of power and privilege that make sexual intimacy unwise and often deeply harmful, at least as long as the teacher-student relationship is ongoing.

I attended many stimulating conferences in these years, such as those of the American Philosophical Association, the American Academy of Religion, and the Society for Values in Higher Education. For one of these, I flew in a plane for the first time, to Boston from Philadelphia, and took my first trip outside the country in 1968. At the end of a stiflingly hot summer in Philadelphia studying for exams, Jack and I drove up to Canada. We went to Montreal and saw what was left of Expo 67. Not inclined to the anti-technological romanticism coloring sections of the emerging counterculture, I was instead excited by the futuristic atmosphere and wondered what sort of world I would live to see. We also saw Pete Seeger play a concert there, and he projected such an aura of human warmth and solidarity that I glowed with it. Later, as we walked down a dark alley, we spotted him walking a bit ahead on the other side, carrying his banjo, humble and alone. I wanted to speak to him, but wasn't sure what to say, and didn't.

I felt alive, engaged, and happy. The convent seemed to belong to another era of history. It was hard to believe I ever put up with it or hesitated to leave. One day I returned to Chestnut Hill for the first time since I had left four years earlier. I was going to the college, rather than to the mother house, having been invited by a professor there to participate in a seminar. On campus I ran into some nuns who entered with me, who were now wearing a modified habit. The skirt had come up a few inches, the veil was shorter, the guimpe was abandoned, and their chins were bare. They excitedly told me how they could now drive and go bowling. They said I should have stayed, because it was all different now. It was hard to tell them how far I had moved from it all. I was glad to see them, but the gap between us was wider than ever.

I was still ardently seeking meaning, but felt less isolated in my search. At the same time that I felt a burning need for change, both in the world and in myself, others expressed similar needs, and the times were truly a-changing. Perhaps there was no better time for someone to endure a crisis of worldview, because such crises seemed to be the agenda of the times. I had a sense of call and answer, a longing to know the world that seemed to echo all around me. The big questions were in the air and sometimes the answers were too, blowing in the wind. The folk music of the time resonated with such force. Over and over I played the songs of Bob Dylan, Leonard Cohen, Simon and Garfunkel, Joan Baez, Tom Paxton, and Pete Seeger, and pondering their words and voices. These songs seemed such a fitting soundtrack to the world as I was living it. The words seemed so much more profound than the tunes we heard when we were young, such as "By the Light of the Silvery Moon" or "Stranger in the Night," or even those to which our own generation rallied in adolescence, such as "Hound Dog," "Heartbreak Hotel," or "Blueberry Hill." They were not just about romantic relationships. They seemed to reach down into the psyche and out into the social order.

Movies, too, vibrated with meaning. The films of Ingmar Bergman, especially those dealing with faith and doubt, such as *Winter Light*, captured my inner dilemmas so artfully and appropriately. At a Bergman festival held at the art house cinema that Jack and I frequented, I was awed by the films' intellectual, emotional, and sensory intensity. Some of the other iconic movies of the era, such as *Easy Rider* and *Midnight Cowboy*, excited me less. I didn't identify with drug-dealing bikers and street hustlers as symbolic of the era as I lived and understood it. I didn't see much television during these years, but I didn't agree with academics who disparaged television as "the idiot box" and boasted of not allowing one in their house. I felt television was a medium with great potential, even if I didn't have much time to watch it.

There were so many questioning and challenging books appearing then. I read everything by Loren Eiseley, who had just published *The Unexpected Universe*. I incorporated his work into my doctoral thesis, citing him as an example of the powerful use of metaphorical language in dealing with cosmological questions. His writing wove together autobiography, philosophy, science, literature with grace and eloquence. As he was not far away, teaching physical anthropology at Penn, I asked to interview him. As I soon learned, meeting authors whose writing you admire does not always work out. He was cordial and helpful, but less articulate in speech than in writing. (I wondered if this had roots in his childhood, much of which he spent in relative silence and solitude, with a deaf mother and an often-absent father.) There were also older books that I was only just discovering. Helen Waddell's *Peter Abelard* was another example of writing about big ideas that were exquisite as literature. The book's themes of reason and dogma, teachers and students, and forbidden love resonated strongly with me.

By summer 1970, I was nearing the end of my three years of PhD coursework, having passed my comprehensive examinations with distinction, as well as my language exams and oral defense of my thesis proposal. I was ready to move on to the next phase: writing my doctoral thesis. This would take further my exploration of the naturalistic analysis of religion, focusing on metaphor as a way of relating to mystery, on the role of myth and the function of paradigmatic stories. I had been nominated for two national fellowships by my supervisor so that I could work on my thesis full-time, and was awarded both. Temple mobilized their publicity department to advertise these awards, which brought me an unexpected flurry of local media attention. The *Philadelphia Inquirer* sent a reporter and photographer to profile me. The article was well-intended, but my views got garbled in the writing and editing. The story of an ex-nun questioning the foundations of religion and joining the new intellectual movements of the time stirred much interest. I was then asked to go on a popular television talk show, where I gave a long interview telling my story and explaining my views. The station forwarded to me a huge bag of letters in response, many of which could be categorized as hate mail. Not long after, I gave a public lecture at Villanova on women's liberation to an audience packed with hostile nuns. My invitations to give public lectures multiplied. All this took me by surprise, and I had to learn to deal with it as I went along. The experience pushed me toward becoming a (minor) public intellectual. I still believe that academic voices should be heard in the mass media, and that academics should learn to distill their views in widely accessible ways. I only wish that someone more experienced in this area had been around to advise me before I was plunged into it.

One of my fellowships came with a requirement to attend annual conferences with other fellows over a three-year period. The first was in Santa Fe and was most unusual. As well as some talks, there were many sessions built around "encounter groups" and experimental games. One day we were divided into teams, deposited on the side of a mountain, and told to invent a culture from scratch. I didn't think it worked, but it was certainly an experience. The emphasis at the conference was on our role as a new generation of university educators. We discussed the novel ideas challenging every academic discipline and the relation of the university to the many movements bursting forth both within and outside it. Politically, everyone there was on a spectrum ranging from liberal to radical. Some really got on my nerves, as I thought that they wanted to be radical in a way that was too cozy and involved no real risk. One woman responded to a remark Jack made about draft and tax resistance (spouses were also invited to attend) as if these were no more than lifestyle choices. Others, however, seemed to be genuinely seeking a new way of life, with much talk of a "new man" and the relationship between psychic and political liberation. I kept in contact with some people I met there, such as Marilyn French, who became famous as a feminist novelist, and Julius Lester, later a provocative speaker about the "Woodstock Nation" he claimed we were building.

After the conference, we explored the Southwest, which I found amazing. I could hardly believe we were in the same country. The vast open spaces, the warm, dry air, the aboriginal cultures, were all in such contrast to the East Coast. We saw a stunning sunrise at the Grand Canyon and sunset in the Painted Desert. Most memorable was Mesa Verde, where I had an ecstatic experience beholding the pueblo cliff dwellings and felt a visceral sense of an animistic worldview and the long, hard struggle to conceptualize the universe of which the cliffs' long-dead inhabitants and I were all part. We drove to the wilds around Los Alamos, visiting activists from Philadelphia who had retreated there for a time. We passed right through Las Vegas, but lingered in Albuquerque as long as we could. Then we returned to Philadelphia, where I was free to spend my days writing my thesis. I had much of it drafted already. I expected to submit it by 1972 and become a university professor shortly thereafter.

That was yet another plan that went awry.

4

The Times They Are A-Changin'

Ever since the day I heard that girl in the alley singing "The Times They Are A Changin'," something stirred in me that would not be suppressed. As the 1960s unfolded, this feeling grew ever stronger. It stepped up its tempo, deepening and expanding with each passing year. The soundtrack of the times was full of songs that captured my sensibility, quickened my pulse, challenged my perceptions, and spurred me to action. Sometimes their meaning shifted. When I first started singing "We Shall Overcome," it was to defy cosmic evil generally and Southern racism specifically. I saw the Kennedy and Johnson administrations as basically on "our" side and the political system as basically sound, if in need of serious reform. With time, it became the administration and even the system itself that I hoped to overcome. Before too long, it was not only "Faith of Our Fathers" that I could no longer sing, but "The Star-Spangled Banner" as well. At the ceremony where I received my master's degree from Temple, I refused to stand for it, as did others scattered through the hall.

The consensus that characterized our youth was rapidly disintegrating. The discordant notes became more frequent and furious. Questioning that began in response to particular injustices swelled into a critique of capitalism, which no longer saw racism, sexism, poverty, and war as isolated phenomena that occurred in spite of the system, but as interconnected manifestations of the system itself. Movements for specific reforms converged and adopted the rhetoric of revolution. Peaceful protests erupted into increasingly bitter and violent confrontations. Opposition to the war in Vietnam turned into active resistance to the military-industrial complex and all its works. For those of us who joined this emergent New Left, life changed suddenly and dramatically. There had been a profound shift of mood, reaching into virtually every corner of American life. No one could remain untouched by it. Families were torn apart. The American dream had become a nightmare, ironically at the peak of its material fulfilment (at least for the white middle class). The polarization intensified as each of the mass movements spawned increasingly radical successors. Some who started in simple opposition to US policy in Vietnam came to support the other side. Protesters did not just chant "Hey, hey, LBJ, how many kids did you kill today?" but also "Ho, Ho, Ho Chi Minh, the NLF is going to win." Flags of the National Liberation Front, the Viet Cong, began to appear at antiwar demonstrations. At first, I was shocked, because I was against the war, but didn't support the other side. Before long, I did.

Despite my preoccupation with philosophical matters during my university studies, I was evolving politically as well as philosophically. I was struggling to understand the social order as well as the cosmic context. One day in the mid-'60s I saw a television interview with SDS leader Tom Hayden in which he articulated the vision embodied in the *Port Huron Statement*. I got a copy and read it. It said almost exactly what I thought or was on the verge of thinking. It spoke powerfully to my estrangement from what had been familiar and my longing toward something unfamiliar but irresistible: "We are people of this generation, bred in at least modest comfort, housed now in universities, looking uncomfortably to the world we inherit."

Students for a Democratic Society was founded in Ann Arbor in 1960 and the *Port Huron Statement* was adopted in 1962, though neither was on my radar at the time. By the time I got clued in to these developments, I felt I had missed something important. By the mid-'60s, SDS had spread to many campuses, but not Chestnut Hill or St. Joe's. By the time I got to Temple in 1967 and joined SDS there, the best of it was over. I expected to find people like Tom Hayden, Paul Potter, Todd Gitlin, and Carl Oglesby, who wrote powerfully of a political sensibility, and whom I admired from a distance. Instead the dominant atmosphere at Temple seemed more old left than new, increasingly dogmatic and riven by factionalism, giving off an air that felt somehow alien. I was moving further to the left, but I was not a Marxist.

For many of us, the Vietnam War opened our eyes to the nature of the system under which we lived and provoked a breach that would never be healed. On my first or second date with Jack, he launched into a brief history of Vietnam, with special emphasis on the role of US foreign policy. It wouldn't have been everyone's idea of a good time, but it was mine. Protests against the war became an integral part of our lives. We marched not only in and around Philadelphia, but wherever mobilizations called upon us to go, especially to Washington. We marched on the Pentagon in 1967. It was like nothing I had ever experienced. There were more people than I had ever seen in one place, a sea of faces as far as you could see, in every direction. I thought the power represented by the Pentagon had to crumble in the face of the power of the people who were converging upon it that day. However naive that came to seem later, it was how I felt on that day. It did not come as a surprise that the Yippies failed to levitate the building, but it was a source of disillusionment over time that our voices had so much less impact than we felt they deserved. I still thought that truth and justice would somehow prevail. I did not understand power.

The draft was a difficult issue. University teachers and students had deferments and women were exempt. Refusing to accept this privileged status, we engaged in draft resistance along with those in the front line of the draft, who were disproportionately poor and black. One slogan in vogue was "Girls say yes to guys who say no." Draft cards were burned at rallies, often held at symbolic sites such as Independence Hall. Others returned their draft cards or refused to go when drafted, often resulting in imprisonment. Although he had a teacher's deferment, Jack sent his draft card to his local board with an explanation of his opposition to the war. We held our breath waiting for the consequences. I saw friends sent to federal prison as conscientious objectors. I often visited them there or took part in demonstrations of solidarity inside the courts and outside the prisons. One of my first acts of civil disobedience was at Lewisburg federal prison, where we trespassed and broke through a line of guards. We could hear prisoners cry "Freedom!" from the other side of the wall, and it was exhilarating to feel the shared struggle between those of us on both sides of the wall. We also had joyous celebrations welcoming them home when they were released. I remember a particularly happy night at the party thrown by Philadelphia Resistance for Bob Eaton upon his release after three years.

My family was hostile to draft resisters and my father was particularly offended that my husband was one of them. My brother Gene volunteered rather than be drafted. My brother Mark came of age when the draft lottery was introduced and put his plans on hold until the draw was made. His birthday was not drawn and he instead went to teacher training college, where he became more critical of the war. At one family gathering, an argument broke out on the My Lai massacre, one brother called the other "Lieutenant Calley," and they tumbled around on the floor until they were torn apart. On another occasion, at a protest at Fort Dix, we were confronted with troops wearing helmets and gas masks, pointing guns with bayonets at us. I wondered if one of them was my brother, who was stationed there at the time. We affixed leaflets to their bayonets.

Most family contact was fraught during these years. My aunt's husband was an accountant and a graduate of St. Joe's, and he liked to use his college degree to his advantage in an argument. He was from a working-class environment where few had degrees. He often referred to the logic course he had taken, as if that copper-fastened his authority, even when he was being completely illogical (aided by alcohol). He did it even when arguing with me and Jack, although I was also a graduate of St. Joe's and Jack was a teacher there. My aunt deplored my feminism too, particularly the fact that I insisted on being Ms. Sheehan and not Mrs. Malinowski. "I'm proud to be Mrs. Charlie Smith," she would declare. It never ended well.

It was nearly an atmosphere of civil war. Civil society was torn apart. Families were split down the middle. At times, we even shocked ourselves by how far we had come, and how quickly. A slogan of the day was "We are the people our parents warned us against." We could no longer sit down cozily to dinner together. At one Thanksgiving, it all erupted furiously. It was not only the tension between my brother and me on opposite sides of the barricades (he was in a chemical and biological unit of the army, and, as far as I knew, transporting nerve gas to Thailand). It was a total clash of worldviews, with one fault line after another opening, with most of my family on one side and Jack and me on the other. I reached a breaking point when my father raved about Frank Rizzo, a right-wing police commissioner who became mayor of Philadelphia, and my grandmother chimed in to praise him for "putting those Negroes in their place." I called them cozy, conformist, and cowardly. I stormed out. I didn't speak to anyone in my family for months after that.

A battle of ideas and a struggle for power was raging, and we who had grown up together, sat in the same classrooms, even formed strong bonds of affection, were on the opposite sides. I was particularly conscious of Ken James, so important to me in my high school and convent years, who had joined the Marines. I wondered what he was thinking and doing about it all. It made me terribly sad to think of him on the other side. Some of my early mentors were likewise on the other side. One who had taken me under his wing during the Kennedy campaign, met me for lunch one day and expressed racist views that made me feel deeply disappointed. I had to face the fact that those who helped me to grow along the way would no longer be walking further along with me. One day, while demonstrating against Richard Nixon's appearance at a convention of Catholic educators, I saw Nixon himself pass by in his car. I looked at him with revulsion and clenched my fist, while all around me were priests and nuns, some of whom had been my friends in the novitiate, waving and cheering him. It was an experience I was destined to repeat many times in these years. The confrontations between them and us were becoming more and more extreme. It was a time increasingly marked by marches and occupations, denunciations and arrests, trials and prisons.

The election of 1968 was the first presidential contest in which I could vote. I had longed to vote in 1960 and 1964, and supported Kennedy and Johnson wholeheartedly. By 1968, my enthusiasm for electoral politics was well past its peak. The voices expressing my sense of the world were all outside the electoral arena. Those inside it sounded so myopic, compromised, and bland by comparison. Nevertheless, I could not abstain. I supported Eugene McCarthy in the primary. I did not think Robert Kennedy's entry into the campaign was a good idea, as it split the antiwar vote, but I was stunned and saddened when he was assassinated. I beheld the protests on the streets of Chicago during the Democratic Party convention and wished I were there.

I found it amazing and appalling in that wondrous year of 1968 that our political system presented us with a choice between Hubert Humphrey and Richard Nixon. It was also the year where we beheld the ferment we felt at home taking fascinating forms abroad. We cheered on the events of that spring in Prague and Paris, although we sadly saw their efforts overtaken, as were ours. Their inspiring slogans, such as "Power to the imagination," lived on in our minds. In Prague, we watched an experiment in "socialism with a human face" unfold, which broke down our prejudices and raised our hopes, only to see it falter as well. Nevertheless, the global momentum continued to build.

I felt increasingly impatient with liberals, even or perhaps especially those who were against the war, but took little personal risk to oppose it. On the night Nixon announced the invasion of Cambodia in 1970, we streamed into the streets in spontaneous demonstrations. During a midnight vigil at St. Joe's Jack gave an angry speech around a fire. I kept thinking of Joan Baez singing "Children of Darkness," which captured my mood on the night. The next days saw massive protests and much disruption on campuses throughout the country. Students were shot dead at Kent State and Jackson State. We held a requiem march to City Hall in Philadelphia and a mass mobilization of 200,000 in Washington. Amid all this, I had an oral examination at Temple to defend my PhD proposal. The faculty on the examining committee were all very sympathetic to my project and against the war. On the day of the examination, I was tired from staying up all night and caught up in a sense of apocalyptic upheaval. Sitting there as the committee engaged in academic nitpicking, well rested from not being out in the streets, I lost my temper and told them that the world was burning while they talked trivia. They were remarkably indulgent of my outburst, and I passed. I had been fighting a battle within myself. I felt guilty for giving my previous exams precedence over the Chicago '68 protests. Over several years I struggled to balance my PhD course work and teaching duties with my growing involvement in political activities on and off campus. For a time, I prioritized my intellectual search and academic pursuits, but my conscience nagged at me as I realized what a privileged life I led, while our cities were in flames and hamlets abroad were being bombed.

The mood on campus was becoming ever more radical. Even those who did not join left groups came out to support numerous ad hoc activities: speak-outs, teach-ins, sit-ins, bitch-ins, draft counseling, brown bag boycott, building occupations. The university felt the full pressure of the world upon it, not just in distant North Vietnam, but in its immediate surrounding community in North Philadelphia. Temple became increasingly conscious of itself as a white island in a black ghetto. Both black students at the university and the black community outside it made increasingly militant demands, such as the creation of a black studies program, academic credit for community work, and an end to university expansion into the neighborhood. I felt the gap between "town and gown" acutely, perhaps because of my earlier experiences as a primary school teacher and poverty program worker.

Consciousness of the racialized character of poverty was rising. It had consequences in crime and punishment: it was not by accident that the population of our prisons was so disproportionately black. Those of us who realized it were often defensive about it, even in minor matters. One day, I was mugged as I went to unlock the door of my car after class. I was roughed up a bit by a group of locals and my bag was taken. As I no longer had my keys to drive home or to get into my apartment or even money to make a phone call, I went to my academic department. The secretary called the police against my wishes and I had an awkward encounter with them, as I refused to answer the racial question. Jack arrived to rescue me along with his keys to our car and apartment. Another day it was put up to me in a more positive way, when I was heading home after a seminar, wearing my professional best. As I went to get the subway home, I came across a group of black activists I knew from my political activities off campus, who invited me to join their protest against transport fare hikes. The action "to liberate SEPTA" involved jumping turnstiles. I joined in, the only white person to do so. We were arrested and spent the night in jail. I shared a cell with a black prostitute from whom I learned as much in that jail cell as in the seminar earlier.

The day after Martin Luther King Jr.'s assassination, I was teaching at Temple. The atmosphere was fraught. Students, especially black students, wanted to talk about it and not go about business as usual. It was impossible to do otherwise. Indeed, it was hard to talk about anything else anywhere on that day. We articulated our common grief in a cathartic class. I wasn't always so amenable to student demands, although I always discussed them and never dismissed them. Some wanted to turn every class into a freewheeling rap session. Some wanted to dispense with grades. One teacher was denied tenure at Temple at this time on the grades issue. I joined the protest to support him, although I did not believe in refusing to give grades. We had a great teach-in, raising searching questions on the nature of the education system, with speeches by Carl Davidson of SDS and Paul Goodman, author of *Growing Up Absurd*. Even more problematic for me were failing students who, knowing I was active on the left and thinking I was a soft touch, appealed to me to raise their grades to save them from being drafted. I didn't do so. I told them to up their work if they wanted to up their marks. I was always for defending high academic standards, even if I was open to radical scrutiny of those standards. I pondered *Pedagogy of the Oppressed* by Paulo Freire and *The Wretched of the Earth* by Frantz Fanon. I wanted my teaching to be liberating and transformative. I realized that decolonization of consciousness was a primary aim.

An organization at Temple that suited me better than other campus groups was the New University Conference, considered the "grown-up SDS," as many involved had been in SDS as students and were now teachers. The NUC was formed in 1968 for radicals pursuing academic careers who wanted both to address issues within the university and to mobilize academic resources to address issues in the wider society. It was a group for those who worked "in, around, and in spite of universities," organizing discussions, teach-ins, protests, and publications. It provided both intellectual and political support to those seeking to transform both universities and society as a whole. NUC promoted critical examination of curriculum and research priorities and of relations with local communities, as well as support for antiwar initiatives, such as the people's peace treaty. Such activities were not without risks. At the University of Chicago, Richard Flacks was battered in his office and Marlene Dixon was denied tenure. In 1970, there were over two thousand members on sixty campuses.

By 1970, I could no longer treat my political commitment as a part-time supplement to my full-time academic work. I couldn't keep up the pattern of business as usual, punctuated by sporadic meetings and demonstrations. I felt that more was demanded of me. I needed a new level of integration between my intellectual and political commitments. Others were putting their lives and careers on the line, and I was haunted by those who went to prison for draft resistance. I also had the example of Jack, who was taking greater risks and giving greater priority to politics. He had been arrested several times in acts of organized civil disobedience and was considering another form of resistance to the war that would put his position at further risk. Jail and bail were everyday matters in our circles.

Although I was supposed to be writing my PhD thesis, and I did try to keep on track, I became virtually a full-time activist. The movement became a whole way of life. I joined meetings, marches, protests, strategic brainstorms, and tactical tête-à-têtes morning, noon, and night. I gave talks to small community and student groups, as well as rabble-rousing speeches at mass demonstrations. I did a lot of writing, but less for my thesis and more for meeting memos, searching letters to other activists about the nature of the movement, articles for left publications, and notes for a book I never wrote. My social life too revolved around the movement. I was in and out of communes. I bought food from a co-op. I also changed my look: no more hair curlers, lipstick, mini-dresses, or high heels. I now wore no makeup, with long straight hair, jeans or long skirts, loose tops, and boots, loafers, or sandals.

Jack and I helped launch a national campaign for war tax resistance, urging people to refuse to pay the percentage of their taxes that went to support the war. The agreed mechanism for doing so was to claim additional dependents. Those who did not earn enough to be serious tax resisters arranged to become "dependents" of those who did. The money withheld was put into a fund that went to progressive projects. Jack decided to withhold part of his taxes, and we held our breath, waiting to see what would happen. We had a menacing visit from IRS agents, as did others in our group. Then, one morning in 1970, I went to pick up the *Philadelphia Inquirer* from the doorstep and saw a front-page headline announcing that Jack had been indicted by a federal grand jury. I shook him awake with the news. He lost his job. The trial began in June 1971. We had both been in court before on civil disobedience charges, but *US v Malinowski* was a high-profile federal trial. More people came to attend than could be admitted into the courtroom. I took a defiant attitude to the marshals and the judge and it is a wonder that I was not held in contempt of court when I shouted at the judge. After a three-day trial, the jury returned a guilty verdict. We burst into song in the courtroom, singing "We Shall Not Be Moved." There were motions for a retrial in the coming months, and the day for sentencing finally came in April 1972. The mood was tense in the packed courtroom, and we feared that Jack would be sent to federal prison. Before the sentence was pronounced, Jack gave a resolute statement saying that the war tax resistance movement was growing and he would continue to be part of it and refuse to pay war taxes. The judge then delivered the sentence: three months' probation. We could hardly believe it. The crowd clapped, burst balloons, and sang songs of solidarity. The following year another member of our group, Henry Braun from Temple, was prosecuted on the same charge and also got probation, plus a fine.

We were deeply involved in city politics by 1970. The movement in Philadelphia had some distinctive features. It was the center of Quaker activism, which gave most of our organizations and coalitions a certain tone of resolute moral witness and a tradition of pacifist civil disobedience. I was moved by this Quaker approach, especially by those who put their careers on the line and welfare at risk. Sometimes I became impatient with what seemed like a bland, least-common-denominator humanism, but on the whole their staunchness and simplicity was a force for calm in the overheated atmosphere of the times. I had a lot to learn from them, particularly about coalition-building. I needed to understand when to be maximalist and when to be minimalist in my goals and demands in any time and place.

Aside from the Quaker influence, religious activism from other traditions also played a big role. Radical Catholics featured strongly, some of them part of the same network as Daniel and Philip Berrigan. They engaged in risky acts of civil disobedience, such as breaking into draft boards and destroying files. Among their many incarnations were the Camden 28, the Harrisburg 7, and the East Coast Conspiracy to Save Lives. I knew some of them well, and we formed strong bonds. Some were modest and funny, while others were elitist and self-righteous. Some disdained antiwar activities, even illegal ones, that did not involve the same level of risk as theirs. They had a distinctively Catholic approach that saw suffering not just as a necessary risk, but as itself redemptive. Others took part in many kinds of movement activities and I respected their diversity of tactics.

Two of the most prominent political figures of the Philadelphia left were Protestant ministers. David Gracie was an Episcopal priest who had served in military intelligence before attending divinity school. His ministry was in effect full-time political organizing, which he pursued in many directions. He had unwavering support from his bishop, although many conservative church leaders took grave exception to these activities. He was embroiled in constant controversy in and out of the church. Strikingly handsome as well as intelligent and inspiring, his presence lifted any gathering, and his analysis of any situation carried enormous weight. He was involved in almost everything: antiwar, anti-racism, and anti-poverty activities. Never afraid to risk arrest, he was an indispensable presence in our left lives, moving with ease through the counterculture of the times, even as he remained more conservative in lifestyle than most of us. He had a wife and three children and didn't live in a commune, smoke grass, or sleep around. Jack and I became quite close to him, working together on many projects. Even when he and I argued—which we did often, about everything from the truth value of religious beliefs to political tactics—there was a deep, strong, and warm bond between us. He also had a wry sense of humor. On one political occasion where ideological debate was particularly rife, he proposed a toast: "To the long march. We may be going down different roads and moving in opposite directions, but at least we are all marching."

Then there was Muhammad Kenyatta. Born Donald Jackson,

he was a Baptist minister. As a leader in the Black Economic Development Conference, he made headlines disrupting church services and demanding reparations for black people from white churches. He was also involved in many other organizations and coalitions, and we worked together on several projects, particularly political education programs and a proposal for a movement center that would provide a base for such programs. I had a strong but spiky relationship with him, too. We had long talks, sometimes dealing with difficult topics, such as racial and sexual guilt tripping in the movement. He told me I would end up hating him, because he was a "manipulative bastard." He did turn out to be manipulative, though I never came close to hating him. Another BEDC activist I got to know well was named George Washington, a serious student of Marxist texts. We talked about the theoretical grounding of our movement, and while I remained skeptical of Marxism, listening to such activists made me think about it more deeply. Mo was moving toward Marxism, too, though I wasn't sure how he reconciled his growing inclination to dialectical materialism with his theological convictions.

Led by the formidable Cecil Moore, the NAACP also had a strong presence in the city, as did the Black Panther Party. On the whole, relations between the black and white left were reasonably good, even after the turn to black power. Black activists were often more separatist in their rhetoric than in practice. I often got a jolt listening to the incendiary rhetoric of those who I knew acted differently in private settings. There were, however, points of tension. Although Muhammad Kenyatta and David Gracie had fought many battles together, they fell out over the former's ill-fated run for mayor of Philadelphia in 1975, which facilitated the reelection of Rizzo, the most racist mayor in the city's history. Mo accused Dave of racism, which was utterly unfair.

SDS was not so strong in Philadelphia as elsewhere, although there were chapters at Swarthmore, Penn, and Temple. Resistance, a national draft resistance organization, was the primary prototypically New Left group in the city. It was involved in much more than draft resistance, with a core group who formed the office staff and lived in a commune, but beyond them a much wider community. Almost anyone active on the left in the city seemed to be somehow involved with Philadelphia Resistance, as I certainly was. The core group, mostly recent Penn graduates from liberal Jewish backgrounds, were inclined toward anarchism, and introduced me to that tradition as a serious political philosophy. I started reading Bakunin, Kropotkin, Goldman, and Bookchin. I was especially charmed by Emma Goldman's *Living My Life*, which many of us were reading at the time. She was a brilliant and passionate writer, making a compelling case for anarchism and embodying a life lived to the fullest. One ritual I rarely missed was the Monday night Resistance potluck dinner, where I ate amazing foods I would never have tasted otherwise. The meal was always accompanied by a speaker, film, or performance, followed by stimulating discussing and socializing. The group hosted local speakers as well as nationally prominent ones, such as Paul Sweezy, Philip Foner, Rennie Davis, and Noam Chomsky.

There was much mixing of liberals and radicals, old left and new left, in various coalitions, but particularly in antiwar activities. Many of my generation on the new left were "red diaper babies," who were often politically and theoretically more sophisticated than those of us without a left background. They tended to take a critical but sympathetic view of our political elders, while I was more sharply critical of the old left. Having grown up in the shadow of Cold War anti-communism, I was at first astonished even to find myself in the same room as communists in antiwar coalitions. I constantly clashed with older left activists—liberals, Stalinists, and Trotskyists alike—whom I saw as stodgy, manipulative, unimaginative, overcautious, and reductionist. For their part, they were forever counterposing what they called "bread and butter" issues—wages, prices, and working conditions— to the worst excesses of drug culture, flower power, and free love.

Once I was invited to be a guest speaker at a retreat of the National Lawyers Guild in New Jersey. Founded in 1937, the NLG was a progressive association that provided legal representation to labor unions, the civil rights and antiwar movements, and various new left groups. The FBI accordingly considered it a subversive organization and a Communist front. The NLG sometimes struggled to understand the tactics and motives of younger activists, and an argument opened up over the relationship of lawyers to the movement. We relied on NLG lawyers to represent us when we were in legal trouble. Many of them believed that their job was to defend us as clients, albeit pro bono, more or less playing by the rules of the game. I argued in my speech that they should be organically part of the movement, joining us in the streets as well as defending us in court—and that they should do that in a way that challenged the nature of the system and role of the law within it. I got a barrage of caustic criticism. Who was I to speak for the movement? Who had invited me and why? Didn't I throw their deliberations way off course? It was their job to stand between the oppressed and the law, but also to keep personal and political considerations to a minimum. They had been around for years and knew how the system worked. I was young. What did I know? They were doing their best to understand us and they would protect us, but movements came and went, while the NLG remained. They would deal with it all case by case, and all this talk about a long-range vision was a luxury. I thought the point of a retreat was to focus on long-range vision. It was a bit overwhelming. Then David Kairys, a lawyer and NLG member, probably the one who had invited me, came to my defense, saying, "She is not alone." He, too, articulated an alternative view of lawyers' relation to the movement. Other younger lawyers spoke along such lines, and some of the older ones took positions that sought to bridge the gap. We talked through these issues into the early hours of the morning.

The prime "movement lawyers" in my circles were David Kairys and David Rudovsky. The Davids were young public defenders, who decided to set up their own law firm to specialize in civil rights cases. The tiny office of Kairys and Rudovsky was in a city center office building and movement people streamed through it constantly, not just to seek their help on legal matters, but to confer with them on many projects in which they participated as activists. They not only advised and defended us, but protested, planned, and partied with us. They were as angry against injustice as any of us, but had a quirky way about them and were always great fun as well as utterly dependable and practical. I often wondered how they earned a living from it in those early years. As the years went on, they continued in their law practice, to ever greater national prominence and acclaim, as they took many groundbreaking cases, and even argued before the US Supreme Court. They took on the FBI, the Department of Justice, the Philadelphia Police and many powerful forces. They both became professors of law as well, Kairys at Temple and Rudovsky at Penn. I liked the way that the Davids behaved in court. They wore suits and argued their points in astute legalese. However, they were never obsequious, as some lawyers were.

Although clashes constantly erupted between older and younger activists, their relationship on the whole was benign, even essential. A rock on which many projects depended for their logistics and funding was Joe Miller. A genial investment banker with a wiry frame and white hair, he was always attending to the practical details that made many of our plans possible. His long experience and expertise were crucial to our activities. He was also sensitive to our generational insights and patient with our myopia. He didn't talk much about struggles of past decades, and I wish now that I had probed him about that, but we were so caught up in the moment. One time, though, when I was in tears after a rough meeting where I had been opposed by some of my closest allies, it was Joe who comforted me and spoke of his many years on the left and the toll it took on people. Despite our moments of mutual incomprehension, we most often found common ground with our elders and learned a lot from them. In academe, too, there were those who had been joining radical critiques with political activism for many years. At Penn, for example, professors such as Ed Herman and Bob Rutman contributed to many of our projects.

Many of our activities took place in Powelton Village, just north of Penn and west of Drexel. The proximity to Penn was especially convenient, as many of our events took place on that campus. We sided with local activists, however, in fighting the encroachments of both Drexel and Penn into the neighborhood, entailing evictions of local residents. A racially integrated area, it was a site of communes, coffeehouses, and co-ops, a hub of left activity and a center of alternative culture, including many parties. The whole country was then full of such enclaves and experiments. The texture of our everyday lives was transformed by a vibrant counterculture of communes, co-ops, collectives, speak-outs, sit-ins, teach-ins, be-ins, die-ins, vigils, consciousness-raising, street theater, underground press, and independent cinema. Together these formed a vast network of alternative institutions, which we saw as the embryo of a new society germinating within the shell of the old. I was very into the prefigurative politics of the time, in which we sought to live as far as possible according to the norms of the sort of society we wanted to create. We saw politics as not just about seizing the commanding heights of economic and state power, but about everything—a revolution in consciousness, a transformation of everyday interactions and relationships. We talked long into the night about everything from food choices to free love, in an atmosphere in which everything seemed to be up for grabs, all philosophical assumptions had to be rethought, and all social arrangements renegotiated.

There was some tension between politicos and hippies, though the boundaries between them became increasingly fluid. Photos of left meetings and marches through much of the '60s show a clean-cut look, with men wearing suits and ties and women in dresses and high heels. As time went on, it was sometimes hard to tell males from females by the length of their hair. Clothing became looser, wilder, and certainly more colorful. A new vocabulary also came into use. We said: *Let's rap. Dig it. Right on. Far out. What a rip-off. What a bummer, man. That movement heavy was ego tripping big time. I'm splitting. Why do women do all the shitwork?*

We also had a different way of occupying space. We sat and slept on floors and on the ground. We papered our walls with political posters. We collected books and arranged them in makeshift bookcases cobbled together from planks and cinder blocks. We played music that defied the existing order and incited to rebellion, rather than mooning and spooning and finding one true love and living happily ever after. We danced together, rather than in couples, to celebrate a wider love and larger vision.

Although elements of the hippie lifestyle, even including drug use, began to permeate the culture of politicos, a notion still prevailed that it was important not to sink into self-indulgence to the point of losing perspective and social commitment. Timothy Leary incited our generation to "turn on, tune in, drop out," but Tom Hayden warned of the danger of "creating islands of post-scarcity hedonism far from blood and fire of the third world." I was on Tom's side there. Nevertheless, I was surrounded by drug taking, primarily grass, from which I mostly abstained. I thought people on it talked awful, muddy nonsense, while thinking they were lucid and brilliant. I wanted to be *compos mentis*, which made me reluctant to get into the drug culture surrounding me. I did feel I was missing something, though, and thought I should try it, just to be properly clued in. I did try a few times, but nothing really happened. Jerry Rubin, Yippie superstar, once took it as a challenge to get me high on his best hash and coached me on how to inhale, but it still didn't happen. Another time, someone slipped mescaline into my drink and I had a terrible night of paranoia, a "bad trip." After that, I affirmed my resistance to drugs, even as it set me apart in a way I disliked. Even some serious activists got heavily into drugs, while others just went for a bit of grass now and again. I did drink, though only at parties, and talked nonsense myself when I had too much.

The Youth International Party (Yippies) aimed at a particular fusion of politics and counterculture. They had done their time in serious left politics and moved to a more theatrical zany style of politics. They were into anarchism, rock and roll, psychedelic drugs, guerilla theater, crazy costumes. They specialized in pranks, such as throwing dollar bills from a gallery onto the floor of the New York Stock Exchange and nominating a pig to run for president. They invaded Disneyland and occupied Tom Sawyer's island. They applied for a permit to blow up General Motors and, when denied, argued that it just showed that you couldn't work within the system to change the system. The most famous were Abbie Hoffman and Jerry Rubin, especially from their roles as defendants in the Chicago 8 trial. Stew Albert ran for sheriff in California and challenged the incumbent to a high noon duel. Phil Ochs and Judy Collins sang at their events. Some Yippie women, such as Robin Morgan and Judy Gumbo, founded WITCH (Women's International Terrorist Conspiracy from Hell), bringing guerilla theater into the feminist movement. I met Abbie Hoffman and knew Jerry Rubin, Stew Albert, and Judy Gumbo. Stew asked me to go with them to Chile to check out what was happening there. I didn't go, but I organized some speaking gigs for him in Philly when he got back. By the end of one of his sojourns in Philly, where I was putting him up, I felt a strain on my sanity after prolonged exposure to Yippieness. One of the problems was that he was pulling me into involvement with someone with whom I did not want to be involved, Ira Einhorn, who was the embodiment of everything that made me uneasy about certain forms of the counterculture. He presented himself as a guru who had fathomed the secrets of the universe and expected everyone else to listen in awe. He talked about living in an anti-environment and continued in a discourse that violated all my logical and empirical standards. He invited me to his apartment to see for myself. I went and saw an empty room and listened to more of his New Age nonsense. He claimed to be creating a paradigm-changing international information network. He exuded narcissism and inauthenticity. He also thought he was irresistible to women, although he was very resistible to me. He floated around the edges of the left, periodically demanding center stage to dispense his pseudo-profundities, but he was not a part of the movement when there was actual work to

be done. He got money from various patrons, including corpora-
tions, who paid him to explain the movement to them, even if his
claims to speak for us were dubious. Whenever he was proposed
as a speaker, I opposed it, as I thought that he sowed confusion. I
didn't vote for him when he ran for mayor. However negatively I
thought of him, I still didn't see how destructive he actually was.
He later became even more notorious and not in way that any of
us foresaw at the time.

Another project I was involved in was an initiative for a community of learning. We had been discussing the need for something
that would allow us to go beyond ad hoc meetings and explore
the larger and deeper questions of our times together. Some of us
wrote our thoughts and proposals and circulated them in advance.
The proposals ranged from a series of seminars to a movement
center to a communal living arrangement. The latter was quickly
shot down as impractical, and though there were grandiose
notions of a Philadelphia Liberation Front in play, what came
out of these discussions was something more modest, but quite
successful for a while. It was called Philadelphia Book Club—a
name I didn't like, both because it was too bland and noncommit-
tal and because it seemed too narrowly focused on books, instead
of themes, projects, philosophies. Inspired by the Left Book Club
of the 1930s, which had 57,000 members in Britain by 1939, the
group's leaders held regular meetings about choosing books and
speakers and evaluating results, but also intense discussions of
the ideas involved. There was also a monthly meeting open to the
public that would begin with a speaker reviewing a book, followed
by a group discussion. The books we debated included *Vietnam
Will Win* by Wilfred Burchett, *Soledad Brother* by George Jackson,
The Dialectic of Sex by Shulamith Firestone, *Labor's Untold Story*
by Richard Boyer and Herbert Morais, *Bury My Heart at Wounded
Knee* by Dee Brown, *Ireland Her Own* by T. A. Jackson, and *Red
Star Over China* by Edgar Snow. We hosted various speakers with
a national profile, such as Rennie Davis and Arthur Kinoy, and our
most popular meetings attracted audiences of a hundred or more.

The core group was old left and new left, black and white, male and female, anarchists and feminists and socialists and communists. The discussions we had among ourselves challenged me and left a lasting mark on me, sometimes more so than I realized at the time. Perhaps the person who most provoked me was Ron Whitehorne. A few years older than I was and a former member of VISTA and SDS, he was then arguing strongly for a turn toward organized labor in strategy and Marxism-Leninism in theory. I found many of those who took this line unappealing to varying degrees, and some struck me as almost zombie-like in their dogmatism. They were often an aggressive presence taking the floor at broad coalitions, where they displayed a rigid fixation on the "correct line," often delivered via a guilt-tripping tirade. Ron was not like this at all. When engaged in ideological debate, he was persuasive rather than derisive or divisive. His face readily broke into a disarming smile. He often had his guitar slung over his shoulder and sang labor songs at many events. We had real differences: one night we had a debate on the Soviet invasion of Czechoslovakia, and I was shocked to hear Ron defend the action on the basis of the need to defend the socialist bloc. Nevertheless, while he and I often stood on opposite sides of debates, especially the ongoing one between Marxism and anarchism, we never fell out over it. Often I found myself thinking about his arguments afterward.

Another person who provoked me, although in a different way, was Peter Countryman. He studied at Yale and Princeton, but had trouble relating his studies in philosophy, literature, or political science to the real problems he saw on the streets. He was involved in the early SDS and founded the Northern Students Movement in 1961, which sent books and money to the South to support the civil rights movement and then turned to organizing tutorial programs in the inner cities of the North. He thought that racism was the primary problem of US society. He was sometimes overwhelmed with guilt at being white, male, educated, first world. He said that he sometimes longed to have black skin and calloused hands. At the same time, he felt that he had been screwed up by the society in which we had all been reared and that we had a right to seek our own liberation, but he could never quite believe in the legitimacy of his own struggles. Whatever he did, it seemed never to be enough to legitimate him in his own eyes and he entered into a dark downward spiral. He became interested in Reichian therapy and started explaining many things, too many things as I saw it, in terms of sexual frustration. He was always intelligent and stimulating and sincere, but increasingly dark and depressive. Every conversation we had seemed to sink into despair at a mass of insoluble contradictions. He lived in a commune called Any Day Now, which struck such a hopeful tone, but I rarely left it after my long talks with Peter without a feeling of hopelessness.

Many of us in the movement felt an acute guilt about our privilege that played out in many ways, sometimes very destructive ones. Weatherman played a crucial role in breaking up SDS, raged through the streets, and then went underground, bombing buildings to exonerate themselves of their white skin privilege and bring on revolution. At many meetings the guilt was also a source of ugly accusation and counter-accusation between conflicting factions. It intensified with the rise of black power, with black activists sometimes denouncing all whites, and then women's liberation, with radical feminists denouncing all men, even those who stood shoulder to shoulder with them. However, it was most often well-educated white men denouncing one another for their privilege, part of a pattern of more-militant-than-thou, macho posturing.

We talked a lot about the relation of psychological and cultural liberation to political and economic liberation. We all felt it was a problem that we had to resolve both personally and collectively. We believed that the personal was political, and accordingly sought to avoid the pitfalls of both apolitical individualism and impersonal politics. There was strong sense on the New Left that we were legitimate agents of the historical process in our own right and not just allies of the wretched of the earth. We needed to liberate ourselves to be of any use to the liberation struggles of others. We knew, however, that we were children of privilege, especially when we looked at the lives of the oppressed, whether in our own cities or in the third world. Paul Potter's book *A Name for Ourselves* was an honest and moving attempt to articulate this tension and find a way through it. We had to name the system, name ourselves in relation to it, he argued, and break out of it through our own analysis and in our own name, by integrating autobiography and politics. For example, we had to stop feeling so guilty about having resources that the Vietnamese lacked, that we threw away what we did have, shrinking our own lives as well as making us less effective allies for the Vietnamese. Other New Left writers, such as Tom Hayden, Todd Gitlin, Carl Oglesby, Marge Piercy, and others, also addressed this tension and developed an exemplary style of writing that blended the personal and political.

We felt like aliens in our own land, shaken by an overwhelming revulsion toward the culture that had nurtured us. We didn't want to live as our parents had. We didn't want their homes, jobs, or ambitions. We rejected their gender roles, cultural conformity, and political passivity. All had to be overturned: economics, politics, culture, psychology, philosophy. Moreover, we had to prefigure it in our lives and organizations. The new man would not emerge *ex nihilo* the day after the revolution. We had to create a new society in the struggle for a new society. A liberation movement should bring people together in a way that was itself liberating. We believed in continuity of means and ends. We were creating liberated zones in our communes, co-ops, street theater, alternative media. We lived by different norms, making us put flowers in the barrels of guns, practice free love, and renounce or suspend careers.

We sometimes matched the dominant culture's moves with our own countermoves. The Nixon inauguration provoked a counter-inauguration. Federal grand juries incited people's grand juries. We issued "Wanted" posters for the president, the attorney general, the special prosecutor, and the police commissioner. If the police could not be trusted to protect and serve, we set up structures for community accountability of police. If the government would not make peace with Vietnam, we organized a peoples' peace treaty.

We formed our own foreign relations, as we built networks of connections with liberation movements abroad. Some governments, such as those of Cuba and North Vietnam, dealt directly with our movement. If their newspapers and magazines presented a distorted view of the world, we published our own. We had *Distant Drummer, Free Press, Ramparts, Liberation*, and many more. As the mainstream wire services wouldn't convey our truth, we had the Liberation News Service. If the whole range of their media failed to represent the world as we saw it, we made our own films and found openings to make our voices heard on radio and television. If they persisted in parading women in beauty pageants, we crowned a sheep Miss America in Atlantic City.

We embarked on a "long march through the institutions" of society: homes, schools, workplaces, governments, neighborhoods. It was not simply a matter of seizing control of factories or government buildings. It was a slow, hard, intricate process. It was building the new in the shell of the old. I was most attracted to this positive side of it. Although I was into confronting the old order at every turn, as we did in all our protests, what I most wanted to create was a new order by building alternative institutions. We formed intense bonds with each other in this cauldron of purposeful activity. We had long, meaningful conversations where we told our stories, conceived of our projects, and articulated the nature of our movement. All human emotions and desires came into play: love, hate, generosity, sympathy, anger, anxiety, resentment. Sexuality ran through many of these encounters, and the prevailing ethos was one of free love. We questioned the emphasis on once-in-a-lifetime, male-female, one-and-only relationships. We saw ourselves as part of a web of relationships more than as a series of singles and couples. Even where there were marriages and couples, these tended not to be traditional and exclusive. Although I continued to live with Jack and we were on good terms, I no longer believed in marriage. I had close relationships with many men and this sometimes expressed itself sexually. I did not regard our ethos as "promiscuous," as we were not indiscriminate or uncommitted.

Nevertheless, our relationships were fraught with many problems. We didn't like everyone equally, and some thought others were arrogant, egotistical, irresponsible, or timid—tensions found anywhere people come together, but sometimes heightened by the intensity of our mission. We also faced a problem particular to our communities. The movement was heavily infiltrated. At meetings, it was always likely that someone would be informing on us, even when our activities were legal, which most of them were. Yet we disliked thinking that some among us were not what they seemed. It was a breach of trust, a virus contaminating our relationships. Furthermore, not all our activities were legal, and here the question of who could be trusted was more consequential. There were levels of illegality. Some of it was minor and routine. We often made long-distance calls and charged them to IBM, GE, or Dow Chemical. We specialized in defense contractors, and it was easy, because we had the code that would translate their phone number to their credit card billing number. Some of our activities were illegal but not secret. We would protest without permits or trespass on private property—and we were often arrested. Other activities, such as breaking into draft boards and destroying files or entering defense installations and vandalizing equipment, had to be done in secret. Afterward we claimed collective responsibility, but gave no individual names.

One action that intensified the pressure on the left in and around Philadelphia was a raid on the FBI office in Media, Pennsylvania, in March 1971. A group calling itself the Citizens Commission to Investigate the FBI seized over a thousand documents detailing years of systematic wiretapping, infiltration, and media manipulation designed to suppress dissent. These files, which the group systematically released to major newspapers, uncovered the existence of COINTELPRO, a secret counter-intelligence program aimed not only at investigating but also disrupting radical left groups. COINTELPRO sought to discredit and demoralize and "enhance the paranoia endemic in these circles." They sent anonymous letters to parents, employers, and university administrators.

They recruited informants and agents provocateurs, cultivated journalists, spread rumors, sent notices cancelling meetings, lobbied against use of venues for conferences, and fanned the flames of hostility within and between groups. Unsurprisingly, the FBI director, J. Edgar Hoover, and the US attorney general, John Mitchell, were furious and went all out to discover who was behind the break-in. However, even with two hundred agents assigned to the case and after accumulating a 33,698-page file, they never discovered who did it. In the immediate aftermath, all of us who were active on the left in the area came under intense scrutiny.

Pages that the FBI released to me confirm I was a "MEDBURG suspect." They got my fingerprints from the Philadelphia police and failed to match them to a fingerprint found at the scene. I didn't need these files to know that I was a suspect, because it was obvious at the time. When we emptied our trash, someone came to retrieve it. People who knew me were interviewed about me. Some told me so, but there may have been others. FBI agents visited the apartment building where we lived and asked how long I had lived there, what kind of person I was, whom I knew, whether I was away a lot. FBI agents even visited my father at work and my family at home. My brother Mark recounted their home visit to me. They asked the same sorts of questions about my character, associations, and travels. They asked if I would do anything dangerous. My mother told them I was a person of extremes. My father told them about our blow-up at Thanksgiving, six months before, which was the last they had seen of me. I also received a call from an FBI agent, identifying himself as Brian Masterson, requesting an interview. I refused. A diary was taken from me, presumably by the FBI, during a demonstration in New Haven.

It wasn't only me, of course. Many others around me endured the same sort of overt and covert surveillance and harassment. Our movement lawyers, David Kairys and David Rudovsky, asked us to write down all that we knew about these activities, and they brought a case against the FBI in *Resistance v. Mitchell*. Kairys was also involved in the Camden 28 case, which was won on the basis of the FBI's role in enabling the raid aimed at destroying draft files. There was also a trial in the case of the Harrisburg 7, charged with conspiring to kidnap Henry Kissinger and to blow up utility tunnels in Washington, in which an FBI informant featured prominently. The FBI believed that these three cases were connected to a Catholic left conspiracy. We organized protests and teach-ins surrounding these trials and I spoke at several. On a lighter note, we also threw an anti-FBI street party in Powelton, where liberated files were on display. It was fun until a fight broke out later in the evening—down to provocateurs, perhaps, or just ourselves being our own worst enemies, as we sometimes were.

The FBI was perplexed by our lifestyles. Some of the tactics they used to blackmail or discredit the old left would not work with us. Uncovering non-marital liaisons was hardly something that would intimidate those who rejected marriage and embraced free love. "Whereas the Communist Party and similar subversive groups have hidden their indiscretions," one report noted, groups "flaunted their arrogance, immorality, lack of respect for law and order" and "communal living quarters for unmarried male and female members." In another, they spoke of how we "did much to jeopardize established morals and diminish long-prevailing concepts of femininity." We gloried in our revaluation of traditional morality and rejection of traditional femininity. One document had a paragraph subheaded "Immorality" that observed that activists lived together at a house "where thirty persons often spend the night . . . sleeping on the floor or on torn, bottomless couches." I can't remember ever seeing a bottomless couch, whatever that was, but otherwise it was accurate enough. It was polymorphous perversity, to go with Marcuse's reversal of Freud. The FBI also sought to exploit a tendency toward New Age mysticism by using a "propensity for symbolism . . . to send a series of anonymous messages with mystical connotations . . . to subject these individuals to . . . mental anguish, suspicion, distrust and disruption." It wasn't just the FBI. Other agencies were on our case as well. The Philadelphia police had a special civil disobedience squad that maintained records on all of us and kept an eye on many of our activities, whether they involved civil disobedience or not. Agents' questions about my travels and associations were not related only to my activities in and around Philadelphia. At the time, I was also deeply involved in national politics. I was constantly on the road from city to city, representing Philadelphia groups at the meetings of the national ones. My work was primarily antiwar organizing, but also alternative academic and feminist activities.

The national antiwar movement was then undergoing major shifts and splits. In January 1971, Joe Miller and I attended the meeting of the National Coalition Against War, Racism and Repression (NCAWRR) in Chicago. This soon became the People's Coalition for Peace and Justice (PCPJ). Both PCPJ and another antiwar group called the National Peace Action Coalition (NPAC) were descended from previous national antiwar coalitions, resulting from splits in the National Mobilization Committee to End the War in Vietnam (the Mobe), which organized mass antiwar demonstrations in 1967. The great divide was between groups advocating a single-issue (end the war), single-tactic (mass march) approach and those who supported a multi-issue (connecting the war to systemic racism, poverty, and repression) and multi-tactic (mass marches, plus a variety of other forms of protest) one. NPAC wanted to keep bringing out the maximum number of people in national demonstrations against the war, while NCAWRR was known as the "coalition against everything." PCPJ wanted not only to broaden the focus but to engage in more varied and more militant tactics to build pressure against the war. It wanted to go beyond repetition of the reactive mega-march to more active tactics that would up the ante against the government. It was a coalition of many antiwar, anti-poverty, anti-racist groups, old and new. NPAC and PCPJ continued to negotiate to form a united front, at least on some activities.

The January 1971 meeting was a new experience for me. It was the first time I met a number of national figures, such as Dave Dellinger and Rennie Davis, whom I had only admired from a distance. There were many tensions between different forces and references to past events that I didn't quite understand. I was determined to get up to speed, though, and more experienced activists put me in the picture. We agreed on a spring offensive that would center on the people's peace treaty, include a people's lobby in DC in April, and culminate in a series of nonviolent but militant protests in DC in May. The degree of militancy was a point of debate. Dellinger and Davis were arguing for mass civil disobedience that would threaten to stop the government if the government didn't stop the war. This line was strengthened after another conference, in Ann Arbor, which I also attended, after a long drive in stormy weather, followed by meetings in other cities where I began joining the fray and taking positions in debates. After each meeting, I reported back to Philadelphia, where we were planning our own spring offensive coordinated with the national one. We opened a PCPJ office in Philadelphia. I spoke at rallies, visited many groups and campuses to mobilize support for the people's peace treaty, and organized our participation in actions in DC in April and May. We showed a film called *Time Is Running Out*, a powerful documentary about the struggle of the Vietnamese people and the necessity of our spring offensive, featuring Rennie Davis and Judy Collins—until our copy was unwittingly handed over to someone who was probably an FBI agent, and it disappeared.

Within PCPJ there emerged a Mayday collective, spearheaded by Rennie Davis, of which I was part. I got to know Rennie during these months and was moved by his untiring commitment to the movement, his personal warmth, and his searching conversation, which often went from practical tactics to cosmic reflections. From mid-April to mid-May I was based in Washington, making occasional visits back to Philadelphia. I stayed at a Mayday commune on Lanier Place and worked at the Mayday office on Vermont Avenue. It was a hothouse atmosphere, with people coming and going at all hours, some sensible and hardworking, others eccentric and with questionable intentions. Obviously, some were informers and provocateurs, and others were "freaks" (a term used affirmatively at the time). Some, such as myself, represented the antiwar movement in other cities, whereas others just showed up representing nobody but themselves, though they had the same voice as those who represented many others. There was much talking, partying, drug-taking, momentary mating. I got on best with those who were more mature and serious about organizing, such as John Froines, a scientist and one of the Chicago 8, and Mike Lerner, a philosopher and one of the Seattle 7. I was coordinating the regional participation from Philadelphia as well as working on national actions, particularly political education during the ten-day encampment at West Potomac Park. There was a reverential way of referring to "the land" and what we were doing there, part of a romantic back-to-nature tinge to New Left culture. Many people were more into blissing out on the land than into teach-ins about political strategy or critical pedagogy, so my efforts on this front met with constant frustration.

The Vietnam Veterans Against the War (VVAW) set up an encampment in DC as part of the spring offensive. For Operation Dewey Canyon 3, "a limited incursion into the country of Congress," they wore military fatigues, engaged in guerilla theater (including mock search-and-destroy missions), and threw their combat medals on the steps of the Capitol. They marched to the Pentagon and demanded to turn themselves in as war criminals. I attended their events and visited their encampment, and felt that they made a powerful and distinctive contribution to the antiwar movement by bearing unique witness to what they had seen and done in Vietnam. On April 23, there was a mass march co-sponsored by NPAC and PCPJ bringing 500,000 to DC and 125,000 in San Francisco to demand an end to the war. We leafleted for Mayday at the event. Many went home after the big march, but many stayed for an all-night concert. There was great atmosphere of planning, dreaming, singing, and bonding, especially around the campfires in the dark. During the following week, we participated in the people's lobby by day and had town meetings at the encampment by night. Various groups presented petitions or staged sit-ins at government departments. On Monday morning, I went to a hearing of the Senate Foreign Relations Committee, where we made our points by speaking from the floor and were removed by the police for disrupting hearings. We were roughed up a bit, but not arrested, and were later invited to send a representative to testify before the Committee. Our town meetings in the park provided an open mic to allow anyone to say what was on their minds, as well as to make announcements and plans. Some were focused on the war and how to give our actions maximum impact. I spoke about the people's lobby and the different tactics that different groups were employing. Others wanted to discuss sexism in the movement, including there in the park. Some of these interventions were very acrimonious, and at one point a group of lesbians stormed the platform to make their point.

Meanwhile, pressure and paranoia in the office and commune were intensifying. One day there was a bomb threat in the office. One night the commune was raided by FBI agents, who took away Leslie Bacon, a nineteen-year-old suspect in the March 1971 bombing of a lavatory in the Capitol building, for which the Weather Underground later claimed responsibility. She was taken to Seattle, where she had no connections, and brought before a grand jury. The atmosphere at the house was full of tension, distrust, and fear. Some split, but I stayed the night. I didn't sleep much and felt quite sick. In the morning, the place was crawling with agents and reporters. When I went out, I saw Leslie on the front pages of all the newspapers. The following nights I stayed at the encampment, where there was discussion, debate, and music all night long, and not much sleep. I met with members of Science for the People in their tent, and we talked about prospects for an international people's university. We celebrated May Day, which fell on a Saturday, with another all-night concert that swelled the camp to around 50,000 people. Early Sunday morning, the authorities revoked the permit and police evacuated the park. Groggy and bewildered, we awoke and did our best to regroup at various centers around DC. The heavy military presence around the city gave it the feeling of martial law. About half of those evicted from the park headed home. I felt edgy and angry, but still defiant and determined. I felt a sense of catharsis when singing along with Pete Seeger "This Land Is Your Land" that day. The only photo I have from that week shows me on a platform clapping while Pete Seeger was singing. I spent Sunday moving frenetically from one meeting to another: a PCPJ meeting at the Ambassador Hotel, a Mayday regional reps meeting in Georgetown, an organizers' meeting in the Mayday office.

The main action was to start early morning on Monday, May 3, when we were to engage in mass civil disobedience, militant but nonviolent, to obstruct traffic, block buildings, and ultimately bring the government to a halt. We rallied under the slogan "If the government won't stop the war, we'll stop the government." Though a tactical manual was issued outlining our targets, it was a decentralized operation based on regional organizing and affinity groups. The 25,000 unarmed demonstrators were met by 14,000 armed police, National Guard, and federal troops. As protesters began to block bridges and intersections, they were tear-gassed, clubbed, and arrested. Over 7,200 people were arrested that day, including Jack. Separated from my Philadelphia group, I spent the day wandering the streets, assessing the situation, and holding meetings. The city felt eerie and tense. At a meeting of regional reps who had escaped arrest, we sensed that we had survived a disaster. Nevertheless, we decided to carry on the next day. After a press conference in the afternoon, Rennie was arrested and charged with conspiracy. There was a warrant out for John Froines, and on Tuesday, we marched to the Justice Department, where Froines spoke and was promptly arrested and charged with conspiracy. The rest of us, about 3,500, were arrested too. I had connected with Philadelphia people again and was arrested with them. On learning that we were from Philadelphia, the police handled us with added roughness, saying we were "used to it." The police under Rizzo had become notorious nationally for their harsh treatment of protesters. The jails were grossly overcrowded.

Many were rounded up in the car park of a stadium with no food or sanitary facilities. I was crowded with twenty or more people into a cell meant for two. We kept our spirits up, singing "Power to the People" and other songs all night. On Wednesday, we were arraigned, released, and resumed our meetings and protests. Over 1,200 were arrested at another big demonstration at the Capitol. Overall there were 13,500 or so arrests in those three days, setting a new record for mass arrests.

On Thursday I went back to Philadelphia with my regional group, but on Friday I returned to DC again. We held a meeting in the office, followed by a weekend retreat. We set out for a big house in the country where we were to evaluate Mayday and make plans for further actions. It was the weirdest weekend. Someone served punch laced with acid or mescaline or both, and this was the occasion of my bad trip. I was overcome by paranoia. All the arrests, conspiracy charges, and infiltrations already made for a mood of paranoia, but the drugs intensified it to a terrible degree. I cried for much of the night. At separate women's and men's meetings, there was heavy criticism and self-criticism of sexism in the movement, particularly around Mayday. Many participants lashed out against the male movement heavies, especially Rennie and John, who might have had their blind spots, but some of these people castigating them represented nobody, did not really think politically, and were too self-indulgent in too many ways. Some were undoubtedly informers and provocateurs. A big conspiracy trial could be looming and a number of us, as well as Rennie and John, could be indicted as co-conspirators.

I returned to Philadelphia for a meeting of the city coalition as well as meetings of smaller groups to evaluate the spring offensive. I spoke at each of these meetings as a national and regional representative. I thought we had succeeded in disrupting the government, setting records for mass nonviolent civil disobedience and dramatizing the intense disaffection with the war, both at the mass demonstration organized by NPAC-PCPJ as well as the VVAW and Mayday actions. It had rattled the government and shown them that they could only carry on the war at the price of massive and militant civil unrest. Some federal workers and troops even supported the actions, as did many in the local black community. Evidence later emerged that the government was shaken by having to show such massive force to keep public order in the nation's capital, and that these demonstrations helped hasten an end to the war. However, some protesters had taken our threat to stop the government too literally and were in thrall to a romanticized paramilitary model of physical confrontation. I argued for a way forward that would involve more than physically converging, either in one big demonstration or in disruptive tactics. I thought that we should mobilize scientists, teachers, factory workers, and others to oppose the war and even to link with their counterparts in Vietnam. The whole thrust of the people's peace treaty was to make peace with the Vietnamese ourselves, rather than just petitioning the government to do it for us. It was effectively entering into foreign relations on our own, which was considered treasonous, as those who had traveled to North Vietnam had been told by the US government. It was the same with the Venceremos Brigades going to Cuba. Projects such as Science for Vietnam and Medical Aid to Indochina carried the movement on in this direction. I returned again to DC for a demonstration on the steps of the Capitol where we read the names of those who had signed the people's peace treaty.

Then I headed to New York and New Haven, where Black Panther Party leaders Bobby Seale and Erika Huggins were on trial, accused of conspiracy to murder a fellow party member, Alex Rackley, suspected of being an informer. Big demonstrations had been held when the trial had begun a year earlier, with many Yale students joining the protests; even the university's president, Kingman Brewster, voiced doubt that the Panthers could get a fair trial. We kept vigil on New Haven Green while the jury deliberated. After a week, the jury was deadlocked, a mistrial was declared, and the defendants were set free. During the week, all through the day we took turns going into the courtroom, but otherwise we were outside having intense discussions on the movement and where it was going. One day I was sitting on the green on a bench caught up in a discussion with Dave Dellinger and discovered that my bag was gone. I was particularly upset, because I had been keeping a diary that was in it. I searched the area in case it was an ordinary thief, who took the money and ditched the rest, but it probably ended up in the hands of the FBI. New Haven was crawling with agents. That week I stayed in the apartment of John and Ann Froines, as did a number of others, including Tom Hayden. I was excited to meet him, especially in a setting where there was time to talk. He took the measure of me quite quickly, handing me a drink and saying, "Here, this will carry you into the next era of history." David Kairys likewise once called me "World Historical Helena." Tom thought on a world-historical scale, too, which he thought had something to do with growing up Catholic. He told me I had a "very Catholic sort of mind, very synthetic, very passionate." One night in New Haven we all stayed up all night discussing the Berkeley Liberation Program. Tom was going through a difficult time with Red Family, the commune in Berkeley where he lived, and from which he would soon be expelled, accused of male chauvinism, bourgeois privatism, and political elitism. Much of the anger had to do with his celebrity as a movement leader, but the incident reflected tensions playing out throughout the movement: feminist reactions against sexism and a drive for self-purification, which together resulted in organizational purges, implosions, burnout, and bitterness, as well as an unresolved attitude to leadership, leading to delusions and confusions of leaderlessness.

These issues exploded into view at a Mayday conference in August 1971 in Atlanta. The agenda was to plan further antiwar actions and more generally to build the movement against poverty, injustice, racism, sexism, and imperialism. As it turned out, sexual identity politics overshadowed everything else. The registration process set the tone: the form asked participants to declare if they were gay or straight. When I objected at a midnight meeting of organizers, an acrimonious debate ensued. Workshops

about class, welfare, health, poverty, and peace turned into endless
consciousness-raising, criticism, and self-criticism—talking about
talking about talking. Gay participants made sweeping denunciations of straight people, mirroring some of the black nationalist
rhetoric about whites and radical feminist rhetoric about men. A
plenary turned into an all-night torture session. I spoke at several sessions, pleading for perspective. Gay liberation swamped all
other themes. Anyone who wanted to focus on anything else, was
accused of being oppressive. At one point, I was confronted by
a guy in drag with whom I had worked well, I thought, during
Mayday. I confessed that I didn't see how it was liberating for men
to parade around in the sort of ultra-feminine clothes and makeup
that feminists were then rejecting. He argued that it dramatized the
arbitrariness of gender stereotypes. I listened to these arguments
and to stories of growing up and coming out, making a sincere
effort to understand, accept, and integrate these struggles into our
overall struggle for liberation. One night we danced around a fire
in the dark, singing a song about revolutionary love, and felt some
of the tensions of the day dissipate. At the same time, I worried
that the war, our ostensible focus, was getting lost. Every person
returning from Vietnam spoke of how seriously the Vietnamese
took our movement, how urgent was the need to end the war and
how important our role was. For the first few days of the conference, I was in touch by phone with Muhammed Kenyatta, who
was back from Vietnam and was headed for Atlanta to be part of
the discussion. I didn't think that Mo would find the atmosphere
at the conference very congenial. Black activists tended not to be
very sympathetic with feminism and even less so with gay liberation. I felt caught in the middle. I was a feminist and I supported
gay liberation, but thought that much of what was going on was
indulgent, even ugly, and that we needed a more disciplined movement to end the war. Mo was predictably appalled by the scene
in Atlanta. I did my best to mediate, but Mo and I argued about
it then and for some months afterward. There was a group called
Radicalesbians in Philadelphia who wanted to be included in our

activities, but he countered that this would give political legitimacy to something he saw as a sickness. The conference didn't sort anything out. After twelve days, I left Atlanta feeling frustrated and exhausted, with no plan for antiwar activity for the autumn. The movement's problems felt more acute and more insoluble. The Mayday organization, such as it was, died shortly after that.

Sexual identity was a constant theme in all our movement organizations at the time. I did believe that sexism had to be addressed seriously, both in the wider society and within the movement. In the latter, it took more subtle forms. Men didn't realize it, but sometimes, when making what they thought was a serious point, they addressed only other men, as if the women weren't even there. This could be especially oppressive when in the company of aspiring heavies who played up to the already heavies and made women feel invisible. Much of the tension was tied up with questions of leadership. The movement's most visible leaders were mostly men: Tom Hayden, Rennie Davis, Dave Dellinger, Bobby Seale—the Chicago 8 featured particularly—and down the line Angela Davis or Bernardine Dohrn might be mentioned. There was a consequent push to recognize the leadership capacity of women. At the same time, pulling in the other direction, was a rejection of leadership altogether. Meetings often included much trashing of movement leaders and a feeling that any drugged-up eighteen-year-old who showed up for the first time had as much right to speak for the movement as Tom or Rennie. It could be confused and chaotic at times. One feminist, Jo Freeman, called the resulting disorder the "tyranny of structurelessness," arguing that this apparent lack of structure or leadership often disguised an informal, unacknowledged, and unaccountable leadership that was all the more pernicious because its very existence was denied.

On the whole, however, the rise of feminism was a healthy current, both in the movement and in the wider society. Some pushed for a separatist women's movement, but I saw the women's movement as a movement within a movement. I saw patriarchy as a powerful force, but not the sole or primary form of oppression. I focused instead on the interrelationship of gender, race, and class within capitalism, convinced we had to look for the intricate interconnections and to fight on all fronts at once. I had rebelled against received ideas of masculinity and femininity and yet so many people still conformed to them that I still took men more seriously than women. Under the impact of feminism, I began to take women more seriously and form better relationships with them. I was not, however, prepared to break off in a separatist direction, though I saw the value of women's caucuses in some cases. Feminism for me represented a challenge to become whole, in opposition to the traditional division of labor, as relevant for men as for women. To be fully human was to be both rational and emotional, logical and experiential, political and domestic. Because of our upbringing, there was still a long way to go. Men still tended to speak in a more distant, abstract mode and expected women to do secretarial or domestic work. Many women still spoke more from their own experience and let men dominate the public discourse. It was changing, though. Reconceptualizing was the first step toward reconstructing.

During this time, I was moving between the academic world and the movement. The resulting tensions and contradictions came into particularly sharp focus during academic conferences, where I participated in forming radical caucuses. The annual conventions of the American Philosophical Association were sites of acute confrontation between the academic establishment and radical scholars. Initially the radical caucus was focused on passing resolutions protesting the war, prohibiting defense research, and supporting Angela Davis. Such resolutions, we now argued, were not enough. It wouldn't do just to get philosophers to denounce the war and then keep on doing philosophy as before. We had to engage in a radical analysis of philosophy itself and a critique of the sort of philosophy prevailing in academic departments. Then as now, the profession in American universities was dominated by analytic philosophy, which we found increasingly sterile, irrelevant, even repressive. At a plenary session of the APA in New York in 1971, the renowned philosophers Arthur Danto and Sidney Hook insisted on the political neutrality of philosophy. I exploded. I stood up and argued that there was no neutral ground, that the whole capitalist economy, the entire bourgeois social structure was grounded in certain thought patterns. Danto replied that it was necessary to separate a philosopher's work in his profession from his moral concerns as a man and a citizen. I argued back. I was applauded enthusiastically from the floor and crowded after the session by others who supported my position. Hilary Putnam of Harvard embraced me, which surprised me, as I didn't find his philosophical or political views particularly attractive. He was a member of the Progressive Labor Party at the time. He became APA president in 1976. Years later, I would confront him at a philosophy conference in polemical opposition almost as fiercely as I did Hook and Danto at that time.

While in New York, I also managed to look in on a meeting of the American Historical Association, where another radical caucus was stirring. The 1969 convention had seen dramatic confrontations, including a melee in which the AHA president fought to wrest the microphone from Howard Zinn. At the same time, the American Association for the Advancement of Science was meeting in Philadelphia and I got back in time for the last two days. The scientists were having the same arguments as the philosophers and historians. Some thought that politics should have no part in proceedings, while others thought that scientists could take political positions, and perhaps work against war and injustice as citizens, but could not let it interfere with the "objectivity" of their research. The recently formed Science for the People brought a more radical critique to bear. Founded in Boston by Harvard scientists Richard Levins, Richard Lewontin, Stephen Jay Gould, and others, it was quickly gaining members and influence. Two University of Chicago scientists I had met at NUC and Mayday, Bill Zimmerman and Len Radinky, were keen on using the AAAS conventions to spread the word about the group. At the previous AAAS convention, in Chicago, they had been refused permission to sponsor a seminar on the official program or even set up a literature table. Undaunted, they distributed copies of their manifesto and rented a suite in the hotel where they held unofficial seminars and strategy meetings. At official sessions, particularly those on weapons research, they interrupted from the floor and continued speaking even when ruled out of order. Their actions attracted national publicity, and the organization grew. This year their efforts were supplemented by demonstrations organized by the Philadelphia antiwar movement against scientific support for the war. Throughout the conference, radical scientists held their own workshops as well as engaging in debate at mainstream sessions.

So it went in other professions. The sociologists, economists, psychologists, litterateurs, and the rest were all arguing for and against "value-free discourse" in their disciplines. There was a Sociology Liberation Movement that opposed "fat cat sociology," value neutrality, and the discipline's emphasis on consensus and de-emphasis of class. The group published several radical sociology readers, and produced a counter-convention newspaper for a convention of the American Sociological Association, which became a journal called *The Insurgent Sociologist*. I met its editor, Al Szymanski, a big, energetic, intellectual powerhouse of a guy, who held up a sign reading "bullshit" in response to any particularly objectionable statement made by a speaker at an ASA convention. It was, he explained, "an experiment in ethnomethodology." To the surprise and sorrow of those who knew him, he committed suicide in 1984. Radical caucuses continued, supplemented by overlapping ones: women's caucuses, black caucuses, gay caucuses, third world caucuses. Journals multiplied: *Radical America, Critical Sociology, Rough Times, Radical Teacher, Review of Radical Political Economics*. The Union for Radical Political Economics, founded in 1968, still exists today, as do successor organizations of these various radical caucuses, such as the Radical Philosophy Association.

From the humanities to the sciences, we came together under multiple auspices and in various venues to probe the interface between the movement and the university. We wanted our teaching to be truly transformative: to bring students to the point of liminal experience, inspiring them to question received dogmas and work out their own worldviews. We wanted to write books that would scrutinize the foundations of knowledge and advance our disciplines in new directions. Our ambitions were boundless, even if our achievements, while considerable, came up against many limitations. All this ferment left its mark on the mainstream curriculum. The demands for "history from below," for black studies and women's studies, gave rise to labor history, gender studies, subaltern studies, and many more. These advances were not easily won, but they transformed academe, so much so that they have come under waves of attack in the decades since. The "culture wars" resulted in real intellectual liberation as well as a lot of nonsense. I was uneasy with some ideas that took hold in the New Left, particularly with the tendency to New Age mysticism. I understood the need for a cosmic perspective, but I was critical of the gravitation toward Eastern religions as a panacea for all that was wrong with Western culture. I was regularly asked what was my star sign, as astrology got a grip. Some feminists got into a cult of goddesses. When some who had a track record as serious organizers, such as Julius Lester and Rennie Davis, began to drift in this direction, I worried.

I pondered and polemicized on these matters, from gender to geopolitics, and scurried from city to city, campus to campus, group to group, trying to build our movement. I sometimes pursued it all with an almost unbearable intensity surging with revolutionary exhilaration before plunging into apocalyptic despair, and back again. I felt the tide of history cascading through me. I was often emotionally overwrought and physically distressed. The constant movement from place to place, sleeping on floors and in cars, sometimes talking all night and not sleeping at all, eating whatever I could grab, all while maintaining a number of intense relationships, took its toll, but I kept going. I still had a strong sense of vocation, even if it didn't emanate from above anymore.

Jack and I moved to Powelton at the end of August 1971. He

joined a commune while I rented an apartment around the corner. Although I participated in communal life, I decided to live alone, so that I would be better able to write. Although Jack and I separated, we remained close. We traveled together, and whenever I needed help or talk, he was my first port of call. When he moved from teaching college to high school, I continued to give guest lectures to his classes as I had done before.

That fall I attended my second Kent fellowship conference in Maine. It was intense. At one point, after twelve hours of continuous talking, listening, and debating, I participated in a panel on "alternative lifestyles." I spoke about the need to build the movement inside and outside academia, about scrutinizing the very structures of knowledge and overturning oppressive structures of power. The next speaker boasted of a lifestyle that was in no sense political, arguing that individual problems required individual solutions. When the panel opened to the floor, many speakers commented on the contrast, but saw both as individual "lifestyle choices" of equal value. This sort of bourgeois complacency made me furious, and I wasn't shy about saying so. Clearly, we had to address pedagogy of the privileged as well as pedagogy of the oppressed. After the conference, we gave a lift to Sandra Levinson of the Venceremos Brigades to the country home of Richard Goodwin, a famous JFK scriptwriter, who had a shooting range there. He put a rifle in my hands and gave me an elementary lesson in firing it.

I continued my travels, moving, often on short notice, to wherever the revolution called. When political prisoners led an uprising at Attica Correctional Facility in upstate New York in autumn 1971, I made my way there to demonstrate in support, seeing many people I knew from other protests, trials, teach-ins, and conferences. I saw the same people again and again wherever I went, but there were always many others I didn't know, giving a strong sense that the movement was reaching into all corners of the society. We were everywhere, it seemed. When back home, I participated more in the Powelton community and spent more

time on the Penn campus, where I sat in on a course on Marxism.
It was about time I studied it seriously.

On Christmas Eve 1971, the radio played "Silent Night" under
a montage of news from the year: the riots in Attica, the arrests at
the Justice Department, and so many other news stories in which
I had participated. Jack and I went to a VVAW ritual at Valley
Forge, where Dave Gracie preached and Vietnam vets were testified in the crisp, clear air around a fire. Joe Bangert had testified
at the Winter Soldier investigations earlier that year, and I had got
to know him during our spring offensive. On this night, he told
his story from the start. He and his twin had been raised in an
orphanage staffed by SSJs in Philadelphia. The day he arrived in
Vietnam, he saw a group of children who made defiant gestures
at American troops blown away. He saw corpses mutilated and
hung on wire fences. He saw a woman stripped, cut open from
her vagina to her breasts, disemboweled, and then skinned. He
was a helicopter gunner. He fired until he could fire no more. He
was a very disturbing person. I was quite haunted by the vets and
their stories. They were conscious of themselves as both oppressed
and oppressor. Even as they sought and found redemption in their
antiwar activities, they knew that those they killed were forever
dead, a burden they would carry for the rest of their lives. I rang in
the new year of 1972 in Times Square with VVAW. At midnight,
they lowered an antiwar banner from a high building as the rest of
us released black balloons into the air. The revelers reacted angrily,
and a nasty scene ensued.

Meanwhile, my brother Mark had brokered a fragile truce
between my parents and me. It nearly broke down immediately
when my father arrived one day to pick me up and met Joe Bangert
in my apartment. Like many Second World War veterans, my father
was intensely hostile toward VVAW vets. The latter's revelations
about the reality of the war—ranging from criticism of policy to
fragging to desertion—revealed a breakdown in military discipline
unthinkable to vets of my father's generation. VVAW reminded
the American public that the lines between "them" and "us" were

porous, ever permeable, ever shifting. Even before VVAW came on the scene, the GI movement had been built around this possibility of persuasion and redemption. Those who took up arms against the Vietnamese came from the same culture as the rest of us. None of us came fully formed into the movement. Typically, vets faced more stumbling blocks in their paths—poverty, trauma, despair—than did the rest of us.

Nevertheless, some were impervious to the movement's influence. The legendary "sixties generation" also included George W. Bush, Donald Trump, and our own siblings, cousins, and classmates, who seemed oblivious to the tides of history that flowed so powerfully through our lives. There were the fraternity brothers and sorority sisters, the jocks and the bikers, the "hard hats" who cat-called feminists, the Young Americans for Freedom who organized counter-demonstrations. The New Left may have defined the decade, but there were still flag-waving citizens who wanted the 4th of July to be the same as ever. Although we spent much of our time in our own enclaves and subcultures, we could hardly ignore the mainstream culture, which was still all around us.

It was especially in our faces on television. The decade from 1962 to 1972 was the time in my life when I saw the least television, first because of the cloister, and later because of my studies and political activities. It has been said that, if you didn't come home for the sixties, you didn't miss much good television. I was too busy to watch it much of the time, but when I did, I was furious. We saw television as the terrain of the enemy. It was deeply implicated in the "credibility gap" between official ideology and social reality. The police we encountered bloodying the heads of peaceful demonstrators bore little resemblance to those in *Car 54 Where Are You?* The military, who now pointed their guns at us, hardly endeared themselves to our generation in the way that those in *No Time for Sergeants*, *West Point*, or *Men of Annapolis* once had. The judicial system, as we saw it in the farcical trial of the Chicago 8, was far from the inevitable triumph of truth and justice that prevailed in the world of *Perry Mason*. Television did in its way convey something of the insistent questioning and sweeping unrest that was changing the social order, at least in news and current affairs broadcasts, where it was impossible to ignore the death toll in Vietnam, the massive demonstrations at home, the draft resistance, the constant disruptions of virtually every institutional function in the country—even if these were often reported in a hostile and distorted manner. In contrast, television drama continued much as before. As priests and nuns left in droves, draft cards burned, and black power militancy and feminist fury flared, *Bonanza*, *Bewitched*, and *Beverly Hillbillies* seemed like something from another planet. In contrast to the dizzying kaleidoscope of images unfolding in the streets and on the news, it seemed absurd that *Search for Tomorrow, Family Affair*, and *I Dream of Jeanie* should go on and on as before. Television drama completely ignored the war in Vietnam, but it did come out with a rash of period war dramas, many of them vain attempts to recapture the Second World War consensus for the war in Vietnam. Finally, by decade's end, in the face of devastating criticisms of the vapidity of American popular culture, the networks began to cancel long-running series and make at least superficial concessions to social change in new series like *The Mod Squad* and *Storefront Lawyers*. Programs like *The Smothers Brothers* and *Rowan and Martin's Laugh-In*, with their mildly irreverent humor, went as far as network television dared to go at this point.

Within the movement, many of us sensed the need for a new direction. Manifestations of this shift included the New American Movement and the New Communist Movement, born of the fracturing of SDS. I gave NAM a hearing when Mike Lerner came to town to see about the possibility of a Philadelphia chapter. It didn't quite gel with me, but Resistance pursued matters further, and did eventually form a chapter of the organization. Ron Whitehorne went in the NCM direction, forming the Philadelphia Workers Organizing Committee, whose members got jobs in factories and doggedly pursued what they called the "correct line" on political and strategic questions. Others withdrew from activism altogether and sought rural retreat in New Mexico or Vermont. I was also looking for something different, but wasn't sure where to find it.

This account breaks with the dominant historiography of the New Left in several respects. The story told in the memoirs of some of its most prominent players—*Reunion* by Tom Hayden, *The Sixties* by Todd Gitlin, *Ravens in the Storm* by Carl Oglesby, to name a few—as well as from more academic histories, privileges the narrative of the rise and fall of SDS, whose dissolution as a mass organization is taken to mark the end of the New Left itself. These are excellent and authentic accounts, but it is not accurate to see the demise of SDS or the end of the 1960s as more or less the end of the New Left. It would be impossible to tell the story of the new left without focusing on SDS, of course, but there were other points of focus, nodes of entry, and patterns of development. There were many who were active in the 1970s who knew very little of SDS. They were younger and became involved later, or they had been otherwise occupied in the 1960s, even on the other side or at war. Even if what happened in the 1970s somehow seemed less "real," the fact is that the movement was in some ways stronger than ever. It brought more people into the streets and toward alternative projects and communities. New organizations such as VVAW brought a changed dynamic into the movement. Why, then, should Chicago 1968 be so much more widely chronicled than May Day 1971? Activist and historian L. A. Kauffman has observed that "the largest and most audacious civil disobedience action in American history is also the least remembered, a protest that has slipped into almost complete historical obscurity. . . . It wasn't part of the storied sixties, having taken place in 1971, a year of nationwide but largely unchronicled ferment." I have thus tried to take the story into the 1970s and testified to other points of entry and to less chronicled events and players. Not that I am alone in this, as others have done so in their own way. Bill Zimmerman's *Troublemaker* deals with May Day and other important projects of the time, such as Science for the People, Medical Aid to Indochina, and Wounded Knee. Bill Ayers's *Fugitive Days* takes the post-SDS narrative into the Weather Underground in the '70s.

It is a different story emanating from the right or center. It is conveyed more in media images than in full-scale history or memoir. The twenty-year anniversary of 1968 prompted a flurry of superficial and spurious assessments of the New Left in 1988. Jerry Rubin's exhibitionist trip from Yippie to yuppie received more media attention than the more serious work of so many others in the years since, as we made our "long march through the institutions." The enduring impression left by it all was one of spoiled kids running on a rampage and getting high on the action, who grew up to become prosperous entrepreneurs and respectable matrons, or else did not grow up at all, basking in nostalgia for the 1960s irrelevant to subsequent decades. I did a study of images of the 1960s in the 1980s as played out in television drama, and all of these tropes were in play.

So what did we accomplish? Not what we intended, obviously, but not nothing, either. We defined the era. We transformed the terrain in many respects. We were responsible for many reforms that have endured. We did not, however, make the revolution we envisaged. So many years later, knowing all that transpired in subsequent decades, it may seem crazy that we ever thought otherwise, but many things seemed possible then, even if they were not. A revolution was necessary, but not possible, we had to conclude eventually. We were not even able to trans-late massive social upheaval into a sustained political force. We were deserted by the opportunistic, the cowardly, and the faint-hearted, the flotsam that flow with every tide. We had our casualties and tragedies. We had our traitors, too. Nevertheless, most of us who were really committed then remained so, and found ways to advance the ideas and ideals formed in the sixties into subsequent decades. Sadder but wiser, we carried on. The system against which we set ourselves turned out to be far more formidable than we thought. We seized the intellectual and moral initiative. We shook up a very smug and stable social order, which would never be the same again. We challenged the dominant ideology and shattered forever the consensus of the 1950s. It is true that we then lost that initiative, and witnessed the aggressive reassertion of all that we sought to undermine: the primacy of the free market, imperialist domination, traditional definitions of male and female roles, fundamentalist religion. However, the pendulum has nevertheless not swung back to where it was, and these areas remain disputed territory. In this disputed territory grew crops we did not intend to plant, not expecting postmodernism to sprout from the seeds of disaffection that we sowed. Some have suggested that the new right was the real beneficiary of what was set in motion by the new left.

No Western government fell, but no government has since ruled in such an uncontested way as before. Capitalism has prevailed and has shown itself to be a far more resilient system than we ever imagined, capable of restructuring itself and regaining lost ground on an unanticipated scale. However, our critique of capitalism has not been refuted, and massive disaffection remains ready to rise up again. The legacy of the New Left is contested and complex. It is a story of both victory and defeat. Our defeats were due not only to the strength of the system, but also to our own limitations and blind spots. Our movement splintered into bitter and opposing factions, each with its own shortcomings. I myself took issue with the movement's strain of anti-intellectualism, the cult of violence, the shambles of structurelessness, the romanticization of the third world, the indulgence of drug culture, and the ethos of consumption versus production. I did, however, share the general rejection of the old left, naïveté about power politics, ignorance of economics, and suspicion of science and technology. I would reevaluate my thinking on these fronts as the next decade unfolded. It unfolded in a very different way from anything that I had foreseen. Another stark turn was imminent.

P.S. ON IRA EINHORN: I had no further contact with Ira Einhorn after I left Philadelphia in 1972, but I heard the news that he had been arrested for murder. The decomposing body of his ex-girlfriend, Holly Maddux, who had gone missing in 1977, was found in a trunk in his Powelton apartment. He claimed that the CIA had murdered her to frame him, because of his research on psychotroics. He skipped bail on the eve of his trial and was on the run for twenty-three years. He lived as Ben Moore in Dublin for a time, but I never ran into him. His book *Prelude to Intimacy* gave a characteristically narsissistic account of his life in those years until he was found living under a pseudonym in France. There was a movie made about him in 1999 called *The Hunt for the Unicorn Killer*. He was extradited to the United States in 2001. He is now in prison serving a life sentence without the possibility of parole.

P.S. ON THE MEDIA, PENNSYLVANIA, FBI FILES: On 7 January 2014, there was an international news story that made my heart thump as I read it. It was like the denouement of a crime fiction, but enhanced by the long period of mystery and the intensity of my personal involvement. I always knew that those who broke into the Media FBI office were people I knew, without knowing exactly whom. I always wanted to know and wondered if I ever would know. I was not surprised to learn that it was instigated by Bill Davidon, a tireless and fearless activist, who was also a professor of physics at Haverford. I was surprised to discover that John and Bonnie Raines were part of it. John was my ethics professor at Temple. I saw him as the sort who signed petitions and came to major marches, but I never imagined that he did this. John and Bonnie told the story to Betty Medsger of the *Washington Post*, who wrote about it in a book called *The Burglary*, triggering the international news story. There was also a documentary film made about this called *1971*.

5

Four Green Fields

As the New Left developed, we looked abroad more and more and saw ourselves as a liberation movement among other liberation movements. Vietnam and Cuba were our primary points of reference at first, but we gradually began to look toward other nations and peoples. A great tide seemed to be sweeping over the world, and we wanted to be fully a part of it. Some of us took a particular interest in Ireland, both because of our own Irish roots and because the "Troubles" were in the news. We also felt a deep alienation from America and a sense that we had become unmoored, inspiring us to seek roots in a history longer and deeper than that of America. I turned toward Ireland. I read many books on Irish history and literature. I briefed myself on the current political situation. I listened to traditional and contemporary Irish music. I lectured to Jack's class on eight hundred years of struggle while playing "The Rising of the Moon." Others were going this way too, Tom Hayden among them. He wrote about the Irish together with the Indians and the Vietnamese, seeing them as peasant cultures of communal people living in a seamless web of interdependent relationships with one another and with the earth, disrupted by Anglo-Protestant imperialism. It was a highly romanticized vision, but such was the mood of the time. We longed to reconnect to primal sources of life. During one of our conversations in central Pennsylvania, Tom evoked the spirit of the Molly Maguires, Irish-American labor activists in the anthracite coal mines who were hanged in that area in the 1870s. Deeply disappointed that he had been turned away for "security reasons" when he tried to enter Ireland, he suggested that we form a group called Friends of the IRA.

I began to frequent Irish centers in and around Philadelphia. I went along to a St. Patrick's Day party with some friends who were also into Ireland, trying to get a feel for the community and discern different points of view. Joe Bangert's Yippie behavior and Vietcong t-shirt made it a bit difficult from the start, but our New Left sensibilities were bound to set us on a collision course with some types who frequented these centers. We did establish a rapport with some people at the centers. The whole scene seemed very old-fashioned—a culture clash in so many respects, even though it was the culture from which we had come. People danced only in couples, which we hadn't seen in a while. I was asked out on a date, which by then seemed quaint. At the end of the evening, the Irish national anthem, the "Soldier's Song," was followed by "The Star-Spangled Banner," which we found alienating. This tension played out over the next months. At demonstrations demanding the British leave Ireland, some insisted on waving the US flag alongside the Irish flag, to which some of us objected.

The tension arose not just from our New Left sensibilities, but from conflicting political positions in Ireland and the Irish-American community. The major divide was the split in Sinn Féin/ IRA, dating from December 1969, when the IRA convention voted to end the policy of abstentionism and open the way to take seats in parliaments in Dublin, Stormont, and Westminster, with the Sinn Féin Ard-Fheis making the same decision in January 1970. It was about much more than that. Influenced by global left currents, Sinn Féin/IRA had been moving left: studying Marxism; engaging in social agitation on such issues as civil rights, housing, natural resources, and employment; and seeing the movement as a national liberation front in the struggle against global imperialism. More traditional elements were uneasy about this. They saw it as a move away from Catholicism and nationalism toward communism. They were preoccupied with armed struggle against British occupation and feared the dissipation of organizational energies into agitation for social justice and "eyes elsewhere" politics. They didn't want the national struggle to be diverted into class struggle. This defeated faction split off to form the Provisional Sinn Féin and IRA, while those who remained were called Official Sinn Féin and IRA.

Much of the discord also had to do with each group's attitudes toward the United States. The Provisionals tended to be Catholic and conservative, even supporting the United States in the Vietnam war. It therefore seemed a natural choice for the New Left to support the Officials, though some, including Tom Hayden, favored the Provisionals, because they seemed more vigorous in pursuing armed struggle. I sided with the Officials. The split played out not only across Ireland, but also in Irish republican networks in the United States and Britain. There were scuffles at Irish centers over the sale of newspapers, with the Officials promoting the *United Irishman* and the "Provos" pushing *An Phoblact*. I became active in the James Larkin Irish Republican Club in Philadelphia, which distributed the *UI* and other movement publications. I learned to use the word *republican* in a completely different way. It meant rule by the people, not a monarchy or oligarchy, through representational structures, as distinct from direct democracy. More than anything, it was opposed to everything the American GOP represented. It became weird to hear the word used in the US way.

As Irish politics took ever more of my time and attention, I started thinking about going to Ireland. I wanted to see it for myself and I weighed the pull of Ireland against my projects in America. One day in April 1972, I boldly bought a one-way plane ticket and started preparing for a leap into the unknown. At the same time, I helped organize Philadelphia events for the US speaking tour of Liam McMillen, a member of the IRA Army Council and Sinn Féin national executive, and O/C (officer commanding) of the IRA in Belfast. I distributed leaflets for his lecture at Penn and arranged for a party in his honor the following evening in

Powelton. He spoke straightforwardly of the need for a thirty-two-county democratic socialist republic, answering questions about the movement in Ireland and asking many questions about our movement, not just the Irish republican movement, but the whole spectrum of the US left. He was particularly struck by our idea of "liberated zones," which he said they were trying to achieve with "no go areas" in the north.

Then forty-four, Billy was a scaffolder by trade. He left school and joined the IRA at sixteen, and was later interned for five years. He had stood in parliamentary elections. He advocated the revival of the Irish language. A strong supporter of the left position leading up to the split, he had narrowly escaped further internment in 1971. He was charming and warm and funny. For a major player in an internationally high-profile armed struggle, he was strikingly non-macho. After a few days in Philadelphia, organizers panicked because they had lost track of him, imagining the nefarious fates that could have befallen him at the hands of MI6 or CIA or the Provisional IRA. However, he was with me. We spent a day together and talked about everything. Breaking that day was news from Belfast that Joe McCann, an iconic IRA figure, had been shot dead. A silhouette of him in battle had appeared on the cover of *Life* magazine, as well as on a cover of the *UI*, and was made into a poster I hung on my wall emblazoned with the words "Army of the People." It underlined for me the dangerous world in which he lived. Nevertheless, I felt drawn into it. Before he left the United States, I met him again in New York, attending his final lecture and seeing him off to Ireland.

Meanwhile, I was tying up the loose ends of my life and saying my goodbyes. The book club held two events on Ireland, one a seminar among ourselves and the other a big public meeting. After the second one, there was a surprise going-away party for me, with a number of dramatic fare-thee-wells. The next day, Jack drove me to New York and saw me off on my flight to Ireland. We promised to stay in touch, no matter what. During the overnight flight, I thought of my ancestors crossing the Atlantic in the opposite direction, of how I was shielded by the comfort of the airplane from the cold and dark and hunger they must have suffered on those coffin-like ships during the Famine. Surveying the landscape from above, especially after a stopover in Shannon, I thought of Johnny Cash singing "40 Shades of Green." It was so green.

When I got to passport control and customs, I felt apprehensive, knowing what happened to Tom Hayden, but all went well. I wasn't famous, which was in my favor. At the same time, I was already connected to an illegal organization, which could be a problem. When I emerged, Billy was waiting for me and gave me the warmest welcome. He brought me to the house in Ranelagh, on the south side of Dublin, where I would be living. I met Mick Ryan, who owned the place but didn't live there, and Sean Garland, who did. Sean lived upstairs and I lived downstairs. It wasn't properly divided into flats, so we shared certain areas. Sean, Mick, and Billy were members of the Sinn Féin Ard-Chomairle as well as the IRA Army Council. Sean was national organizer of Sinn Féin and adjutant-general of the IRA. Billy advised me to make the most of my proximity to Sean, to elicit his political views and to learn all I could about the political situation.

Unlike Sinn Féin, the IRA was illegal. Almost all IRA members were also members of Sinn Féin, but not all Sinn Féin members were members of the IRA. Despite the illegality, the leaders of the IRA were widely known, although it was less apparent who the ordinary members were. There were certain ranks: chief of staff, adjutant-general, quartermaster, commanding officer, but most held the rank of volunteer. The leaders moved around Dublin and the rest of the twenty-six counties freely and openly enough, even if they could not do so in the six counties of the north. *Hibernia* ran a cover story on the IRA, showing the chief of staff, Cathal Goulding, and his son, also Cathal Goulding, looking heroic and handsome in military berets. There was, however, a sense that this freedom of movement was threatened. Only days after my arrival, the government brought in special criminal courts under the Offenses Against the State Act. There were fears that the office of Sinn Féin and the publication of the *United Irishman* were at risk. In the north, both Sinn Féin and the IRA were illegal, and the *UI* was banned. Republican Clubs had been set up as a way around this.

After settling into the house, the next stop was O'Connell Street, to see the General Post Office, site of the Easter Rising in 1916. From there we went to Sinn Féin's national headquarters at 30 Gardiner Place. On the ground level was a spacious bookshop, with a wide range of left books, creating an atmosphere of intellectual buzz, as did all the notices of lectures, protests, and cultural events. Billy introduced me to all around in the head office. I met Tomás MacGiolla, president of Sinn Féin—tall, dignified, reflective, professionally dressed in suit and tie. It was not the way revolutionaries looked in the United States, I thought, but why not? He worked as an accountant, but had educated himself in political theory and history and was taken seriously as a political thinker. Also tall and dressed in suit and tie was the vice president, Derry Kelleher. He was a chemical engineer, but presented himself as an all-purpose intellectual. He seemed anxious to impress, citing in one conversation Descartes, Teilhard de Chardin, Engels, and Bernal, all to no coherent effect. Then there were the joint general secretaries of Sinn Féin, Máirín de Burca and Tony Heffernan, both welcoming and down-to-business, dealing with the practical details of my joining Sinn Féin. I applied there and then. I would be notified of new members classes and assigned to a *cumann*, a local party branch. Also present was Eoin Ó Murchú, editor of the *UI* as well as author of *Culture and Revolution in Ireland*, which I had recently read, seeing revolution as connecting roots in ancient Gaelic culture to international socialism, an idea I found very attractive at the time.

I still hadn't met Cathal Goulding, the IRA chief of staff, but on my fourth day I was awakened from my sleep and answered the door in my nightdress in the early hours of the morning, and there he was. I was a bit tongue-tied, but we said a few words and he proceeded upstairs to find Sean. This happened regularly afterward, as he often arrived in the wee hours to see Billy or Sean. Cathal was an attractive figure. The description "charismatic" was coming to be used too loosely by this time, but it truly applied to him. Speaking at meetings or events, he was compelling in both analysis and rhetoric. You could see how people might follow him through thick and thin. When he was socializing, he was full of fun, with a mischievous tilt. He was forty-nine, having joined the IRA in 1939 and been chief of staff since 1962. He had been imprisoned and interned. He had moved to the left through observation, reading, and reflection, interacting with Marxists, including Klaus Fuchs, the notorious nuclear spy, when they were in prison together in England. He led the radical turn within the republican movement. He had children by three different women moving between different houses. He worked as a jobbing house painting contractor, although he was under pressure to give it up and work full-time for the movement.

The pattern in my first weeks was to start the day with an Irish language lesson from Billy. I spent the rest of the day reading books, magazines, and newspapers to expand my knowledge of Irish history, culture, and politics and talking to people in the head office. In the evenings, I went to meetings or lectures and then to a pub, often followed by a party after pub closing. This meant habitually staying up later and drinking more than I ever had before, while remaining the early riser that I naturally was. I was only twenty-seven, so I could do it for a while. I delighted in the pub *craic* and the sing-songs in those days, enchanted by their flair for language. It was particularly riveting when I was a new presence in the company and therefore perceived as fresh eyes and ears for everyone's best party pieces. Everything and everybody was new and fascinating to me. Obviously, I took to some more than others, but working out who was who and who thought what was utterly absorbing.

It was not only a new political organization, but a new country and a new continent for me. I saw everything in such sharp relief. I read the *Irish Times* thoroughly every morning and listened carefully to every item on RTE news, noting what was unclear, so as to ask Billy or Sean. I liked riding on the upper level of double-decker buses. I also had a new currency to manage. I had an income of $2,700 a year, from my PhD fellowship, which worked out to roughly £1,000. Generally, the freshness of food was a pleasure. I was amazed that the yolks of eggs were deep orange rather than pale yellow. The weather was something else. Even in July and August, I could rarely go out without a jacket. Come autumn and then winter, I was really cold. I sent an SOS to Jack to send me my warm clothes, because I couldn't make do with the few clothes I brought with me and couldn't afford to buy new ones. There was no central heating in the house and I had to learn to make a fire. There was no telephone or television either. Sometimes I received calls in a pub, which was where I usually saw television as well. I bought a radio and record player soon after I arrived, along with a few albums that I played constantly. *Mise Eire* by Sean O Riada and *Revolution* by the Dubliners were two of my favorites. I also played lots of rebel songs, both old ones such as "Four Green Fields" and new ones such as "Men Behind the Wire." The continuity between them seemed unbroken.

There were new words to master, mostly Irish terms used in English: Taoiseach (prime minister), Tánaiste (deputy prime minister), Dáil Éireann (parliament, equivalent to British House of Commons), TD (Teachta Dála, equivalent to MP in Britain), Seanad Éireann (senate), Ard-Chomhairle (national executive), Ard-Fheis (annual conference). In English, diapers became nappies and chips became crisps. Sometimes a familiar English word was used with an entirely different meaning. One day someone knocked on my door and asked if she could get me any messages. I asked what she meant. She was going to the shops in Ranelagh and asked if she could collect any messages for me there. Who would be leaving messages for me in shops? Was it some IRA operation in which I didn't know what part I was supposed to play? We talked past each other. Eventually, it became clear that the messages were groceries. I never would have guessed. Another revelation was the identity of J. J. McGarrity, who signed all statements made by the Official IRA. I expected to meet him any day, until finally I saw a statement in the paper that I had earlier seen being written by someone else.

The house was often abuzz with political activity but quite quiet at other times. It was ideal in many ways for me, in that I wanted to combine a life as an activist with reading, thinking, and eventually writing. When Sean and I were the only ones in the house, we kept out of each other's way. I found the arrangement awkward at times, as Sean seemed somewhat dour. He would answer my political questions, but other conversation was hard going. He didn't do small talk. Then thirty-eight, Sean had grown up in a Dublin tenement, the whole family living in one room. At nineteen, he joined the IRA, then enlisted in the British Army as an IRA agent, preparing the way for an arms raid. After deserting the British Army, he led an IRA raid on an RUC (Royal Ulster Constabulary) station in the border campaign, during which Sean South and Fergal O'Hanlon were killed and Sean was seriously wounded and then imprisoned. The incident was memorialized in several ballads, such as "Sean South" and "The Patriot Game." He was subsequently imprisoned and interned a number of times, while becoming a leading voice in the movement's leftward trajectory. Although his conversion to Marxism was forged in the furnace of political practice, he took a particularly studious approach to it. The house was full of Marxist books and he spent as much time as he could reading them.

There were lots of other people coming and going. One day a stranger, who had obviously started drinking early in the day, came into the kitchen, sat in a chair, pulled me onto his lap, and started singing to me. I soon discovered that it was Dominic Behan. I knew his song "The Patriot Game," which had apparently influenced Bob Dylan's song "With God on Our Side," both of which were favorites of mine. Dominic was forty-five, living in Britain and working for the BBC. He was the author of books and plays as well as many songs. That night Sean, Billy, and Dominic stocked up on six-packs and took me along to an all-night session of talking and singing. Although he remained quiet, it was good to see Sean relaxing, drinking, and laughing. Not like Billy, who was always laughing. More people kept appearing in the house and office, some of them just released from internment. A colorful one was Des O'Hagan, who had studied at LSE and been a member of the CPGB, and still took a strong pro-Soviet line. Within the next months he went on to the Army Council and became director of education.

Although I landed among the leadership of this movement and I was honored to be in their company, I wanted to make my way in the grassroots too. Many rank-and-file members were closer to me in age. I attended lectures for new members run by Tony Gregory, a teacher who later became a TD. Thereafter I went to Wednesday evening meetings of the Pearse cumann. Because it was in Ranelagh-Rathmines, a district with many houses divided into flats, many members were people up from the country to study or to work. No one in the cumann, as far as I remember, owned a house. A number were students, mostly at University College Dublin, including Pat McCartan, who was later elected as a TD and subsequently became a judge. There was always a packed agenda. There were many political questions and organizational arrangements to be discussed. The *UI* was usually on the agenda: not only organizing sales, but analyzing its content. There was also a local newsletter to be produced and distributed. We mobilized our members around various national issues, such as special courts, as well as local initiatives, such as a flat-dwellers' association and a boxing club. I understood the need for agitating on rights of flat-dwellers, but I was puzzled by the boxing club when it first appeared on the agenda. I thought it must be like "messages" and have a different meaning than it appeared to—but no, in this case it was what it seemed. What, then, was our role in it, I asked. To assist the local community in doing what it wanted to do, I was told. I wondered if this was perhaps stretching it too far. The cumann sometimes seemed to be flailing about for local issues and initiatives to latch on to, instead of seeing clearly what our role and priorities in the area should be. It was all well intended, though, and I learned a lot about everyday life in Ireland from these discussions and activities. In addition to the weekly meeting and activities, such as paper sales, the cumann also organized educational sessions, including Irish language classes. We also discussed resolutions and amendments, as well as the election of delegates for the Ard-Fheis. As time went on, I was elected education officer for the cumann and delegate to the Ard-Fheis.

Political education was the area in which I felt I had most to contribute. There were educational activities at the local, regional, and national level, with introductory, intermediate, and advanced courses, weekend schools, and conferences for education officers. I was asked to coordinate national educational programs at Mornington, County Louth, where there was a complex for residential educational courses. I was flattered, but I had not been there long enough to feel ready to take it on. There was also the matter of my PhD. I was still registered for it and receiving fellowship money and I needed time to do it. I did become involved in organizing, lecturing, and attending courses at Mornington, branded by a British tabloid as a "school for terrorism," though the courses were more about philosophy, history, and political economy than anything military. There were also monthly general members' meetings in Liberty Hall, where there was usually a central issue for discussion: civil rights, political prisoners, national wage agreements, the development of Dublin Bay, the future direction of the UI. All meetings at all levels spilled out into the nearest pub, where the same agenda was discussed in a freer and often funnier way.

I was always thinking about the contrasts between America and Ireland in general and about differences in their left movements in particular. The biggest contrast lay in the structure. Sinn Fein/IRA had clear procedures for joining, moving from one stage to another, deciding policy, and electing leadership. I found the structural clarity of this refreshing after the chaotic structurelessness of the

New Left. It was not only structured but hierarchical. There was no problem about recognizing the role of leaders. This did not trouble me at the time. I thought Goulding, Garland, and MacGiolla had earned the weight given to their voices. I might argue with them in time, but first I had much to learn from them. The culture of commemorations was another point of contrast. The annual Wolfe Tone commemoration in County Kildare was in honor of Theobald Wolfe Tone, leading figure in the United Irishmen movement, who sought to unify Catholics, Protestants, and dissenters to fight for an Irish Republic. The turnout was huge, with a very disciplined march to Wolfe Tone's grave, led by a color guard and men in black berets, followed by bands, then followed by people, from old men to young girls, all in their Sunday best, marching in columns and in step to the rhythm of pipes and drums. The generals walked with the people. At the grave, a party leader would give an oration. In 1972, it was by Sean Garland, on the theme of building a revolutionary party. Afterward there were drinks and dinner in Osta John Devoy, and then a *ceili* in the Mansion House back in Dublin in the evening. Another commemoration I attended around the same time was for Martin O'Leary, an IRA volunteer who had died accidentally the year before in an explosion in support of labor struggles in Tipperary. We marched through the streets of Cork to his grave, and Cathal Goulding gave the oration.

I was also keen to connect with the women's liberation movement in Ireland. Soon after I arrived I went to a meeting of an organization called the Irish Women's Liberation Movement. It didn't go well. Some of the most vocal participants were hostile toward the left in general and Sinn Fein in particular. Any mention of anything to do with class or economics or even politics was denounced as something "out of Gardiner Place." Someone even proposed a picket on Gardiner Place to protest against an IRA tar-and-feathering of a fifteen-year-old girl accused of fraternizing with British soldiers in Belfast. They had a point about that. Even within the movement, the act provoked a sharp response. Máirín de Burca criticized it and Máire Woods shaved her head in protest.

At the time the republican movement lacked a strong feminist consciousness. I felt it was time for this to change, and I could be part
of it. Some women in the movement were very traditionalist and
felt no need to be liberated from traditional gender roles, but as
time went on, there were more women like me, bringing a feminist
perspective to bear. For me, feminism was an integral part of my
worldview, but only a part of it. I was acutely aware of the differences within feminism as defined at the time—liberal feminism,
socialist feminism, and radical feminism. I was a socialist feminist.

Billy was back and forth between Dublin and Belfast, after staying in Dublin for ten days when I first arrived. The first time he left
for Belfast I got a shock, as he changed his appearance, dying his
hair and shaving off his moustache. He looked over his false identity papers and memorized the details of a biographical sketch that
he then destroyed. It sent a chill through me, as it brought home
to me the dangerous life he led, which was sometimes easy to
forget, with his lighthearted manner and the freedom with which
we moved around Dublin, despite the dangers lurking there, too.
When he was on the run in Belfast, the only way I could communicate with him was to leave a letter in head office, which would by
some route be delivered to him by hand. His letters to me came via
head office or sometimes just appeared in my flat. In the top right-
hand corner, he wrote "Belfast, no fixed abode," which reminded
me of the letters my father wrote to my mother during the war.
His letters were funny and full of concern for the minor details
of my life, as well as discussion of the political situation on the
ground in the north. Making light of the real dangers, he wrote of
his journey in mock cinematic terms: "After many hair-raising and
breath-taking adventures, narrow escapes, frantic car chases, near
misses, furious confrontations, two or three beers and a plate of
mixed fruit salad with ice cream, I arrived safely, without so much
as a strand of hair out of place."

Before long, he would be back in Dublin again and we would
walk by the sea and go to concerts, meetings, socials, restaurants,
and pubs. We spoke of how and when I might visit Belfast. When

he was there, he wrote that he was glad that I was not there, as he fell asleep to the sound of gunfire and exploding bombs. At the same time, he wondered what I would make of his scene. So did I. I mixed with a lot of northerners on the run in the south. Many weren't able to settle into jobs, education, or political activity, spending all afternoon and evening in the pub expressing their frustration and disaffection. After some military activities had gone wrong or failed to win public support—particularly the bombing in Aldershot, which was aimed at British officers, but instead killed five female cleaners, a gardener, and a chaplain—a ceasefire was called in May 1972. Many of these volunteers fiercely opposed the ceasefire, with complaints about not equipping northern units adequately or pursuing armed struggle vigorously enough. The official policy was defense and retaliation, as opposed to offence. This still left a lot of space for IRA activity, as there was a lot of defending and retaliating to do.

On a Thursday evening in July 1972, I traveled alone by train to Belfast, a scenic journey by the sea. When it crossed the border, I saw Union Jacks flying and soldiers stopping cars, guns at the ready. When I arrived in Belfast, I followed Billy's instructions. I saw boarded-up shops, rows of burned-out houses, bullet-riddled walls, and lots of barbed wire. The city was full of graffiti: angry, defiant, ironic, reflective. One wall posed the question: "Is there life before death?" I met IRA volunteers sent by Billy to show me around. Belfast seemed very different from Dublin. It was much more tribal. Here the houses seemed to open out on to the streets, where there was a lot happening. The next day I was in the Falls area, having tea in one of its little houses, when we began to hear one bomb after another going off and the house began to rock. Everyone went out into the streets as ambulance after ambulance raced past. Billowing black smoke and wailing sirens filled the air. People tuned into the police and ambulance radios and heard reports of dead bodies at one place and then another, then requests for more plastic bags for the severed limbs that were scattered all around. A jeep came up the road with bags of body parts. Word went around that Provos had warned their own people not to go into the city center and left everyone else to take their chances. We had been heading there ourselves but were delayed, and it dawned on us how narrowly we had missed being blown to bits. People coming from the center of the bombing said they didn't know if they were running away from the next bomb or toward it. Their nerves were shattered. Bombs had been planted at bus and railway stations, banks, hotels, pubs, garages, bridges. Nine people met their deaths that day and 130 were injured, some horrifically mutilated. That day became known as Bloody Friday. All through the night, I heard nonstop gunfire. The next day no one talked of anything else. Things went from bad to worse, as this gave the British Army excuse to enter the no-go areas of Belfast and Derry and clamp down even further. Many more people, both Officials and Provos, were arrested.

I couldn't see Billy when I was in Belfast, as it was too dangerous, but he kept tabs on me. After a few days, he got word to me to make my way back to Dublin, and we could talk there. We walked and talked for many hours that night. Although I had already firmly taken the side of the Officials, I turned still more adamantly against the Provisionals after seeing so close-up the brutality of armed struggle as they were waging it. One night, I was having a late dinner in a restaurant in Rathmines with Cathal Goulding and Billy McMillen. At a nearby table were Ruairí Ó Brádaigh, Dáithí Ó Conaill, and Maria McGuire. McGuire accompanied Ó Conaill on arms-buying trips and was in the news as a glamorous face of the Provisional IRA. Only a few months later she fled under special branch protection and wrote a kiss-and-tell memoir, in which she claimed that Bloody Friday had been the turning point for her. Many years later, she emerged as a Tory councilor in Croydon. But back on that night in 1972, the two tables kept eyeing each other oddly and uneasily, though nothing notable actually happened. The same could not be said about the streets of the north. Some northerners told me they thought Billy should have a bodyguard, even when in the south.

Everything was so new to me that it was sometimes hard to interpret the nuances and assess the dangers. Seamus Costello was the IRA director of operations, and was the prototypical IRA hard man. He not only planned operations, but executed them as well. He instilled both respect and fear. Not just a gunman, he was also a successful local politician in Wicklow. He had joined the IRA as a teenager during the border campaign in the 1950s, when he was nicknamed the "boy general" for his physical courage and leadership skills. Like so many others, he had been imprisoned and interned. Internment was his university, and he became a serious student of socialist theory. He had been a strong advocate of the move to the left in the 1960s, but not of the 1972 cease-fire. Much of the discontent around the ceasefire was crystallizing around Costello. He could be eloquent enough when he spoke, but most often he just listened and watched with a steely gaze that gave me a chill. One night, it was all cozy and almost comfortable when I was in a pub with Billy and Seamus drinking, talking and laughing for several hours. I would think back on it later with a strong sense of pathos, in light of what happened later, in light of how they both died. On that night, however, we were comrades, and all seemed well.

I was eager to see as much of the country as possible, and was especially keen to discover rural Ireland. I had read Daniel Corkery's *The Hidden Ireland*, a panegyric to centuries of Gaelic culture, and to the worldview embodied in the peasantry, surviv-ing despite the colonizing Anglo-Irish mentality. Corkery exhorted his readers to find the hidden Ireland of Gaelic culture by "leaving the cities and towns behind, venture among the bogs and hills, far into the mountains even, where the native Irish . . . still lurked." Sean Ó Faoláin's *The Irish* stirred this feeling in me too, this desire to reconnect to ancestral memory. However, my romantic vision of the country soon came face-to-face with the real Ireland. There was no pure point of contact with ancient Gaelic culture, which I came to realize was much messier and less poetic in reality than I would have found congenial anyway. Rural people seemed to me much like urban people, surrounded by prettier scenery but concerned with most of the same issues of modern life as anywhere else. There were still thatched cottages, but those who lived there had electric cookers and televisions and sometimes even central heating. There were no pigs in parlors or kettles boiling on open fires. After a while, my initial euphoria and fascination with every little detail wore off and I began to settle into Ireland as someplace I might live and work for a long time to come.

Many of my travels around the country were to attend political and cultural events. Eoin Ó Murchú often invited me to accompany him on trips to *Gaeltacht* areas, places where Irish was still the primary language. He acted the bard and seemed to have an endless knowledge of Irish legends. He spoke the language fluently and sang in the *sean-nós* style. Born Owen Murphy in London to Irish parents, he came to Ireland to study at Trinity College and stayed. Since graduating, he had worked full-time for the movement, first as an organizer for the Gaeltacht, and now as editor of the newspaper and a member of the IRA's GHQ staff. A hardline Marxist-Leninist, when he wasn't reciting ancient lore he was polemicizing about contrary ideological tendencies inside and outside the movement. The primary target was Trotskyism, but he denounced all varieties of "ultra-leftism." I didn't find his stageist approach very convincing, and some of the anarchist positions he deplored were not far from my own. Nevertheless, it was a challenging dialogue, and gave me a sense of the range of positions and players on the Irish left.

Eoin was also somewhat insensitive to issues raised by the women's movement, mostly because of lack of exposure to feminism. He did listen to my arguments on such matters. For some months, there had been controversy brewing about the *United Irishman.* Many members thought it reflected the personality of the editor too strongly, arguing it should be overseen by an editorial board, to make its contents more representative of the movement. All this came to a head when Eoin published a poem in the paper in both Irish and English. It was on a theme of famine, emigration, and return, and it was dedicated to me. Many who objected referred to it as a "love poem." I was present at many of the meetings where it was denounced, which I found acutely embarrassing. It was the final straw. Eoin was removed as editor, although he continued to work full-time for the movement.

After a few months in Sinn Féin, I was invited to join the IRA, and I did. I was not attracted to guns and did not feel I had much to offer to the military side of the movement. I did still have a touch of a romantic idea of armed struggle, though it was erod-ing steadily, especially after Bloody Friday. Besides, we were on ceasefire, which I supported strongly by this time. So why do it? I joined because it was the way to be fully a part of the movement. The organization had parallel structures, so decisions discussed at the level of the cumann, region, or Ard-Fheis would have already been addressed in army structures. Nevertheless, I had reserva-tions. I would not follow any instruction blindly. I would not kill, except in some life-or-death situation. I would not lie, though I might refuse to speak or refrain from telling the whole truth in certain circumstances. I was instructed to go to an address in Cabra for induction. Upon arriving, I discovered it was a house divided into flats. I had been cautioned to be vigilant, as it was an illegal assembly. I stood by the door for a few minutes, wait-ing for someone inside to see me and let me in. No one did. As I didn't want to be late and it seemed ridiculous to just stand on the doorstep, I started ringing bells. As each occupant came on to the intercom, I spoke vaguely. Finally, I found the right one. Several people who came after me did the same. It didn't inspire confi-dence. Someone later told me that when they went for induction, they were instructed to stand in a bus queue in Amiens Street in the city center. Bus after bus went by, with the same few people hanging back each time, not boarding any bus. Finally, the person in charge came and led the recruits away from the bus queue. Not exactly the most discreet way to conduct an illegal assembly with-out attracting attention. During my next recruit's class, I was given an address to go to in Finglas. We assembled in the front room of a council house where we were solemnly read the army constitution by a member of the Dublin brigade. Prohibited activities were spelled out in a long list, and after each one, as if in a litany, the same refrain would be spoken: "Penalty: death." It was an autumn evening and darkness was falling, but for security, the lights could not be turned on. Every time a noise was heard from outside—often neighbors putting out trash bins—the person in charge would jump to the window and scan the street. It was all quite chilling. The next step was to go for arms training in the Dublin mountains, which I never did. I was, however, asked if I would use my passport to travel abroad and liaise on certain matters. I was kept on standby on several occasions, once to pick up a sample of a Czech submachine gun in Italy. I wondered if I was the right person even for this, since I was so openly active in the movement, coming in and out of Gardiner Place and living in the same house as Sean Garland. Someone must have had the same thought, and I never did go.

I often went to political meetings and parties with Billy or Eoin or both, or in larger company. My feminist and New Left mores made me averse to presenting myself as part of a couple. At one social, a woman called me aside and warned that "remarks" had been made about me. I resisted such pressures, but found my room for maneuver narrowing. While life on the left was bohemian in comparison with that in the rest of Ireland, it was still more traditional in some ways than in my American circles. There was a bit of a double standard in evidence at times, and the gossip and humor could be quite cutting. A female author's book based on interviews with movement leaders, titled *On Our Knees*, was often referred to as *Between Our Knees*.

I also was going through a phase where I wanted everything to be as "natural" as possible. I had already renounced makeup, and then turned against processed foods and pharmaceuticals, which meant that I went off the Pill. I tried and failed with the rhythm method of contraception, perhaps due to the stressful transition through which I was living. I had one pregnancy that ended in a miscarriage, and then another pregnancy. Both times my feminist friends assumed right away that I needed advice about getting an abortion. It was illegal in Ireland, and the usual route was to go to Britain for the procedure. While I was very radical about marriage and monogamy, I wasn't so radical about abortion and I could not do it. I had never thought of myself as a mother. It might have been the most "natural" thing in the world, but it was a major shock to me. At first it was traumatic, and I was nauseous morning, noon, and night. At one point I had to be hospitalized and fed intravenously. Still I continued on as best I could.

Life became more difficult for other reasons as well. The Fianna Fail government was growing more repressive. The offices of (Provisional) Sinn Féin were shut down, and prominent members were arrested and brought before the special criminal courts, set up to try political "subversives" without juries. A ban on broadcasting the voices of members of illegal organizations led to the imprisonment of an RTE journalist and the dismissal of the RTE Authority. The broadcaster's employees went on strike for three days, followed by a one-day strike by newspaper staff. There were also work stoppages in the power and transport sectors. In December 1972, the government had proposed an amendment to the Offenses against the State Act that would have made a statement by a *garda* superintendant sufficient evidence to convict anyone suspected of IRA membership. It completely transferred the burden of proof onto the accused. While the bill was being debated in the Dail two bombs went off in the center of Dublin, killing two transport workers and injuring many others. Jervis Street Hospital was overwhelmed. No one has ever taken responsibility or been charged for the attacks. Most people I knew believed the bombings were the work of either the Irish special branch or British forces, designed to provoke repressive legislation. If so, they had their intended effect. Opposition to the bill collapsed. The taoiseach, Jack Lynch, went on television at midnight and announced its immediate enforcement. We expected a police roundup at any moment. Sean rushed downstairs, where Eoin was, and together

they fled into the night. I waited for a knock on the door, worried I
might be deported. Several Americans associated with the Provos
had recently been sent back to the United States. I had already
noticed that my incoming mail seemed to have been opened before
I got it. The whole experience made me less dismissive of liberal-
ism as a milieu in which to struggle for socialism. I learned not to
take basic civil liberties for granted. A British intelligence report
looked at Officials versus Provisionals in terms of security threat,
observing that the Officials were not so well armed, but were more
vocal and politically sophisticated, having support in universities
and media, concluding that we were the greatest subversive threat
in the long term.

The expected dragnet didn't happen, and those who had gone
into hiding resurfaced for the Ard-Fheis in mid-December at
the Mansion House. Seven hundred delegates came from around
the country, plus journalists, visitors, observers, and fraternal
delegates from left organizations abroad. Over three hundred resolutions were debated, dealing with all aspects of "how to organize
the Irish people for a successful socialist revolution." We considered motions on economics, organization, culture, international
affairs, even gender. I was a delegate and spoke on political education and gender. I thought by this time I was starting to blend in,
but one delegate who encountered me for the first time there later
told me how I had stood out with "your long flaming red hair and
multicolored poncho, looking and talking like no one I had ever
seen or heard before."

I also made several trips to Britain, particularly London, and
began to inform myself about the British left. I spent hours in the
bookshops along Charing Cross Road, returning to Dublin laden
with as many books as I could afford. In London I also met Eoin's
family, who didn't really know what to make of me. Though we
would see each other many times, our encounters never got beyond
awkward politeness. They were working-class Londoners who had
been born in Ireland but lived and worked for most of their lives in
Britain, a country they hated. They were living to retire in Ireland.

I kept up with what was going on in the United States as best
I could. I sent and received many letters discussing life and politics here and there. One day I received a piece of a parachute
from an action where some activists I knew had broken into an
air force base in Willow Grove and damaged several aircraft. The
mail was slow and liable to be intercepted, but it was all we had
in those days. Jack was very good about sending news clippings
and taking care of various practical matters for me. Sometimes he
and others would record and send audio cassettes—an exciting
new technology at the time—of themselves talking to me, often
including music as well. There was much to discuss. Rennie Davis
had gone off to India and come under the spell of Maharaj-ji, a
fifteen-year-old charlatan guru who spoke of "divine light" while
wearing expensive clothes and driving luxury cars. Rennie set out
to convert our whole generation to his vision and was organizing
an extravaganza at the Houston Astrodome, promising it would
be "the greatest event in history." Many of us felt that the stress of
the movement had somehow brought him to the point of mental
breakdown. Tom Hayden, who had been close to him, was especially distressed. Tom had married Jane Fonda and continued with
antiwar work. Others took a different path. Even some in Powelton
who had been on the anarchist side of the Marxism-anarchism
debate now leaned toward Marxism, as did I. Several were
involved in the New Communist Movement and went to work
in factories (even though they had university degrees), became
active in trade unions, studied Marxism intensively, formulated
a "correct line" on everything and struggled against all contrary
tendencies. Nationally this was expressed in the Revolutionary
Union, the October League, the Black Workers Congress, and in
the pages of the *Guardian*. In Philadelphia, the movement centered on the Philadelphia Workers Organizing Committee. All of
them endured excruciating criticism and self-criticism.

I started thinking about visiting the United States. I missed my
friends and the New Left milieu. After all my talk about it, Eoin
was keen to see it for himself, and got approval for a US speaking

tour. I did much to organize it, adding my own university and left contacts to the movement's existing network. I was by then in my second trimester and feeling better. I even began to find pregnancy an interesting, grounding experience. Eoin and I were in the States from January to March 1973. As international secretary of the IRA, he spoke to various university and political gatherings and gave media interviews on the political situation in Ireland. My family took the news of my pregnancy surprisingly well. They had also started to get involved with Irish-American culture, and my radicalism didn't seem so bad if it was Irish. They didn't probe too much into the politics. One night we threw a party in Springfield where my family mingled with my New Left and Irish Republican friends. Ron Whitehorne brought his guitar and played labor songs, and my parents spoke quite civilly with Dave Gracie, whom they knew only from news reports, which had elicited their disapproval. My brothers and sisters even attended demonstrations against British imperialism. After living in Ireland for seven months, I found many Irish-American images of Ireland naive, romantic, and even ridiculous. One guy always wore a black beret, combat jacket, and belt buckle with big brass letters spelling "IRA." I heard him tell his girlfriend: "My mother is first. Ireland is second. You are third." I hope he grew out it.

I returned to Ireland in March 1973. At passport control, I was given a visa only for three months, which raised fears of deportation just as I was due to give birth. I was told that the best way to circumvent this was to marry, which I hesitated to do. In any case, I asked Jack to initiate divorce proceedings. Since there was no no-fault divorce in Pennsylvania then, we agreed that he would sue me for desertion. Movement lawyers sorted out the details. While we were away, a snap election had been called, and when we returned there was a new government, a Fine Gael–Labour coalition. It was even more committed to repressive legislation. I moved into another flat in Ranelagh that quickly became a hub of political activity. I continued with all my political activities, even after my due date came and went. I was keen on natural childbirth.

In my last month, I had by chance witnessed two births. I was in Leeds to visit activists there when our hostess went into labor late at night. The midwife arrived and I rushed to assist her, and in the process I saw a child born in a way that was totally natural and deeply moving.

It didn't go so well for me. There was no NHS service to assist with home births. I could not risk doing it anyway, given the dangers: my baby was in a particularly difficult breach position, with feet presenting. Two weeks before I ultimately gave birth, I had been taken to the hospital and given a general anesthetic while they tried unsuccessfully to turn the baby. A young woman in a bed next to me was there for the same thing. As we chatted, she lifted the sheets and saw a huge amount of blood. She lost her baby in her ninth month, right in front of me. Afterward I often saw her in the local shops; she must have found it painful to see me with my child. I was at a meeting of the national education committee on the top floor of Gardiner Place when labor finally began. I didn't say anything until the meeting ended, taking comfort in the fact that it was being chaired by John McManus, a medical doctor, who could help if needed, which it wasn't. Nevertheless, the pain shocked me. I took Christopher Caudwell's *Illusion and Reality* with me into the labor ward, but was unable to concentrate. After thirty excruciating hours, I succumbed to a general anesthetic and caesarean section. I was very disappointed, but happy to have a live, healthy baby, my son Cathal. I thought of the song "Four Green Fields" and the line "But my sons have sons, as brave as were their fathers." I felt strongly that I was bringing forth a son into this struggle, though he would obviously have to make up his own mind, as he eventually would. While I was in the hospital, my divorce papers arrived. Once more the arguments were put to me about marriage and deportation. I consented. Eoin and I arrived at the registry office in Kildare Street along with our witnesses, Eoghan and Anne Harris. It was quite grim. The registrar took Anne to be the bride, as she seemed so much more enthusiastic and I was busy fussing with Cathal. The registrar checked my divorce papers and said that "nothing need ever be said about it again."

I brought Cathal everywhere: to meetings, lectures, demonstrations, socials. When it was time to breastfeed him, I did it there and then, without hiding. This created a stir, especially at meetings. Most had never seen it done before. My parents were keen to meet their first grandchild as well as to see Ireland for the first time. My brother Gene, who was in the US Army, came with them. We toured around Ireland, all six of us packed into Eoin's tiny car. They took in the beautiful scenery and old ruins and did not inquire too much about the politics. Eoin combined our passing through Donegal with conducting an IRA court-martial, although my family had no idea. His work for the movement was quite varied. It often took him abroad. He made several trips with Cathal Goulding to Lebanon to meet with the PLO seeking help in arms acquisition.

We saw a lot of Eoghan and Anne Harris. Eoghan was growing more prominent in the movement while working as a current affairs producer in RTE. Fast-talking, articulate, and colorful, he filled every room he entered, turning every discussion into high drama. He didn't listen too carefully to anyone's personal story, instead taking a few scraps from it and inventing his own bio for each person, fashioning them as characters in his own script. Terry Murphy, Eoin's brother, had briefly been a clerk on the London docks, but in Eoghan's telling he was the prototypical docker, leading strikes and sorting out scabs. His back story for me was that I had been a member of the CPUSA and was bringing an authentic communist perspective to bear on Irish politics. At the time Eoghan often talked about Eamonn Smullen, an experienced communist and trade unionist, who, at forty-eight, had just been released from prison in Britain and was returning to Ireland. Whatever the problem we would be discussing, Eoghan assured us that Smullen would sort it out. He was portrayed as the fount of all proletarian wisdom, steeled in the fire of class struggle. Naturally, I looked forward to meeting him. I was stunned to find him a somewhat pedestrian figure. Whoever he was before, he had since become a character in Eoghan Harris's drama, and I watched as he took on the part in the script written for him. I saw the same happen with other people. Eoghan had a mesmerizing effect on certain people, even some who seemed to have strong characters of their own, but they all became characters in his script, puppets on a string.

One prime plot was the building of an industrial division. The movement had already been paying more attention to trade union work, but now it was to be ramped up. Lar Malone had been spearheading this effort, but after his arrest for armed robbery (a source of organizational fund-raising), he jumped bail and resettled abroad. Now Smullen was made director of economic affairs as well as a member of the Army Council. He went to Sam Nolan, the industrial organizer of the Communist Party of Ireland, for advice on how to approach trade union work. On one level, Smullen came to a general members' meeting and told us all to stand for whatever positions were available in trade unions. On another level, there was a conspiratorial atmosphere surrounding industrial work that went beyond the risk of illegal activities in support of industrial disputes or violations of union rules against factional activity. It was a cult of conspiracy, really. Industrial cumainn were set up, provoking a bit of tussle over their relationship to Sinn Féin and IRA structures. Harris was dismissive of Sinn Féin and insisted on coordinating only with the IRA. Beyond that, certain people were invited in while others were kept out, sometimes for no reason other than Eoghan's flights of fancy.

Another storyline in this drama was a battle to combat Trotskyist infiltration. The actual evidence for such entryism was thin. Nevertheless, Eoin and Eoghan were always going on about it. Gerry Foley, a US Trotskyist, visited Sean Garland several times, and I was in the house once while they talked upstairs for hours. These visits caused consternation and made certain people anxious to curb Foley's influence, as Garland was such a pivotal player. Seamus Costello was also suspected of contact with certain

Trotskyist elements. There were IRA units in Derry and Galway that were thought to have Trotskyist tendencies and associations. Padraig Yeates, who ran the bookshop in Gardiner Place, had been a member of International Socialists in Birmingham before he came to Dublin. The bookshop's inventory was regularly scrutinized for Trotskyist texts. There were some who spoke as if some section of a Fourth International was issuing secret orders on the stocking of our bookshop. There were several Trotskyist organizations in Ireland at this time, but most members never came in contact with them.

Relations with the CPI were strong, and this was essential to the IRA's national liberation front strategy. The CPI had brokered the acquisition of arms from the USSR, via the KGB, in an operation code-named Splash. The request was made by Cathal Goulding and Seamus Costello in 1969 before the split, but KGB chairman Yuri Andropov hesitated, and arms only started arriving in 1972. Michael O'Riordan, CPI general secretary, wrote to Moscow that relations with the IRA were good, that they organized joint political and anti-imperialist activities in public and had a mechanism in place for consultations in secret, adding somewhat patronizingly that they "unfailingly accept our advice." At one point, a meeting was held to discuss an even closer relationship, though that was derailed by O'Riordan's insistence upon the vanguard role of communist parties.

In October 1973, Mac Giolla, O Hagan, and Garland went to a Congress of International Peace Forces in Moscow, which symbolized and strengthened the tendency of the party to align itself with the communist tradition. Garland was especially affected by the Soviet experience and from then on sided very firmly with the communist movement. This pleased Harris and Ó Murchú, who at the time were explicitly Stalinist. Everyone in our circles was enthusiastically reading and quoting Mervyn Jones's *Joseph*, a fictionalized biography of Stalin that gave a gripping account of the struggles and choices facing the Soviet Union. We felt that understanding the USSR, the world's first socialist country, was of primary importance. This meant taking a stand on the debates swirling around it. The contest between Stalinism and Trotskyism was seen not only as the key to Soviet history in the 1920s and 1930s, but was sometimes extended to the whole of life. "Stalinist" was an all-embracing term of praise and "Trotskyist" the corresponding term of condemnation. When someone new arrived on the scene who knew nothing of these debates, but had the Harris seal of approval, Anne spoke highly of her as "a natural Stalinist." When their daughter Constance was naughty, she was "a little Trot." It was even projected back into the past, before Trotsky. In a lecture on the First International, Harris accused Bakunin of "introducing provo-Trotskyism into the working-class movement."

There wasn't much communication or travel between Ireland and Eastern Europe at that time, but we seized every opportunity to learn what was going on there. We joined the Ireland-USSR Society. We read loads of Soviet periodicals and Progress Books titles. We arranged screenings of Soviet and Cuban films. Cuba and Vietnam remained special places on our political map, and we wanted to learn all we could about the history of their revolutions and the nature of their societies. We had a great *grá* for Albania as well. *The History of the Party of Labour of Albania* was a must-read in our circles and issues of *Albania Today* were passed around every month. We were also into China. We read lots of Maoist literature, and though aware of the Sino-Soviet split, we tended to support both the USSR and the PRC. Some members were more Maoist than others. The outstanding voice of Maoism in Dublin Sinn Féin was Patrick Kinsella, who knew the texts well and quoted them with zeal as guides to making decisions in our own situation. He spoke up at meetings with particular precision. There was much serious probing into the history of the left and its different intellectual traditions in the political education programs going on, which were also being ramped up.

Political education in Dublin took place in a real hothouse atmosphere, particularly in 1973-74. I was feverishly occupied in planning and teaching the introductory, intermediate, and advanced courses. I lectured on topics I myself was just learning, such as the October Revolution, debates in the early years of Soviet power, dialectical materialism, and socialist culture. The intermediate course was focused on the history of socialism and the history of Ireland, with a strong emphasis on class and progressive movements. The advanced course was on Marxist theory, divided into sections on economics, politics, philosophy, sociology, and culture. All education officers were required to take the course and to observe rules about attendance, reading, note-taking, and reporting back to cumainn. Every lecture included both required and recommended reading, from classical works by Marx, Engels, Lenin, and Connolly, to books such as *Ireland Her Own* by T. A. Jackson, *The Bolshevik Revolution* by E. H. Carr, *Red Star Over China* by Edgar Snow, and *The Wretched of the Earth* by Frantz Fanon. We allowed time for questions and answers and even discussion after each lecture, but it wasn't an atmosphere conducive to conflicting interpretations. There was a correct line on all questions, and *anathema sit* upon all deviations from it.

The most controversial aspect of the program was the series of essays that students were required to write to enroll in the advanced course. The topics were worded so as to close off any ambiguity or alternative positions: "The four Fourth Internationals and all the groups they have formed are active agents of imperialism. Elaborate." Some members objected, prompting debate at various levels of the organization. On top of the dogmatic tone, some lecturers lacked pedagogical experience or flair. I did know better, as I was an experienced teacher, and I tried to make my own lectures more persuasive than declarative, open to questioning and discussion. Nevertheless, I was very protective of the project, and convinced of the importance of knowing the history of socialism and progressive movements, of mastering concepts in philosophy and political economy. Indeed, I took a strong polemical stance against anyone who came into the debate with an anti-intellectual or relativistic position. There was such a thing as truth, I defensively declared. The Ard-Chomairle eventually ruled against the essays, clipped our wings, and cut back on such intensive educational courses.

There was an influx of new members during this period, but I have to wonder how many we drove away with the mood of heresy-hunting mistrust that pervaded these classes as well as other meetings. Many were just taking their first steps toward the left and lacked well-formed political philosophies. They were faced with a barrage of complex debates and pressed to take sides on issues they had not properly processed. This preoccupation with purging the party was justified by quotes from Lenin, particularly a passage from *What Is To Be Done?* "Better fewer but better," it was constantly said. Anyone who wavered, anyone who exhibited social democratic or anarchist or other tendencies that differed from the pro-Soviet, Marxist-Leninist line was unwelcome. With a convert's zeal, I was part of this, and in retrospect I regret it. Nevertheless, I learned a lot in the process, as did others. We read feverishly, and we did so with a sense that our ideas and the actions they inspired really mattered. We were building a revolutionary party, and we believed that somehow we would make a revolution. This was not based on an astute assessment of the balance of forces that would be required for it to happen, but it was inflamed by a passionate conviction that it needed to happen.

The profile of feminism in the movement was also rising during this time, partly thanks to our political education program. We held a weekend school on Mornington devoted to women under capitalism, women under socialism, and the politics of the women's liberation movement. We believed that socialist feminism was in every way superior to other strains of feminism. We also ran a series of seminars based on biographies of women such as Anne Devlin, Constance Markievicz, Elizabeth Gurley Flynn, Sylvia Pankhurst, Alexandra Kollontai, Rosa Luxemburg, and Emma Goldman, and another based on reviews of books such as *The Feminine Mystique*, *The Dialectic of Sex*, and *Women's Estate*. All these presentations were led by women, all of us young. We debated the relative importance of gender and class. Our weekly tabloid newspaper *The Irish People* carried a column under the byline of Anne Devlin (actually Anne Harris), who attacked feminism for downgrading class struggle. Máirín de Burca responded that it was "Trotskyite bullshit," which raised the stakes, the T-word being the worst possible offense in the Harris universe. De Burca insisted that the distress of battered women could not be shelved until after victory in the class struggle.

In this movement, I became a Marxist. I had already moved far in the direction of Marxism without conscious or direct influence from it. When I did finally come to it, the effect was electric. All that I had been struggling to synthesize suddenly clicked into place. It was as if, having put a fair few pieces of a puzzle into place, I suddenly saw the shape of the whole. It was the difference between seeing each item in a pattern and seeing the pattern itself. It sent me rushing down the corridors of knowledge, with a new key for opening every door, discovering again everything I thought I already knew, making the familiar strange and the strange familiar. It spurred me on both to assimilate new fields of knowledge and to reassimilate old ones. With a newly firm grip on the broad outlines of economics, science, and technology I began to also comprehend philosophy, politics, sociology, history, and literature more clearly, finally seeing them in the fullness of their interconnections. My mind was soaring wildly, yet it had never been so securely anchored.

Amid all of this, I became pregnant again and gave birth to my daughter Clíodna in 1974. It was not so difficult this time. I went into labor on time and gave birth naturally and consciously, an experience hard to compare to anything else. Playing in the background was the radio broadcast of the funeral of the president of Ireland. Birth and death, the natural rhythm of life, I thought. Earlier that year we had moved out of the tiny flat in Ranelagh, which was often overflowing with people during late-night political discussions and sing-songs, including many overnight guests. We moved to a four-bedroom house in Bayside still busy with political activities, but with fewer post-pub sessions, as it was farther from the city center. It was a full house, with five adult activists and my two children, plus many others staying overnight from time to time, along with a continual stream of visitors from abroad. Not only that, but my younger sister had gone missing, and my parents asked if, once they found her, she could come and live with us for a while, thinking of Ireland as a place that would keep her out of trouble. They had their hands full with the younger children, who were in trouble more than the older ones had been at their age, which was a sign of the times. (It was nearly a year before my sister resurfaced; when she did return from Florida, where she had been living, she was diagnosed with cancer and stayed in the United States for treatment and eventually remission.) We were in the O'Leary cumann now, which had a different flavor from the Pearse cumann. There were fewer students and more construction workers, some in trades going back generations. They took knowledge very seriously in the proletarian way that has been a great strength of the labor movement.

These were fertile years for radical cultural expression in Ireland. One memorable experiment was the *Non-Stop Connolly Show*, a twenty-four-hour play by John Arden and Margaretta D'Arcy based on the life of James Connolly, performed at Liberty Hall. I knew lots of people involved and wanted to be affirmative about it, but found it a bit of an endurance test. The agitprop knockabout music hall style jarred at times. However, this mix of music and jokes with serious history and calls to revolt worked brilliantly in the Scottish 7:84 theatre company's *The Cheviot, the Stag and the Black, Black Oil*, an economic history of the highlands, which came to Dublin to raving acclaim. The name of the company referred to the fact that 7 percent of the population owned 84 percent of the wealth. Around the same time, Club Ui Chadhain opened in a basement in Gardiner Place as a center for cultural events as well as nightly drinking and socializing. This also diverted much of the money spent by members on food and drink back into the organization instead of commercially run pubs. Other methods of fund-raising ranged from folk concerts to bank robberies. As a political scene, it combined aspects of international left culture with those of Irish male proletarian subculture, with pubs and pints at the core.

A constant stream of people from various international left groups were coming to Dublin to express solidarity with our struggle and to inform us of theirs. In July 1974, we hosted an Anti-Imperialist Festival in Dublin and Belfast, with lectures, concerts, historical tours, cultural events, commemorations, and lots of drink, stretching over two weeks. Newspaper headlines branded it a "festival of terror." Interpol was on alert, and several would-be attendees were refused entry to the country. In Liberty Hall, they were welcomed to an alternative Ireland to the one in travel brochures, one where 5 percent of the people owned 75 percent of the wealth. All the speeches, whether by visitors from Europe, Africa, or the Americas, ended with the same incantation: "Our fight is your fight. Your fight is our fight." We had special connections to movements in other Celtic regions those days, especially Brittany. During this festival, Gilles Servat, a Breton folksinger who performed during the festival, stayed with us in Bayside. He invited us to come to another such festival in Larzac in August. We traveled to the South of France with five of us packed into his tiny car in sweltering heat. I had Cathal on my lap and was expecting Clíodna, so it was a tough trip, but it was worth it when we arrived. It was stunningly beautiful. The festival was full of music, crafts, fun, talk and a powerful sense of solidarity. The discourse was earnest and defiant, although it put my French to the test and I must have missed many a nuance.

The year 1974 was also full of hardening factions and bitter polemics. Debates at the November 1973 Ard-Fheis on organizational structure, relations with socialist countries, reform versus revolution, and industry versus agriculture were angry, tumultuous, and ultimately poisonous. Moves accelerated against those pushing for increased military action and against alliances with socialist countries, the "Provo-Trots," as Harris and Ó Murchú called them.

Both the IRA and Sinn Féin opened inquiries against Seamus Costello, who was accused of vote-rigging, faction-building, and misappropriation of funds. The Dublin unit of the IRA was summoned to a meeting at the North Star Hotel, where we were read a list of offenses committed by "Volunteer Clancy," some of them dating back to the 1950s. I was astonished. If he had done all these things, I thought, how could he have been such a prominent movement leader for so long, entrusted with the position of director of operations? It was surreal. Soon after came the full IRA court-martial, held at Mornington in April 1974. In a monumental mistake of double-booking, a weekend educational course was scheduled to be held at the complex the same weekend, and though some of us there for the class realized immediately what was going on, others had no idea. The ensuing conversation over Sunday lunch was like walking on eggshells, giving rise to a few unintendedly hilarious double-entendres. It was another adventure in surreality. Costello was found guilty of all charges and dismissed from the IRA with ignominy. The Sinn Féin Ard-Chomairle suspended him. Just days after giving birth, I joined seven hundred others to attend the 1974 Ard-Fheis, where there was a final attempt to prevent a split in the organization. Maeliosa Costello and Nicky Kelly spoke for the reinstatement of Seamus Costello. Ó Murchú and Garland responded with bitter denunciations. In closed session, the Ard-Fheis voted for explusion by a vote of 197 to 15.

If this bitter phase still had its lighter moments, what followed was heavy and brought no laughs and many tears. Those who left in support of Costello and his analysis formed the Irish Republican Socialist Party, with a military wing called the Irish National Liberation Army. I knew many members who left. Unlike other splits, where one side hits out against the other in words, this one backed the words with guns. The polemics became even more vituperative and were followed by resignations and expulsions, threats and counter-threats, assaults, interrogations, tussles over funds and arms, fire bombings and shootings. Some were wounded and survived, while others died. Eoin was a prime target, as he had been explicitly threatened by Costello on more than one occasion and was in the forefront of polemicizing and pushing against this group. Costello had called him a "blue-nose, wine-drinking, Trinity shit" at an IRA GHQ staff meeting. During these months, nights were frightening. We put chairs and irons and anything else that would make noise on the stairs, both to obstruct and to awake. Only the rich had house alarms at the time. I locked the kids in a separate room at night, knowing several children had been shot and wounded during the fighting. With houses being raided and weapons seized, we could not have a gun in the house. We kept kitchen knives in the bedroom, though they would have been no use against guns.

In March 1975, Sean Garland was ambushed late one night in Ballymun and shot six times. He was not expected to survive. I went to see him in the hospital. He had refused the solace of a priest and was willing to face death without any false comforts. I was quite shaken at the sight of him in intensive care. Then came the worst shock of all. In April, Billy McMillen was shot dead in the street in Belfast. I heard it on the radio. It was front-page news in all the national papers the next day. I could hardly believe it. Thousands attended his funeral in Belfast two days later. I could not go, but I mourned him at a distance and in silence. In May, there was an attempt on the life of Seamus Costello in Waterford. It failed. After that, they bided their time, but they finally shot him dead in 1977. There were a series of defiant paramilitary funerals on both sides. It was the most bitter and brutal conflict I had ever seen at such close range.

Meanwhile, now that one faction had left, the remaining members, who had formed a not-so-united front against those who formed the Irish Republican Socialist Party and Irish National Liberation Army, could concentrate on their differences with one another. These struggles not only pitted Marxists against social-democrats, quasi-anarchists, and people without well-developed political philosophies, but Marxists against Marxists. Most of these groups were by then pro-Soviet, but they were divided by personality conflicts as well as ideological nuances. Moreover, differences on the national question opened a new front, with one group, led by Eoghan Harris, veering away from republicanism toward quasi-unionism. It was a common position to move from Catholic nationalism and physical-force republicanism and to try to win progressive Protestants, especially the working class, to a common struggle for civil rights and socialism. However, some became so obsessed with Protestants that they started down a path of conceding everything to them. Harris himself would eventually become a unionist, wear the poppy, and support imperialist wars, past and present. In the intervening years, he wreaked havoc in the republican movement before renouncing republicanism altogether.

It was all falling apart. Even while the guns were still firing from the IRA-INLA split, new battles had begun. My political education work hit a brick wall. I was thirty, with two children to raise. I still had no PhD. I had no job. I had put everything at risk for this movement, and it was in chaos. My political commitment remained strong as ever, but I had to find a new way. In March 1975, I resigned from Sinn Féin, saying that the movement was floundering, without proper discipline or clear ideology, and that serious Marxists were being isolated and undermined. I received a reply from the head office accepting my resignation with regret. I also received a long letter from the O'Leary cumann agreeing with my criticisms but disagreeing that they were cause for resignation. I still considered them comrades, and wanted to move on without bitterness.

I also resigned from the doctoral program at Temple and informed the Danforth Foundation. Aside from the fact that my activism had overtaken my studies, my doctoral thesis had mutated until it disappeared amid shifts in my intellectual priorities, and indeed in my whole worldview. It was time for reorientation, on both political and academic fronts. It was time to move on.

PS ON *THE LOST REVOLUTION*: While there are few first-person accounts of life in this movement, there have been a number of studies, examining the documents and interviewing the participants, including myself. The definitive work is *The Lost Revolution* by Brian Hanley and Scott Millar, published as a Penguin paperback in 2009. It has been widely read, discussed, and reviewed. According to the blog *Splintered Sunrise*: "It's in the quotes from the interviews that you get a sense of the movement through the eyes of the people who were in it, their experiences, memories and impressions. You also come to form quite a vivid picture of the leading individuals. So you have Goulding . . . there's certainly a sense of what an attractive figure Goulding was, as well as what a pain in the ass he could occasionally be. You have MacGiolla as the cautious conciliator, always anxious to avoid unnecessary division, yet resolute once he had picked his side. You have Costello the dynamic, sometimes arrogant hotshot—he almost swaggers off the page—impatient with those who hadn't caught up with his latest brainstorm, and with a fatal tendency to choose drastic action as the first resort. And there's the enigmatic figure of Garland, who may have liked to be the self-effacing behind-the-scenes operator, but whose presence makes itself felt even when he isn't there. The characters come to life, and so do the settings."

6

The Internationale

As some paths closed, others opened. I turned from one party, university, and thesis, to another party, university, and thesis. Indeed, there were a whole series of shifts in the contours of my life. Life in Sinn Féin/IRA had been somewhat turned in on itself. Once I left, I moved outward into Irish society and the wider world. I took part in campaigns for resources protection, against unemployment, for Chile solidarity, and against South African apartheid. I registered at Trinity College Dublin, where I resumed doctoral studies and university teaching. I became involved in trade union activity through the Association of Scientific, Technical and Managerial Staffs. I wrote for national newspapers. I socialized in different circles. I even donned an evening dress and dined and danced on one occasion at the press ball.

Of all the changes, what most shaped by life in these years was my joining the Communist Party of Ireland. The day after I resigned from Sinn Féin in 1975, I went to New Books in Parliament Street and asked Sean Nolan for an application to join the CPI. He smiled gently and gave it to me, but didn't say much. I discovered that he rarely said much. The only party member I had previously met was Tom Redmond, the area secretary, and that only recently. Not long after I joined the party, so did Eoin Ó Murchú and others from Sinn Féin. There was some bitterness at this exodus, which overlapped with the IRSP split. Sean Garland spoke angrily of the variety of those who left as "the opportunists, the instant revolutionaries, the sectarian bigots" as well as "the cowards who fled, not to greener, but to safer, pastures." The last phrase angered me most, because I didn't know anyone who left out of cowardice. Some had lived with quite a high level of risk on the operational side.

Moreover, it wasn't safer at all, but even more dangerous. On top of the INLA threats still hanging over Eoin, there was now an IRA one. Eamonn Smullen, who became Dublin O/C, informed Mick O'Riordan, general secretary of the CPI, that any action against Eoin would target him not as a member of the party, but as an ex-member of the IRA. While not taking elaborate security precautions, Eoin and others checked under cars for bombs and were watchful about being followed. I still locked the children in their room at night. Eoin was working as a sub-editor for the Irish Press and was often alone on dark streets late at night upon finishing a shift. He continued his polemical assault on the IRSP/INLA, but added Official SF/IRA to it, increasingly using CPI publications to do so. Several who left OSF/IRA and joined the CPI were attacked with guns, bars, and hatchets in a Dublin pub. The CPI confronted SF/IRA about these threats and attacks on their members. These were not safer pastures.

Moves toward left unity emerged, flourished, then floundered, for various reasons. In 1976, Left Alternative—comprising Official Sinn Féin, CPI, and Left Liaison of the Labour Party—was launched at a meeting attended by a thousand people in the Mansion House. However, the previously good relationship between OSF and CPI was under pressure on several fronts, not only the exodus of members from one to the other. There ensued a barrage of polemics on the national question, competition for positions and influence in trade unions and various campaigns and for international recognition. Official Sinn Féin, which became Sinn Féin the Workers Party and then the Workers Party, sought to displace the CPI as the embodiment of the international communist movement in Ireland. This intensified from the mid-1970s and continued through the 1980s.

Basically, I joined the CPI because I thought that it was the embodiment of the international communist movement. I felt that

I had become a communist and that I might as well be in a communist party. Initially it was more about the October Revolution, which I saw as a monumental and transformative event in the history of the world. In the world of my youth, it was seen as a triumph of evil. Now, for me, it was the opposite: the world's first socialist revolution, an experiment in building a radically different form of society. It was the triumph of a long struggle from below, a struggle to expropriate the expropriators, marking a massive shift in the world balance of forces. I had read intensely about the Revolution and the early days of Soviet power and I imagined it all vividly. Lecturing on it in Sinn Féin and later in the CPI, I tried to convey its world-historical significance and to incite others to imagine it as I did, in both its sudden opening of possibilities as well as the staggering weight of its difficulties. This was a drastic shift from the cold war view I grew up with in the 1950s and retained even through the 1960s. This alternative vision of the system grew in me until I felt that I had actually changed sides. I delved ever deeper into the grandeur and terror of this stream of history, and my travels and research opened up new layers of its complexities.

I got diverse responses from those I told of my decision, especially back in the States. Most of my New Left comrades were semi-supportive, but dissenting, about it, while others were more approving. My family was not pleased, but restrained, so hostilities would not break out again. My academic colleagues feared it would compromise me intellectually. The most hostile response I got was from Paul van Buren, the supervisor of the PhD thesis that I was abandoning. He wrote a condescending letter referring to my new religion, saying he didn't understand how I could become a communist, but then, he had never been a Catholic either.

Nevertheless, I was looking forward. I still had a lot to learn about the communist movement globally, but first I had to learn of it in Ireland. I moved among a whole new set of people and my life flowed in new routines. I attended party meetings at the branch, area, and national level, including many at party headquarters. I had only been there once before I joined. It was for

an xmas bazaar, an annual event where goods from the socialist countries were on sale: carved or lacquered boxes, wooden
plates, woven bags, matryoshka dolls, children's books—all
endowed with superior significance, because they were made
under socialism. The premises was in the Ballsbridge area of
Dublin, a two-bus journey from Bayside. It was a two-story
mews, entered through an alleyway and then a hatch door. It
was behind a grand house that had been bought by the party
from money inherited from the Goold-Verschoyle estate by Neil
Goold, a colorful communist, who stirred things up in Donegal,
Dublin, London, and Moscow. The party had sold the big house
and made do with the mews by my time. In 1977, the party sold
this premises and moved nearer to the city center to Essex Street.
The bookshop also moved into this premises. This area was a bit
rundown at the time, but eventually underwent redevelopment
and Temple Bar became known as Dublin's Left Bank, which left
the party well positioned.

I had a meeting in April 1975 with Mick O'Riordan to discuss
my party work. Born in the revolutionary year of 1917, he joined
the IRA and then the CPI as a teenager and made his way with the
international brigades to Spain, where he fought and was wounded
in the civil war. Upon his return to Ireland, he was interned. After
release, he worked as a bus conductor in Cork and then Dublin. He
stood for election as a CPI candidate during the worst Cold War
years, when the electorate were threatened by the Church with
the fires of hell if they voted for him. Other attacks, both physical and political, were made on him and his family during these
years. Whatever qualities he may have lacked, he was undoubtedly brave. He was implacably loyal to the USSR and spent much
time coming and going to Eastern Europe. This first meeting was
daunting. I was my straightforward self, except for being a bit too
nervously talkative, but something about him made me uneasy.
I was putting everything on the table, but he wasn't, and I never
knew what he was thinking. During a series of one-to-one meetings, as well as a night when he insisted on driving me home to

Bayside after a meeting, he quizzed me about my background, my motives, and my ideas about party work. We met so often because I had a number of ideas beyond normal branch activity for what I might do in the party, involving political education, the theoretical journal, and university organization. He was pleased that I was learning Russian and doing research into philosophy in Eastern Europe. At this stage, I let my admiration for him prevail and repressed my uneasiness and I had a harmonious working relationship with him during my first years in the party. I met more often with Tom Redmond, the area secretary, to discuss my party work beyond normal branch activities. My rapport with him was much easier than with Mick. He was open to new ideas. He listened with respect to what I had to say and told me much that I needed to know (and then some). We usually met in a pub near Trinity and had freewheeling conversations, although all items on the agenda were duly covered.

I attended branch meetings. Dublin North East branch was almost entirely male, mostly manual workers. Indeed, the whole membership of the party was largely male manual workers. There were also some clerical workers and trade union officials as well as some unemployed. There were few academics. There were few women. There was also an issue of scale. It was a party of only a few hundred members, whereas Sinn Féin had a few thousand. Not that SF abounded with female intellectuals. Branch meetings were driven by political discussion and paper sales. The party produced a monthly paper, the *Irish Socialist*, which was sold door-to-door in the local area and in pubs all the way up to Dundalk on Friday nights. For the lads this was no problem, but it was for me, since I could not go out without a babysitter. As time went on, more and more of the paper was produced in our house, as Eoin became editor and I wrote regularly for it. Beyond that, I was on many committees and involved in other party work in evenings, so I had to get babysitters many nights of the week. However, for some guys, who did little other party work, the pub run was the touchstone of commitment to the party, which created tensions.

Meetings of the party at all levels, especially in the south, were dominated by ideological debate and an impending split during my first months in the party. In 1968, both parties, north and south, before re-forming as a single party in 1970, supported the Prague Spring and condemned the Warsaw Pact intervention in Czechoslovakia. All communist parties, except those in socialist countries, did so as well. In the intervening years, party leaders, who spent much time in Eastern Europe, came under pressure to reverse this position. O'Riordan, who disagreed with the decision at the time, was particularly determined to do this. There was a major debate about it at the March 1975 national congress just before I joined. It was quite bitter. Coming up to the congress, the Ballymun branch did not elect Sam Nolan as a delegate. In retaliation, the Dublin South Central branch did not elect Mick O'Riordan. At the congress, they occupied the top table in their roles as general secretary and vice-chair of the party, but were not able to vote. A resolution, stating that behind Dubček stood imperialist forces dedicated to the restoration of capitalism, was hotly debated. An amendment recognizing divergent positions on the intervention was agreed, but the published version omitted this part, and so appeared to announce the overturning of the previous policy. Also contentious at the congress was a resolution calling for greater freedom of artistic expression under socialism, which was defeated. On elections to the national executive, rival factions voted along the ideological fault lines reflected in these debates. Those of us who joined the party at this time were barraged with one side of this debate. It was already assumed by both sides that we were on the side of the "tankies." (This term came into use to designate those who approved of the tanks going into Czechoslovakia in 1968, but it came to be used for hardline communists more generally.) Indeed some of them were. I wasn't, but I wasn't exactly on the other side either. In 1968, I was totally against the invasion. Now I was working my way through the whole history of the communist movement from a new perspective, and suspending judgment on Czechoslovakia until I got around to looking into it properly. Eventually I did, and I was against it.

Most communist parties in capitalist countries, especially in Europe, were then in the throes of a debate about Eurocommunism. This trend represented a break from Soviet domination of the communist movement from those who were sympathetic to the ideas of the Prague Spring, took a critical approach to the socialist countries, stressed the importance of democracy under socialism, believed that the idea of socialism had to evolve in new times and new conditions, explored the possibilities of new alliances, and took seriously the rise of new social movements, such as feminism. To that extent, I came to agree with Eurocommunism and to be part of it. However, it encompassed a spectrum of positions. Some were taking it in a direction that meant the unraveling of everything that made Marxism what it distinctively was. They began to scoff at concepts such as materialism, imperialism, mode of production, and class struggle. What was left when such crucial concepts were rejected was only social democracy or even liberal pluralism. I became enmeshed in these debates, although I saw them play out far more vividly and vociferously in the CPGB (Communist Party of Great Britain) than in the CPI.

In the CPI, the modus operandi was to refer to anyone who raised any critical questions about the Soviet Union as anti-Soviet. It was true that some who went in a Eurocommunist direction did go so far as to warrant the charge of anti-Sovietism, but in the CPI, with one possible exception, this was not the case. Members who took an affirmative but critical view of the USSR were among the most interesting and respected members of the party. They included Paddy Carmody, editor of the *Irish Socialist*, a colorful and articulate working-class intellectual whose lectures had his audience laughing and thinking in equal measure. He wrote for party publications under the pseudonym A. Raftery. He worked in the public sector as a food inspector and had been warned about his political activities after his attendance at a communist youth festival in Eastern Europe had been exposed by the *Catholic*

Standard. He was an active trade unionist and became secretary of the Dublin Council of Trade Unions. Sam Nolan was the party's industrial organizer, a carpenter, and an active trade unionist in the construction industry. He was also strikingly handsome, and a stirring street orator. George Jeffares had a PhD from Trinity and had worked abroad as a lecturer and high-level translator in Britain and China. In the Cold War atmosphere in Ireland, he was unable to find employment commensurate with his qualifications, so he earned his living as a used car salesman. His dealership was where everyone on the left went to buy used cars—the only sort of cars the left bought at that time. These three were on the national executive and the most prominent advocates of this tendency, but there were others, nearly all of them intelligent and committed party members. The only one I regarded as anti-Soviet was Naomi Wayne, who had been in the CPGB and had only recently become a member of the CPI. I had a number of polemical clashes with her, mostly on the question of women and socialism. She made a particularly big deal of the fact that there were no tampons in the USSR, which I regarded as trivial. I regarded her stance as whiney individualism.

At the area congress in November 1975, the battle lines were drawn once again. There were numerous speeches against both dogmatism and revisionism; indeed I made one myself, a formula on which we all agreed, except that we all meant different things by these terms. The voting for area committee went against the recommended list, and a number of members of the outgoing area committee, targeted as revisionists, failed to be re-elected. Paddy Carmody, George Jeffares, Mick O'Reilly, and Johnny Flood were not reelected, although Sam Nolan was. In December 1975, this group resigned en bloc from the party, citing the contempt for democracy as a concept crucial to socialism as well as lack of practice of democracy within the party. Among them were some of the most active and interesting members of the party. Most, but not all, of those who stayed said "good riddance." I was sorry to see them go, as I found the debates on issues on which my own position was unresolved to be important and challenging. The departing members soon formed the Irish Marxist Society. I often attended their public meetings and lectures and invited them to public meetings and lectures I organized.

The other defining institution of my life at this time was Trinity College Dublin. It was for centuries a bastion of the Protestant ascendancy in Ireland, but by the 1970s it was a more open, liberal, and secular institution. Although its ethos was secular in practice, the remnants of its non-secular origins, starting with its name, grated on me. Degrees were conferred in Latin "in the name of the Most Holy Trinity" regardless of whether those conferring or being conferred believed in said Trinity. The Latin used in its ceremonies became more and more anachronistic, as few academics uttering these words knew what they meant, or even how to pronounce them. As someone who had studied Latin, I found this particularly grating. Latin was also the language of grace at commons, a three-course meal served every weekday and presided over by academics in gowns at high table. I attended commons only when hosting guest speakers, because it was a display of local color. Only once did I process to high table in my gown, as I was invited to do so on the day my PhD was conferred. Even in English, there was a quaint vocabulary to the college culture. The academic year was divided into Michaelmas, Hilary, and Trinity terms.

The campus was located in the city center, with cobblestone squares and old buildings considered architecturally admirable. It was an attractive place in many respects. I liked the campus best in its outdoor aspects where students, staff, tourists, and citizens all went about their business in separate but overlapping orbits, sometimes almost oblivious of one another, but other times setting off interesting or annoying interactions. Maoists would denounce imperialism and the university's complicity with it on the dining hall steps, while tourists asked directions to see the Book of Kells and dons did their best to hurry past both to dine at commons and drink their sherry or coffee in apolitical peace in the senior common room. Outside in good weather there would be a picnic atmosphere at lunchtime and I often found myself in conversation with working people, who thought that the campus was as good a place as any to spend their lunch hour.

Inside those old buildings, it was another story. I hated the ornate chandeliers and the massive portraits of monarchs, bishops, landlords, and scholars, all of an elite born to power and knowledge. Still, the lecture halls and seminar rooms were spaces to be contested, and I was up for the contestation. I registered for a PhD in philosophy. I submitted transcripts for my three years of PhD course work, language requirements and comprehensive exams, hoping that I could proceed immediately to writing my thesis, because I had already been at the thesis writing stage in the United States. To my surprise, I discovered that no course work, foreign languages, or exams were required here. It was possible to proceed directly from a BA to a PhD thesis. This was not only so at TCD, but all of Ireland and Britain. I also discovered that an MA could be conferred a year after the BA for no extra work upon payment of a fee. I was not impressed. All the work I had done for my MA and subsequently for my PhD seemed devalued.

The philosophy department was then located in an old house in Westland Row, although it relocated to a new arts block, when I was halfway along my five-year stint. The academic staff were all male, and most struck me as from another era. The word that occurred to me at the time was "fusty." There were no postgraduate courses to attend, but I was invited to staff-postgraduate colloquia followed by tea or sherry receptions. Genteel older men discussed the meaning of words in the manner of the analytic philosophy of the day, only in less argumentative way than in the United States. Colloquia would be on topics such as Descartes on mind or Hume on evil. Philosophers from past eras were discussed totally out of historical context. It was as if anyone could have thought anything at any time, presuming an essentially ahistorical history of philosophy. The department was also a center for study of the work of George Berkeley, the eighteenth-century bishop and idealist philosopher who had studied and taught at Trinity. At the sherry receptions, there was no piece of Berkeley trivia or paraphernalia that did not seem worthy of detailed discussion among some members of staff.

This was an alien subculture to me and I tried to find my way in it by being polite and finding some way to engage with it, while resisting assimilation into it on its own terms. My responses to queries about my own research and my presentations at colloquia must have seemed from another planet. I constantly responded to papers by a polemic against their most basic premises and articulated an alternative set of premises in my own papers. They responded with polite tolerance. I'm sure that I seemed a very esoteric creature to them. Some of those who came to visit me in the department were even more so. One day a Canadian philosopher named Danny Goldstick arrived in the department, on one of his periodic sabbaticals in which he did world tours meeting with Marxist philosophers. Over tea in the department office, he regaled the faculty with tales of techniques to remove inhibitions, used in encounter groups in America. As Danny spoke, he loudly and hilariously acted out the whole scenario. The clash of cultures was palpable. "Frankly," remarked the philosopher John Gaskin, "I prefer the inhibitions."

The chair of philosophy (originally called mental and moral science) was Professor E. J. Furlong. I believe his friends called him Ned, but I called him Professor Furlong and he called me Miss Sheehan. I had to insist that he didn't call me Mrs. Sheehan, because he knew I had children, but Ms. was too alien, so we settled on Miss. I called the others Mr. Denard, Mr. Gaskin, etc. The number who did not have PhDs was another source of my bewilderment. They continued to call me Miss until the day I got my PhD and then they started calling me Helena rather than Dr. Sheehan. Midway through my time there, the chair of philosophy passed to Michael Slote, an American not much older than I was. The tempo of the seminars stepped up, as he brought all the leading lights of Anglo-American analytical philosophy to deliver lectures at Trinity. We were on tense terms from the start. I thought he was on the make, using the chair to enhance his international reputation, and he thought I was a "tough cookie," who disrupted the discourse, which could do without Marxist interventions constantly querying the terms of the discourse.

I taught some undergraduate philosophy classes, and had to adjust to a very different degree structure and grading system. Seventy, a mark I would have been ashamed to receive in the States, was considered first-class honors. The curriculum seemed narrowly conceived. Philosophy students took courses only in that field, and none in history, sociology, politics, literature, or science. Philosophy itself was taught in the same ahistorical way as prevailed in the colloquia, although I stressed the historicity of philosophy in my own teaching.

Despite all this, I found outlets for organizing. Postgraduates who were teaching were unionized. Soon I was chair of the Dublin Central branch of ASTMS and a delegate to union conferences. On one occasion, there was a conference in Belfast and some members said they couldn't go because they had wives and children. One said he couldn't go because he had a wife and no children and, if he died, she would be alone. So both having and not having children were equally excuses. I found such cowardice hard to take. People lived and worked their whole lives there and lived with considerably greater risk. I didn't think it was asking much to attend meetings there, which I often did, not only in the union, but in party and university work as well. The union's membership was diverse. Some in my branch were insurance salesmen, and I was expected to get involved in disputes over what grades got stripes on their cars, which was a stretch too far. Many other members were solid and dedicated, and I got on best with the scientists. The top union official in Ireland then was Noel Harris, a barrel of a Belfast man, who sang "The West Awake" in grand operatic style. He was also a party member. He once asked me to write a speech for him on the contemporary scientific and technological revolution, although he found it more intellectual than what he had in mind.

I was also involved in the Graduate Students Union at TCD and I was nominated for chair. I didn't really want to stand, as I felt overcommitted, but a communist was supposed to step up in every such situation, so I did. One reason I was asked to stand was to defeat someone named Mary Harney, who was thought to be on the make for an establishment political career. She went on to be a much-hated New Right government minister and tánaiste. I won. I was glad to defeat her, but then I was stuck with the position, which also meant being ex officio on many university committees, including the academic council. I found many of the committees' discussions bewildering, such as whether Trinity should be validating degrees from other institutions or even why there should be degrees in such subjects as catering at all.

Although not required to attend classes or to use foreign languages, I decided that I needed to learn Russian for my research. My registration for a PhD entitled me to audit any classes that were ongoing, so I signed up for a course in Russian. It was really intensive, requiring attendance at six classes a week, including lectures and language labs, with assignments to do between classes. A number of my fellow students were from military intelligence, there to prepare for new tasks connected to the recent opening of a Soviet embassy in Ireland. I kept this up for the autumn term, but found that I couldn't continue beyond that, because of the demands of thesis research, philosophy teaching, party work, trade union activity, as well as child-rearing. It was, however, useful to interact with this department and with Ron Hill in the politics department, who specialized in Soviet studies. The atmosphere was one of critical engagement with the USSR. It was anti-anti-Soviet, but not pro-Soviet. There was usually at least one native Russian speaker teaching the language.

My PhD thesis was originally titled "The Dialectics of Nature Debate," although it came to be "Marxism and the Philosophy of Science: A Critical History," which was eventually published as a book. It focused on the complex interactions between philosophy, politics, and science, as played out in debates of contending positions within Marxism, as well as debates between Marxism and other intellectual currents. It opened to me an audacious intellectual history, full of impressive achievements but also beset with tragic disasters. Facing this dark side and presenting it in proper perspective became a major challenge for me. Trinity was not the most appropriate place for me to pursue my doctoral studies, as there was no base of relevant expertise in the area. It was a flag of convenience, as I had come to live in Dublin for other reasons and, despite its name, Trinity seemed the most secular university for the study of philosophy. University College Dublin (UCD) had a more secular name, but its three (!) philosophy departments were full of priests.

My supervisor, Peter Mew, was a Marxist. He was more into the early Marx than the subsequent history of Marxism, and focused more on ethics and aesthetics than on my own areas of epistemology, philosophy of history, and philosophy of science. I also found it strange that someone who lacked a PhD could supervise one. Nevertheless, he was a congenial conversationalist and signed all the required forms for me to proceed, even if he did not really supervise me. He did not fit in so well with the rest of the staff of the department and spent much of his time on campus in the company of students. He was particularly fond of the female variety. I would often knock on his office door and find it occupied by a pretty undergraduate doing her assignments. He appeared on a national talk show explaining his libertarian views and giving a precise number (in the hundreds) of women with whom he had sexual relations. I was not one of them. At first college authorities were uneasy and gave him warnings about female students being in his rooms when he lived in college and about complaints from female students who said his references to sex during lectures made them uncomfortable. Peter replied that it was not the role of education to make students comfortable. Trinity later suspended him for a time, but he never faced serious penalties.

I also took part in the activities of the university debating societies. The two big ones were the Phil (Philosophical Society) and the Hist (Historical Society). These societies were proud of having attracted the movers and shakers of history as students and speakers. Among previous speakers at the Phil were Winston Churchill, James Joyce, Frederick Engels, and Alexis de Tocqueville. Among student members were George Berkeley, Jonathan Swift, Oliver Goldsmith, Bram Stoker, Oscar Wilde, Ernest Walton, and Samuel Beckett. The first time I was invited to speak at the Phil it was on the question of whether the cause of women's rights was compatible with Marxism. Following in the footsteps of Engels in more ways than one, I argued that the oppression of women was rooted in the social division of labor inherent in class society. It was grounded in private ownership of the means of social production. It was thus necessary for women to emerge from private work in the home and to enter fully into the sphere of social production. Marxism, I contended, was the only approach that conceived gender within a comprehensive worldview, grounded in an analysis of sociohistorical processes and the realities of political economy and that opened the way for the full liberation of women. Radical feminists argued that Marxism was a male theory and that could not explain the oppression of women.

I was on the party's national and area women's committees. One of our activities was to raise the profile of International Women's Day. We filled the Mansion House for this in 1976. The party charged me with writing a pamphlet on the communist approach to women's liberation. The first draft was circulated throughout the party and subjected to a barrage of criticisms, from totally contradictory directions. There was a tendency to economism and reticence to deal with feminism at all. Or, if the party did engage, it was sufficient to quote Marxist classics, support equal pay, and point to advances made by women in socialist countries. Beyond that, it was thought to be petty-bourgeois decadence. One comrade (female) responded to a polemic I wrote against a position put forward by *Banshee*, an Irish feminist magazine, saying, "It is beneath the dignity of our party to even answer such people." Some criticisms were prudish. I quoted Engels against a position regarding monogamy as the highest virtue. They objected to that position, but found it hard to counter a quote from Engels, such was their reverence for the classics. From the opposite angle, others sympathetic to feminism felt that some of my polemics were too strident and should be framed more positively. Some comrades went to lot of trouble writing pages of constructive comments and suggestions, especially to where I could clarify or elaborate. I wrote a memo to the political committee explaining what criticisms I was incorporating and rejecting, and why. I felt a bit battered by the process, but it did prompt a thorough discussion of all aspects of the relation between feminism and socialism in the party. The CPI published *Communism and the Emancipation of Women* in 1976.

I also wrote for the *Irish Socialist* and *Irish Socialist Review*. I did a monthly television column, believing that television production was showing a new level of sophistication and required a nuanced analysis, particularly to excavate the hidden ideological assumptions running through different programs. Sometimes the ideological struggle was not hidden, but right to the fore. I tended to be quite defensive about the Soviet Union and reviewed a whole series of programs aired in 1977 on the occasion of the sixtieth anniversary of the Revolution.

I also reviewed books. Some were published by Progress, the English-language Soviet press. At first I took them to be expressions of a homogenous Soviet line, but found many variations in nuance, quality, and emphasis. I began to see hints of emerging differences in point of view among the Soviet intelligentsia. I was quite interested in debates within Marxism, especially within the communist movement. I read voluminously. One book I reviewed was Adam Schaff's *Structuralism and Marxism*, in which he characterized the philosophy of Louis Althusser as "pseudo-Marxist-pseudo-structuralism." I agreed with Schaff. I was amazed at the influence of Althusserianism. It even had fervent adherents at TCD. I also reviewed for *Hibernia*, which brought me into interaction with a wider audience. I was also reviewed in *Hibernia*. Brian Trench did a review of "tracts for our times," and called me "very spirited for a Stalinist."

Party education was a primary area of my party work. I was involved in organizing and lecturing in new members classes, evening lecture series, and weekend schools. At one stage, we addressed why central lectures in Dublin were not attracting the attendance we expected. So we organized the lecture series to go to the party branches. For me, this meant that instead of giving a lecture on socialism and feminism in Dublin, Cork, and Belfast, I had to go around to every branch in Dublin and give it many times. At one of these, in a kitchen in Tallaght, one comrade, an electrician who had a fair bit of drink before he came, interrupted and insulted me all the way through. Despite its official commitment to education, party culture was too often characterized by a bullying anti-intellectualism, combined with male chauvinism. It pulsed along as a vague undercurrent in ways that were not always easy to confront, but party education sometimes brought it flaring up to the surface. A young female intellectual talking about feminism seemed to be the ultimate provocation. It made me really angry, but at least it was possible to address it when it showed itself so blatantly. At the same time, there were others, including other construction workers, who had an enormous respect for knowledge and I was very moved by their seriousness in reading, thinking, and sometimes advancing to lecturing. It was genuine respect for knowledge that predominated.

Despite the best intentions, however, lectures often tended to be formulaic, even catechetical, starting off with dialectical materialism (the three laws of dialectics, idealism versus materialism), and proceeding to historical materialism (the transition from slavery to feudalism to capitalism to socialism), and then to political economy (the labor theory of value, the falling rate of profit), and finally to the world communist movement and the history and program of the CPI. There was a habit of covering the same ground over and over again. There was a correct answer to every question. In fact, the questions had disappeared. This produced a certain type who was exceedingly smug about having the right answers to questions they had never really asked. I tried to break through this, as did others who were working in the area of party education. We did manage to organize lectures and seminars that pushed out the boundaries and explored problematic areas in ways that opened up real debates. There was great intensity of inquiry and commitment among those who wanted to go in this direction and we did achieve much of what we intended to do. There was still distrust of those who had degrees and had read books not found in the party bookshop. There were also those who had as little as possible to do with party education. Strangely, when people were being chosen to attend the International Lenin School, those who were unavailable to come out on an evening in Dublin somehow could arrange their affairs to go for three weeks to Moscow.

I was keen to be part of an effort to raise the intellectual level of the party, not just in its internal life, but also in its external engagement with the intellectual life of the wider society. I wrote a document sketching out an approach to party work in universities. A central part of this plan was to create a base at Trinity College to engage in discussion and debate with academe and with the wider public. To this end, we had already formed the TCD Communist Society in autumn of 1975. It was registered as a student society, which made us eligible to book rooms and receive expenses, which extended even to airfares to bring speakers from abroad. Unlike most such societies, which were composed almost entirely of undergraduates, we had a preponderance of postgraduates and staff, including academics as well as technicians and librarians, only about half of whom were party members (one was even an ex-party member). Membership fluctuated as people began and ended their studies, but it stood at twenty-five or so for most of its five-year life, which not coincidentally began and ended with my time at TCD and in the CPI. Our primary activity was to organize public lectures, seminars, and debates. They soon became known as a place for robust, open and stimulating debate and attracted a wide cross-section of people who were intellectually engaged with left perspectives. We hosted sessions on economics, history, culture, science, philosophy, gender, religion, and politics.

Some of our topics and speakers were the October Revolution after sixty years, the influence of Ireland on the thought of Marx and Engels, Cuba, and economic crises. Sometimes we co-organized with other groups. With the Hist, we sponsored a session on the Irish left in the 1930s. With the Republican Club, rising above growing hostilities between SFWP and CPI, we held a seminar on Northern Ireland. We held an event on the left alternative with speakers from all of its components. With Christians for Socialism, we organized a two-day seminar on Marxism, Christianity, and atheism, which was a friendly but robust exchange, not the sort of Christian-Marxist dialogue that took place between Marxists who no longer believed in class struggle and Christians who no longer believed in God.

Most of these events fostered an atmosphere of honest interaction and dialogue. But as Communists, we were naturally expected to address the nature of the USSR, as well as other socialist societies, and we did not shrink from it. This was a source of much controversy, as we had arguments thrown at us stemming from the right, often informed only by Cold War clichés, as well as from other sections of the left, with theories about state capitalism or degenerate workers' states. We also faced some unease within the party if we took a nuanced and critical view of existing socialism and admitted criticism where criticism might have been due.

Debates were often polite but sometimes bitter. On one occasion, a public lecture broke out in a physical brawl. We had invited John Hoffman of the CPGB to speak on Marxism and revisionism, the subject of a book he had recently written. A campus Maoist group, the Trinity Internationalists, circulated a long tract headlined "Down with the Visit of Armchair Marxist-Leninist Hoffman." They were particularly incensed with him, because he had been a Maoist previously. This tract denounced the CPI, TCD-CS, CPGB, and the USSR, as well as Trotskyists and bourgeois academics. They claimed that he was invited by revisionists to confuse students about revisionism and the relation of theory to practice. While Hoffman spoke, the Maoists, along with Sinn

Féin (Provisionals) tried to shout him down. John was somewhat shocked. Although he was polemical in print, he was stunned at such vociferous confrontation face-to-face. I was chairing and tried to get them to accept reasonable terms of debate. Then certain party members, as well as some independent leftists, took matters into their own hands and ejected them from the hall. The session then continued, although the controversy was not over. The May issue of *An Phoblacht* carried a big article headed "Muscovite Thugs Attack Trinity Republicans." While they were at it, they attacked the USSR for Soviet imperialism and for infiltrating the republican movement and causing the official-provisional split. The official publication of the CPI (ML) also carried an article titled "Revisionist Ideologue Hoffman Exposed in Trinity." They accused us of "fascist violence."

The most bitter controversy came from within. One of our own members constantly obstructed our activities. From the start, Roy Johnston took a domineering, condescending, arrogant tone, turning every meeting into a battle and constantly being ruled out of order. We worried his behavior would drive people away. Much of his bullying centered on me, because I was doing my PhD in the area of Marxism and science. Although he had never published on this topic, he took a proprietorial attitude to it. He thought that he should be my mentor and he pursued me relentlessly about it. I tried to be polite, but we were not on the same wavelength about it and he would not leave me alone. He often phoned me at home, haranguing me about what I should or shouldn't be doing, and he wrote many memos on my work, both to me and to the party. In one, he accused me of being "up in the air," and argued that every "piece of theory" should be matched to a "piece of proposed practice." If he could not control me, then he would undermine me. He even wrote a memo to academic staff in the sciences saying that what was being done in philosophy of science in the philosophy department should be monitored by scientists in the university. When I submitted a document on party work in universities to the party, he produced a counter-document, which was riddled with distortion and deceit. When I spoke on science at a party school, he sat in the front and heckled me through the entire talk. When I proposed a seminar on Marxism and science in TCD, he tried to take it over and, when that failed, he first appealed to the party to reorganize it as he wanted it and then organized against it. He came to the event and grandstanded from the floor. The Communist Society, in a vote that was unanimous (except for his own), decided to expel Johnston in 1977. Meanwhile, the party had reached the end of the line with him, too. His own branch requested that he be expelled. He was the subject of a whole series of allegations, including his constant demands to be placed in leadership positions, public attacks on the party when he didn't get his way, obstructive behavior in the university society, and failure to fulfill party duties. The party decided to expel him. As he told the story, he was a fearless intellectual anti-Stalinist who stood up to the imposition of a Soviet line. This was not the case. He did not speak up in the debate about Czechoslovakia 1968 in 1975, even though he was a delegate to the congress. Meanwhile he was lobbying the party to help him set up a trade agency to do business with the USSR. When it suited him afterward, he relied on anti-Soviet clichés, but he never interrogated or investigated the USSR in a serious manner.

He subsequently wrote a book called *Century of Endeavour*, aspiring to be a biography of his father and an autobiography of himself. It was ill-organized, badly written, and historically inaccurate (always in a self-serving direction). One of his few allies, Derry Kelleher, also wrote an autobiography, a self-published, egomaniacal, delusional tract called *Buried Alive in Ireland: A Story of a 20th-Century Inquisition*. On the cover was a picture of Christ wearing a crown of thorns with tears streaming down his face juxtaposed on a contemporary cityscape, giving grandiose visual expression to the persecution complex suffusing it. It was a tale of woe over all the editors who refused to publish his articles or review his self-published books. It lurched around from topic to topic to topic with no rhyme or reason.

Another person who crossed my path during this time, who also wrote an autobiography, was Kader Asmal. He was a lecturer in law at TCD and active in many organizations of the left. His primary allegiance was the anti-apartheid movement and he was the public face of it in Ireland. While some undertook dangerous underground assignments or went into the bush for military training, sometimes ending up dead or imprisoned, Kader wined and dined with the elite of Ireland, because this too served the movement and he won wide support for it in Ireland. It was seen as one of their success stories, as indeed it was. Unbeknownst to many of those with whom he mixed, he was also a member of the then illegal South African Communist Party. In his memoir, he revealed his membership in the SACP, and divulged that he and O'Riordan had arranged contact between the SF/IRA and ANC/MK. Whenever I ran into him at Trinity, I never knew if he would be full of chat or somehow not see me, depending on his mood or company. One day, out of nowhere, he threw his arms around me and kissed me, all full of comradely bonding. I gave him a stunned look. "What? Have you never been kissed by a black man?" he asked. I replied, "Kader, I have been more than kissed, and by blacker than you." Then he looked stunned. Then we both laughed. He was a dynamo of activity and loquaciousness. His book *Politics in My Blood* gave an extremely positive, even romanticized, account of his thirty years in Ireland. He was totally uncritical of TCD, which he described as a great liberal institution, a bastion of academic freedom and a stimulating intellectual atmosphere. It was all these things, but such a view missed all complexity and contradiction. The same was true for his version of the Irish left. He went on to be a prominent politician, a government minister in South Africa, where I would eventually encounter him again.

Other accounts of these times overlapping with mine are in diaries, most notably those of Desmond Greaves and Betty Sinclair. Desmond Greaves was a Marxist historian and political activist. He was a member of the CPGB, editor of the *Irish Democrat* and leading thinker of the Connolly Association, based in Britain.

He wrote biographies of James Connolly and Liam Mellows. He came often to Ireland and was for certain people a political guru on Irish politics. His influence was particularly strong in the civil rights movement. In the extracts of his diaries that have been published—with commentary by Roy Johnston, much of it defending himself against disparaging references—he wrote about times we crossed paths. He came to the house on a number of occasions, recorded in his diaries. I took issue with Eoin as well as Desmond on a number of issues, which brought the observation that I "wore the trousers," indicating his lack of advanced thought on gender. I found him interesting and amusing, but irritatingly arrogant. On any subject—including my doctoral thesis on which my research was well advanced, and raising children, although he had none— he tended to pronounce as the world's greatest expert. I did warm to him eventually, and his diaries record that he warmed to me one day on a train journey where I let loose about my frustrations with Roy Johnston and other goings-on in our scene. He was a great gossip, as was I.

Betty Sinclair was a northern trade unionist from a Protestant background and a stalwart of the CPI. Her papers, including diaries, are in the CPI archive in Dublin City Library. A transcript of an interview with Lynda Walker in 1980 covers the basic shape of her life. Born in Belfast in 1910, her father, an agnostic and unionist socialist, worked in the shipyards, while her mother worked in the linen mills, as did Betty. In 1933, she attended the International Lenin School in Moscow for eighteen months. Here she experienced a higher standard of living (central heating, bath, hot and cold running water) and wanted it when she came home. Deciding that the only way to have it was to marry, she married Dan Little for less than three months. She returned to the parental home and gave birth to twins, who died. From then on, she devoted her life to trade union and political work. She was prominent in the early days of the civil rights movement, but ran up against the newer forces, which she did not understand. She had little sympathy for new social movements, including feminism. Even inside the unions and the party, she was uneasy with intellectuals. Her diaries lashed out at Jimmy Stewart, the assistant general secretary of the party based in Belfast, for recruiting young intellectuals and eroding the working-class base of the party, not seeing how the working class itself was changing. She was loyal to the USSR and believed that anyone who raised questions about it needed to be "slapped down." When I came to know her, she had just retired as secretary of the Belfast Council of Trade Unions and found retirement to be "desolation." She then represented the party on the editorial board of *World Marxist Review* in Prague. In Prague, with the Eurocommunism debate in full swing and the aftermath of 1968 still seething, she did not engage meaningfully with any of the issues, only deriding "the boyos of Eurocommunism" and "poor old silly Dubcek." She mocked the *British Road to Socialism* as "the British road to nowhere." She admitted to me on one occasion that she lived in a bubble, but never admitted that it was an increasingly intoxicated bubble. The only time she raised any question about the Soviet Union was when the party in Moscow gave awards to Mick O'Riordan and others, but not to her, on the occasion of the sixtieth anniversary of the October Revolution. She said that she would not forget nor forgive the Soviet Union for this, yet she did. She observed that it was a man's world, but still rejected feminism. She was annoyed at SFWP "playing ducks and drakes" and "queering the pitch at home and abroad." There are many angry comments and negative assessments of comrades, including myself, in her diaries.

Leaders of the party made many trips to the USSR and other socialist countries. They were given holidays in fine resorts, taken to the best restaurants, accompanied to the showcase factories and collective farms and briefed on the party line. As time went on, it made me increasingly uneasy. At first, I thought that the holiday dimension seemed unfair, as these were monopolized by the same people and not appropriately shared. I thought it wrong that the wives of leading party members took precedence over hardworking party members. Some trips were to party congresses as fraternal delegates. I was impressed by Fergal Costello, when he returned from one in Cuba. He worked as a cameraman in RTE and made an excellent slide show that he combined with a talk he gave in various venues. I felt that he shared the experience in a way that others did not. Eventually I began to see how corrupting (in a soft sense) much of it was. I discovered what a distorted sense was conveyed of the realities of life in these countries, and how little they knew or wanted to know about questions being raised, not only in Western communist parties, but in Eastern ones as well. Some became beholden and/or bamboozled. The purpose of some of the trips, especially the many trips made by O'Riordan, was somewhat mysterious, although it was possible to guess. "Moscow gold" was top secret, although most active party members assumed that full-time wages and other expenses were paid in this way. Soviet archives have since revealed that there were massive subsidies to foreign communist parties, particularly compliant ones.

Indeed, many secrets lurked under the surface, some I knew then, some I've discovered since, and some I'll never know. Affairs, arms, purges, espionage: they were all there. At Trinity, there was a Miss MacMackin, who taught Russian, about whom I knew little. She went to the USSR in the 1930s and married Patrick Breslin, who studied at the Lenin School and stayed in the USSR as a translator. She returned to Ireland after becoming pregnant, and never saw him again. Although she died not knowing what became of him, archives have revealed that he perished in the purges in 1942. Another party member of my time, Marian Bragg Jeffares, an artist, was a student of Anthony Blunt, the British art historian and knight of the realm exposed as a Soviet spy in 1979. While living in Britain in the 1940s, she mediated the flow of information to the KGB. She left her husband and child behind and went off with George Jeffares to China in 1950.

Apparently, during my time in the party, the KGB used both the Soviet embassy in Dublin and the CPI to recruit spies. According to *The Mitrokhin Archive*, based on files copied by KGB archivist Vasili Mitrokhin, KGB director Yuri Andropov authorized the

KGB *rezident* in Dublin, Mikhail Shadrin, code-named Kaverin, to approach a leading Irish communist code-named Grum, who agreed to select two undeclared party members for training as KGB illegals in 1977. Spying for the KGB might seem scandalous to others, but in the atmosphere that prevailed in the CPI in 1977, it would have seemed a natural form of commitment to the cause. Spying would not have been so straightforwardly natural for me. Not that anyone asked it of me. It was not only that it was my way to speak and act in the open, but I had a strong commitment to the continuity of ends and means. I perceived many complexities and contradictions about this in the communist movement, even within myself. I admired Kim Philby, John Maclean, and Klaus Fuchs, who spied for the USSR. I reflected upon Brecht's poem "To Those Born Later": "We who wished to lay the foundations for human kindness could not ourselves be kind." Reading the memoirs of the spymasters of that era, such as Markus Wolf and Oleg Kalugin, I can see that Cold War conditions made covert operations necessary in order to assess military capabilities and political maneuvers on the other side. I would defend much that was done by the KGB, Stasi, and other security services, but I find their degree of surveillance of ordinary working people, the use of Romeo agents, the suppression of dissent, the atmosphere of distrust polluting human relationships, to be indefensible. Memoirs have indicated that the evidence of foreign subversion that was used to justify the intervention in Czechoslovakia in 1968 was fabricated by the KGB, not only to foreign communist parties and the wider public, but even to the CPSU Politburo. Once a supposedly necessary lie could be justified in the name of class struggle, the habit of lying became entrenched, and was employed for purposes that did not advance the class struggle. My immersion in the communist movement, not only my activity in its present, but my research into its past, was posing the question of ends and means in ever sharper terms.

It took time for me to get the lay of the land. At first, I gave the USSR the benefit of any doubt and defended it when it came under attack, using the best evidence and arguments I could muster. I read many Soviet books, as well as western sovietological books. I attended events at the Soviet embassy in Dublin, which offered occasions to see Soviet films and to talk to Soviet diplomats and visitors. One occasion was the seventieth birthday of Leonid Brezhnev in 1976. There was a highly hagiographical film shown, featuring lots of tanks, which was very boring. Sitting near me was an old party stalwart who slept through it, snoring loudly and nearly falling off her chair. Awakened at the end by the sound of polite clapping, she sat up and exclaimed, "That was brilliant, wasn't it?" Another memorable occasion was the sixtieth anniversary of the October Revolution in 1977. I could see the logic of the award given to Mick O'Riordan, born the same year as the Revolution and for so many difficult years a leader of the Communist Party, but it seemed incongruous that there was an equal award for the current general secretary of Connolly Youth, who had barely been at it a few years and did not persist in the communist movement.

Naturally, I was anxious to go and see the place for myself. When my first opportunity came, I could not take it, although I would eventually have many opportunities to make my way around Eastern Europe. I was selected to go to the International Lenin School in Moscow in the summer of 1976. I was going to London for the Communist University of London just before that. I asked Mick O'Riordan if I could join the group in London for the Dublin–London–Moscow flight, so I would not miss a session on the dialectics-of-nature debate, the exact theme of my research. O'Riordan said no, so I chose London over Moscow with regret. Nevertheless, the CUL, which I attended for several years, proved fantastic. It offered radical approaches to almost every academic discipline and vigorous debates on every hot topic on the left. It went on for nine days every July at the University of London. There were plenary sessions, weekday and weekend courses (at both introductory and advanced levels), as well as films, concerts, discos, socials, and a publications fair. The hardest thing was making choices among all the simultaneous sessions. There were also lots of area reports on China, South Africa, France, Italy, Greece, and elsewhere. I attended courses on philosophy, history, science studies, Soviet studies—all the converging streams of my own research—but pined for what I might be missing in courses on literature, sociology, psychology, and economics. I took part in debates on Eurocommunism, feminism, culture and ideology, and class. The speakers included eminent authors and scholars, among them Eric Hobsbawm, Stuart Hall, Maurice Cornforth, Margot Heinemann, Bea Campbell, Bert Ramelson, Bob Rowthorn, and Monty Johnstone. Reading lists included not only Marx, Engels, and Lenin, but also Trotsky and Deutscher, as well as contemporary authors across a range of positions. The atmosphere was exhilarating, enlightening, and infuriating. No idea was forbidden; anything and everything could be said and was said. The organizers proclaimed that there was no orthodoxy, no democratic centralism in theory, no such thing as the communist position.

Despite the proclamations against orthodoxy, there was a de facto orthodoxy, at least among those organizing the CUL. It was a revisionist approach to Marxism that tended to be so revisionist that it was questionable if it was still Marxism. There was heresy, too, and that was what was perceived to have been the communist position until then. At one CUL, I made a list of what was in and what was out, according to this trend. Out were economic determinism, labor theory of value, falling rate of profit, historical materialism, dictatorship of the proletariat (or even the more democratically conceived leading role of the working class), vanguard party, one-party state, anti-monopoly alliance, dialectics of nature, realist theory of truth (or sometimes any concept of truth at all). In were pluralism (epistemological as well as political), incomes policy (wage restraint), new social movements, broad democratic alliances, EEC, and NATO. Marx was still in (barely), as was Gramsci, but Engels and Lenin were out. It asserted that all struggles were equal. There was nothing special about trade unions or the working class. Moreover, they were declared "boring."

Gender politics, alternative technologies, and punk rock were so much cooler. One student said that talk about the third world and rent strikes "pissed students off." This trend proclaimed the autonomy of all spheres. It was a pluralist factors theory of history with no pattern, no explanatory core, no particular role played by mode of production. There were constant swipes at economic reductionism, which was fair enough, but it often translated into an impatience with any talk of economics whatsoever, as well as hostility to class analysis. It was the same with the critique of positivism, which sometimes signaled hostility to science, which was far from the same thing.

At the Soviet studies course, there were a variety of positions. A much-cited book was Roy Medvedev's *Let History Judge*, an honest history of the USSR by a dissident Soviet Marxist, who saw Bukharin as the voice of an alternative path for the Soviet Union and advocated a democratic form of socialism. Indeed, my own copy of it was heavily underlined, as was a book by his biologist brother Zhores on Lysenkoism. Dave Purdy articulated a critique of the International Socialists' (Trotskyist) position that the USSR was state capitalist, arguing that the dominant mode of production was not capitalist, but it was also not yet developed socialism. Other lecturers, such as Julian Cooper and Monty Johnstone, gave highly nuanced analyses. Most discussion focused on the lack of socialist democracy. Some thought that the party should allow factions, while others thought that capitalist parties should be able to form and contend for power. The debate became bitter. One party member accused another of being a KGB agent. One of the most vitriolic was Jan Šling. He had reason to be bitter. His father, Otto Šling, was a Czech communist who had been arrested and executed for espionage in 1952. His mother, a British communist, was also arrested when he was a child. He was later arrested and imprisoned himself after the Soviet invasion in 1968. Many of those making the running at the CUL were children of communists who harbored a deep anger toward the communist movement, although few had such terrible experiences of it as Jan

Šling. I wondered why they had to play it out within the party. If they hated it so much, why stay in it? If they were so into rebellion against Marxism and developing positions indistinguishable from those of British liberals, then why not get on with it elsewhere? A session on the family and sexuality, held in a packed room, was actually shocking. It was not that I hadn't seen or heard such things before, but to see and hear them in a communist setting was something else. Bea Campbell, prominent party member, started by dismissing Engels as reductionist and economist, proceeded to denounce vaginal penetration as "phallic colonialism," recommended sexual autonomy (clitoral orgasm by masturbation), and announced that the sexual politics of the future meant getting out of the family. "What about children?" I asked. She responded that bringing children into it only got the discussion bogged down. I then asked, "How is this a Marxist analysis of sexuality?" She replied that Marxist theory was inadequate to theorize the liberation of women. I argued that this retreat from consideration of the economic base, this renunciation of the relational character of sexuality, was a reversion to bourgeois individualism. I was hissed.

Marxism Today, the theoretical journal of the CPGB, was transformed radically during these years. There were lively debates between different positions in the party, and both sides had their say. There was a long-running debate on the dialectics of nature, which I read avidly before deciding I had something distinctive to contribute to it. My article was accepted by the editor, James Klugman. Then he died and was replaced by Martin Jacques, who decided to end the debate.. *Marxism Today* improved its production values and reached out to a wider audience. It became more colorful and influential. However, as it opened out to many positions along the spectrum, to the center and even the right, it began to close down to positions on its left. As Alan Johnson, a later commentator tracing the line from *Marxism Today* to New Labour, put it: "*Marxism Today* theorized a shift in the center of gravity of left-wing politics from the producing class to the consuming individual, and installed a new index of progress, which eroded our critical distance from capitalism." I became very involved with the CPGB, as it was so more intellectually vibrant than the CPI. I read their publications, attended their events, and got to know many of their members. I was also relating to the past of the party as well as the present. My research was leading me into serious engagement with 1930s British Marxists such as Christopher Caudwell, George Thomson, J. D. Bernal, J. B. S. Haldane, and T. A. Jackson. The younger generation of British Marxists were not as interested in them as I was. I found myself forming stronger relationships with the older generation, both living and dead, than with my contemporaries.

At the CUL philosophy course, I spoke to Maurice Cornforth, who had written many books on Marxist philosophy. He had studied philosophy at Cambridge in the 1930s under Wittgenstein, and his work reflected the continuing influence of analytic philosophy, as well as polemical defense of Marxism against it. He invited me to his house in Highgate for dinner, where we continued our discussions. He subsequently invited me to stay at his house whenever I was in London, which I often was, and I took him up on it. I slept in a big attic, which had been the home of James Klugman before he died. His wife was hospitable to me, although I thought I would have got on better with his previous wife, James's sister Kitty Klugman, also a philosopher, who had died. We had long conversations over many dinners, discussing philosophy as well as the history of the communist movement. Because of my interest in both past and present debates and in various thinkers who were by then dead, Maurice was a great source of information, even what could be called historical gossip. He spoke to me honestly and often amusingly about them, which made them more vivid characters in the story I was writing. He himself was reevaluating many positions he had taken in the past, when he was a hardliner, even a Stalinist-Zhadnovist. His critique of Caudwell was nearly as unedifying as Klugman's attack on Tito, both born of the pressures of the last years of the Stalinist era. He earned his living as an editor for the left publishing house Lawrence and Wishart.

Another person with whom I developed good rapport was Monty Johnstone, of the middle generation between the 1930s and 1960s left. Although he was middle-aged by this time, he had a very boyish way about him—tall and lanky, full of knowledge and passion and enthusiasm, forever pushing his badly cut hair away from his eyes. He spoke many languages, knew the politics of many countries, and entered into polemics on all the big issues. He was in Czechoslovakia in 1968 when the tanks arrived and argued in the streets with the tank crews—in fluent Russian—against the invasion. Yet he stood against the abandonment of Marxism in the party and specifically by *Marxism Today*, where he was on the editorial board and fought for the journal to be really Marxism for its day. He was critical yet constructive in his analysis of the USSR and other socialist countries. He was a graduate of Oxford and lectured at a polytechnic for a time, but by the time I knew him he was a freelance left intellectual and activist, raising three children on his own and living in relative and unremarked poverty.

I also got to know the general secretary of the CPGB, Gordon McLennon. I first met him when he came to Dublin for bi-party talks with the CPI and stayed in our house. I often met him in London after that. He had an affable manner, despite the strain of trying to keep an increasingly fractious party together and to maintain good relations between fraternal parties, all without skimming over problems. Tensions between the CPGB and the CPI were ratcheting up over what seemed to be an increasing preference for SFWP over CPI. Gordon believed in the importance of high-level theoretical debate—although he was sometimes in slightly over his head—and was especially impressed by the younger party intellectuals, including his own son, Gregor. He was open to argument, and I took advantage of having his ear to put strongly my arguments against the dominant *Marxism Today* line. When it came to the crunch, he sided with them. I still liked him and enjoyed carrying on the argument with him. Others of this tendency were not so open to argument from this direction, and they were not beyond using administrative measures to sideline their opponents, despite their stated scorn for such tactics.

These debates challenged me to develop my own thinking. I did eventually come to what could be called a left Eurocommunist position in that I came to believe that the grip of the Soviet model had to be broken. It was a strategic position, however, and not a geographical one. I would have preferred to call it a critical communist position. We had to stop imagining a revolution as an insurrectionist seizure of state power that would lead to a one-party state, suppression of oppositional activity, imposition of ideological orthodoxy, and command economy. We instead had to think of undermining the hegemony of capitalism, winning consent for a socialist alternative, forming progressive alliances, and struggling for power in multi-party elections—both on the streets and in all the institutions of society. We had to envision exercising power in terms of facilitating participatory democracy, freedom of intellectual debate, and more diverse forms of economic activity, all while facing up to elections that could be lost. I still believed in public ownership of the commanding heights of production and central economic planning, the core role of class analysis and class struggle, and a materialist theory of nature and history. To the CPGB, I was a hardliner. To the CPI, I was starting to seem a revisionist.

It wasn't just the CPGB debates that convinced me that the Soviet model was not appropriate to imagining a transition to socialism in advanced capitalist countries. More than anything, it was my study of the history of the USSR, particularly my advanced research for my PhD thesis, and my own direct experience of the USSR and other socialist countries. From 1977, I traveled extensively in Eastern Europe and explored these societies. In doing so, I discovered much that I could not have learned in any other way. When, in the summer of 1977, I was chosen for a second time to attend the International Lenin School, I didn't let anything stand in the way. We gathered in Dublin airport and bought whiskey, chocolates, tights, and ballpoint pens to be pooled for gifts to comrades who assisted us. In London, we were joined by our comrades from Belfast, and the twelve of us boarded the flight to Moscow. I was full of excitement about finally seeing firsthand this place we discussed so much.

We arrived at the International Lenin School, a vast unmarked building on Leningradsky Prospect. It was near Aeroport station on the Moscow metro, which made it easy to get around Moscow. It was a semi-clandestine institution. It was also called the Institute of Social Sciences, the name we were instructed to use outside of party circles. There were hundreds of communists studying there, many of them using pseudonyms, as their parties were illegal in their native countries. Most of them were there for long courses of a year or more. The complex included a huge entrance hall with security on duty, a multi-story residence building, classrooms, offices, cafeteria, auditorium, library, polyclinic, bar, and shop, all surrounding an internal courtyard with a big statue of Marx. There were about 600 employees of this institute, of whom 270 were members of the CPSU or Komsomol. All the professors and interpreters were members of the party or youth organization. After arrival on Saturday night, we had a brief orientation meeting, settled into our rooms, and went to a get-together thrown by some Canadian comrades. On Sunday, we headed for Red Square, which was an exhilarating experience, given its iconic significance. We queued at the Lenin mausoleum. It was eerie seeing the body of someone so long dead. On Monday morning, we went through a registration process, filling in long forms, and then we began our studies.

We had lectures from 9 a.m. to 1 p.m., six days a week. Sometimes the afternoons and evenings were free, but sometimes there were special lectures in the auditorium, such as one by Fyodor Burlatsky on Maoism and one on the history of the Comintern by the rector Nikolai Matkovsky. Other days, there were organized excursions to such places as the Museum of the Revolution or the Exhibition of Economic Achievement. In the evenings, we divided spontaneously into two groups. One group, all younger men, headed for the bar. The rest of us walked around Moscow, often gravitating to Gorky Park, enjoying the open air of the summer nights and discussing our impressions of the USSR. The first group claimed to be engaged in more extensive political discussion with foreign comrades, although it was often through such an alcoholic haze that I wondered how much of it they remembered the next day. Some nights we were invited to parties hosted by foreign comrades, and then we stayed in instead of venturing out, and did much talking through an alcoholic haze ourselves.

The lectures were on philosophy, political economy, social psychology, foreign policy, and strategy and tactics of the world communist movement. Basically, it was a short course in Soviet studies from a Soviet perspective. This was what our party had requested. In previous years people were given elementary lectures on dialectical materialism, labor theory of value, and proletarian internationalism that differed little from ones they had at home. We had asked for something more advanced and specific this time. The basic line was this: dictatorship of the proletariat had been necessary to establish socialism and to undermine the power of class enemies to sabotage it, but the USSR had now achieved advanced socialism and the dictatorship of the proletariat had been replaced by a state of the whole people. There were breaches of socialist legality during the period of the cult of personality, but now the state only moved against drunkards, thieves, absentees, and lazybones. The human rights campaign against the USSR in the West was slanderous. Decisions were discussed at all levels in society and not reduced to bourgeois elections. There were lots of statistics. The USSR produced one-fifth of the world's industrial output, one-fourth of the world's scientists, one-third of the world's doctors. Before the Revolution, three-quarters of the population were illiterate, but now illiteracy had been eliminated. There were many more metrics: on production, consumption, prices, wage differentials, infant mortality, educational levels, gender participation, and so on. One of the professors reviewed that day's *Pravda* with us each morning. The atmosphere at these lectures could not have been more different from that at the CUL. Although there was some scope for discussion, even debate, it was a much more one-way process, within far narrower bounds. We took lots of notes and asked many questions. I got particularly involved in discussions in the social psychology lectures. The professor, Yuri Sherkovin, called me into his office to discuss further. As I left, I gave him my pamphlet on women. The next day he quoted it extensively in his lecture, praising it highly as he proceeded. I was quite flattered.

Despite whatever drinking went on the night before, we kept a high level of discipline about attending lectures, meetings, and excursions. One morning, in a rush, I pushed a tampon up too far and had to visit the polyclinic to get it sorted out. Not only were there no tampons produced or imported in the USSR, there wasn't even a word for them in the huge Russian-English dictionary we were using to communicate. Edwina, who came with me, went into maternal mode and finally got the idea across in a somewhat comic mime. I thought back to my argument with Naomi Wayne a few years before, but I still didn't come over to her side. That was the end of tampons for me. I adopted the Soviet method of using ordinary cotton wool after that.

In our third week, we went to Lithuania. The rector and some of our lecturers and interpreters came with us on the overnight train. We had a hectic timetable. We did quick sightseeing tours of Vilnius, Kaunas, and Trakai. We visited a computer plant, a silk factory, a power station, a health center, a pioneer camp, a local soviet, an ancient castle, and a few museums. There was a barrage of information. I was particularly impressed by Mike Kelly, a lecturer at UCD who was writing a book on French Marxism, walking around with a clipboard, noting every detail, putting his face up against every piece of industrial machinery we were shown, wanting no feature to escape his notice. We saw a documentary film about Lithuania, met with members of the central committee of the CP of Lithuania, and ended with a sumptuous banquet, with many toasts to proletarian internationalism in legendary Soviet style. From there we went directly to the night train back to Moscow, where everyone was in merry form after all the drink and no one got much sleep. On our final day in Moscow, we scurried around to buy presents in the Beryozka shops and have a last look at the city. We threw a goodbye party in the school that night. There were sad farewells, especially for those who had struck up romances there. I returned home on my thirty-third birthday, to a great welcome from Cathal and Clíodna.

I promptly resumed my usual activities: political organizing, thesis-writing, and child-rearing. At the same time, I was already planning to go back to the USSR. I felt I had only scratched the surface. Fortunately, I had received an invitation to return on my own for an extended period to pursue my research. When I returned home, I put together a proposal for a program of work in the USSR for the winter of 1978, originally for six weeks, but soon extended to four months. Mick O'Riordan made the necessary arrangements with the Soviet embassy in Dublin. All was paid for by the CPSU. Eoin was also very supportive, although it would involve complications for him in organizing childcare.

When I arrived in February 1978, Moscow was covered in snow, and so it stayed until the spring thaw. My modus operandi this time was different. I surrendered my passport and was issued Soviet identity documents. I still went by my own name, not a pseudonym. I was sent to the polyclinic for medical tests. I lived at the Lenin School, my base for research at the Academy of Sciences and Moscow State University. I was not required to attend lectures or excursions, but was invited to attend lectures, films, concerts, and excursions that they thought would interest me. I was free to move around Moscow as I saw fit. If I required an interpreter, one would accompany me. If not, I went out on my own with no minder. Sometimes I met people in my ever-widening circle of contacts, and other times I just wandered the streets on my own. I assumed I was followed and that my room was searched, but I accepted that. There needed to be serious security at the school, as there were so many people who belonged to illegal parties, and there must have been agents or informers of various security services, such as the CIA, infiltrating it at various stages. In any case, I had nothing to hide. Many years later I discovered on the internet a partially declassified CIA report claiming that, of the 167,000 from non-communist countries to travel to the USSR for education from 1960 on, there was a select group of 10,500 sent to the Institute for Social Sciences, producing 450 graduates a year. Obviously, some of these were CIA agents or informers.

I sought out Soviet speakers who had come to Dublin events that I had helped organize. I often went on Sunday mornings to the home of Boris Kuznetsov, where we drank brandy and fruit juice and talked about the philosophy of science. He spoke lyrically of post-classical physics. To get there, I walked in the snow through a big outdoor market, where people sold private produce. I also met with Zoya Malkova, a leading international expert on comparative education, and in the evening I often joined her and her friends in restaurants and at parties. A range of perspectives on Soviet society opened to me as my contacts expanded. My friend Olga at TCD had asked me if I would deliver a denim suit for a friend of hers, to give as a present to her boyfriend. I met Valentina in the metro on my second day and handed it over, but we chatted for a while and agreed to meet again. We met many times and she introduced me to her friends, who were very different from the people I met through party or academic activities. They were not party members, although not particularly anti-Soviet either. They were young professionals trying to make their way in the world, negotiating the limits of the system, much like people anywhere who take the system as given and don't examine too much the nature of the system. I asked many questions about their everyday lives and they asked me many about mine. Most I could answer easily, but I was always stumped when they wanted to know how many square meters of living space I had. One day I was explaining to Valentina my research and my motivations in doing it. She was amazed that someone would actually choose Marxism in the face of a whole variety of other choices. She had never thought of it that way. In the USSR, Marxism was just there and it was compulsory. The saga of Valentina's own life, as it unfolded, opened to me a window on aspects of Soviet life I might not have encountered otherwise. She married during this time, but not to her boyfriend. Instead, she entered into an arranged marriage to get a permit to live in Moscow. Even after doing that, it was still not enough, because his parents had to sign the form and they were stalling. Through her friends, I learned more about such bureaucratic marriages as well as a black market in flats. Through my expanding circles, I learned many things about everyday life that did not fit the picture that foreign communists had of it. When I told comrades at the school about such things, they were reluctant to believe a lot of it.

My days were full. I woke up early every morning to the sound of the Soviet national anthem on the school radio station. It was not that everyone was required to wake up this way, but I had the radio set to wake me when they started broadcasting every day. I liked the way it focused me immediately on where I was and what I intended to do for the day. I began every day with a great sense of adventure. I wanted to get beyond the clichés of both the Cold War and communist parties. The rules of the game were different from any I had known before, although it wasn't as if they were stated outright. There were nuances and codes that I had to learn to read. There were layers and layers. It was a constant challenge to figure out what might be going on under the surface.

After a month had passed, I felt that every door I opened brought more doors to be opened. Coming from a milieu where Marxism was marginalized, it was great to be in a milieu where Marxism was in power. However, I began to see problems with this unchallenged dominance, and to question whether a philosophical worldview should be an orthodoxy of state. It raised the question of how sincere the professions of Marxism were among those I met. Would those who claimed to be Marxists in the USSR be Marxists if it were not in power, if it were not an advantage, but an obstacle, to their careers? Were they the sort who would be part of a liberation movement struggling for power or were they just the inheritors of that power several generations down the road?

I was constantly sizing people up this way and came to different conclusions about different people, but I couldn't be sure. Only a fall of Marxism from power would reveal this, I thought, but that was then unimaginable.

Most days I worked in libraries or conducted research interviews. I often visited the Institute of Philosophy of the USSR Academy of Sciences and met with philosophers from various sections, especially the one for the philosophical problems of the natural sciences, which was a relatively safe haven for those who wanted to get on with philosophizing that was less subject to the twists and turns of the party line. I also met with those in sections studying Marxist philosophy abroad and critiquing bourgeois philosophy. I asked searching questions, ones that might have surprised some of my interlocutors, especially as I came to Moscow under party auspices. By this time, I knew about Soviet debates of the 1920s: radical debates probing the foundations of philosophy and science as well as economics, literature, gender, and all else; debates about different interpretations of Marxism; debates about different paths to socialism. These controversies had been not so much resolved as suppressed. From the 1930s, there was to be only one valid answer to any question, and it was not necessarily decided on intellectual grounds. I wanted to find out more about these debates, but I also wanted to know how well the debates of the 1920s were known in the 1970s, and how much those ideas were still fermenting under the surface. I discovered that I often already knew more about these debates than those I was asking about them. Another area of discussion was more recent debates within Marxism, particularly in the West. It was interesting to discern how much Soviet scholars already knew and what they really thought. It was the same in my conversations at Moscow State University and the Lenin School. Some recycled clichés. Some were probing but guarded. I often felt they had more to say than what they were saying.

I was getting the measure of the Soviet intelligentsia as best I could, breaking from the monolithic image of it that prevailed abroad, whether rated positively as wisdom personified (the view

held in the party) or negatively as agents of ideological intimi-
dation (the view prevailing in the wider society, including the
university). As time went on, I learned to map the surface, but also
to detect forces bubbling under the surface. I was mixing with the
higher party intelligentsia. Some of them later became famous as
the luminaries of glasnost and perestroika: Fyodor Burlatsky, Yuri
Zamoshkin, Ivan Frolov. Many of those I met were tending that
way and testing the limits of what could be said and done.
There was a coded way of speaking about certain people. When
Vadim Zagladin, number two in the international department of
the CPSU, came to speak at the school, I was told I should go, that
I would like him. If it had been the number one, Boris Ponomarev,
it would have been phrased differently. All visiting speakers were
important, but only some were considered interesting as well as
important. I particularly looked forward to lectures and discussions with Burlatsky, whose style of speaking made clear that there
was a real process of thinking happening, and not just a transmis-
sion of received ideas. In fact, once he said, "I'll tell you a secret.
Not everything is clear. Not everything is settled"—bold words
for that place and time. Zamoshkin was pushing hard to establish
sociology and political science as academic disciplines. He wanted
to engage in empirical research and inductive methods, instead
of depending on formulas of historical materialism. Sometimes I
thought that he was too enthralled by the idea of public opinion
polls and such, as I had seen how myopic empirical social science
could be, and how illuminating broad historical perspective could
be. We were coming at things from opposite directions, but I could
see his point.

    When I asked to interview academician Mark Mitin, I could
see the surprised reaction from other philosophers. He had been
one of the young philosophers in 1931 who had discussed with
Stalin the need for a "new turn on the philosophical front," which
closed down philosophical debate and brought the triumph of
one official line as the true Marxist position. I was writing about
this and wanted to hear about it from him, even though I knew

he personified an old order that had impeded the advance of philosophy in the USSR. The other philosophers remarked that he
was still alive because his wife was a gerontologist. It was a long
and self-justifying interview, but nevertheless it was interesting to
hear his account. He was the embodiment of the Stalinist intelligentsia, the generation who came to power during the purges,
who swept away the older and more sophisticated Marxist intelligentsia. I probed him about purges of philosophers, but he
insisted that no philosopher was purged due to a position taken
in philosophy, only due to political dissidence. I also spoke on
several occasions to Professor Evgeny Sitkovsky, a member of the
editorial board of Under the Banner of Marxism who was arrested
and sent to a labor camp for an editorial mistake made in production of the journal. Stalin's *Short Course*, which was supposed to
be the essence of philosophical wisdom in that era, functioned as
a set of military rules, he said.

I was most interested in the pre-perestroika intelligentsia. As
one thing led to another and my interactions with them became
wider and deeper, I realized that I had a particular role to play in
this scenario. I found myself in situations where I could do and say
things that Soviets couldn't, because I was a foreigner, and things
that other foreigners couldn't, because I was a communist. Once
I became conscious of this, I decided to maximize it. I came to
Marxism freely and I would stand up for it, not only against the
revisionist unraveling, but against dogmatic recycling. This period,
the late 1970s, has been called a time of stagnation in the USSR.
During the early years of Soviet power, there were the vibrant
debates that I was researching, which were suppressed from the
1930s to the 1950s, basically the Stalinist era. Then there was the
thaw, roughly from Khrushchev's revelations at the Twentieth
Party Congress in 1956 to the intervention in Czechoslovakia in
1968. Many of those with whom I was mixing had opened their
minds and spread their wings during this period and had kept
their minds open, although their wings had subsequently been
clipped. They were shuffling between institutes and looking for a

way to advance their still evolving agenda. Some of them had been to Prague and interacted with Eurocommunist thinkers from Italy, France, Spain, and Britain. They knew the Czechoslovak thinkers who were forming the ideas of the Prague Spring. The journal *Problems of Peace and Socialism*—called *World Marxist Review* in the English edition—was a hotbed of political debate in the 1960s, although not all of it actually found its way into the publication. These Soviet intellectuals spoke freely to one another, but somewhat guardedly to foreigners, although there was a coded way of speaking that indicated certain things.

As time went on, I received invitations to speak. First, it was at the Lenin School. Valery Terin, a philosopher who was assigned by the school to liaise with me on my academic program, asked me to give a lecture to his philosophy class, which he taught to members of the South African Communist Party. After this, I interacted often with the SACP. They were all young black men, very earnest about their studies, who would come knocking on my door asking me questions about philosophy.

There were periodic theoretical conferences at the school. One was a three-day conference on the working class. Most talks were clichéd and boring, full of ceremonial language about the virtues of the proletariat, with lots of quotes from Lenin. Then there were "The situation in my country is . . ." with facts and figures about their parties and their superiority to other parties in that country. Mine was about the changing character of the working class under the impact of scientific and technological revolution, rising levels of education, and the entry of more women into the workforce. I outlined debates about the definition of the working class and made a strong argument for a broad definition of the working class as those dependent on wage labor to live, thus including scientists, engineers, teachers, and others. This was very controversial and provoked much response, affirmative and negative. Even those who were negative, in the sense of disagreeing with my position, were positive about engaging in the argument and enlivening the conference. At another conference, on the ideological work of communist parties, I spoke about the contemporary debate about humanism, identifying the various conflicting positions, particularly those underlying the current human rights campaign against the socialist countries and outlining a Marxist theory of human personality. Lots of people wanted to speak to me afterward, saying it was a breath of fresh air. As a result, I was invited to the monthly meeting of the Department of Social Psychology to discuss further my argument that Marxism was underdeveloped in the area of psychology, although it alone had the capacity to generate a superior psychology, that is, one that did not divorce psychology from political economy, properly situating the psyche in a socio-historical context. This generated an affirmative response and lively discussion among psychologists.

A further result of this was that the head of this department, Yuri Sherkovin, recommended to Moscow Radio that I do a series of broadcasts. I was hesitant at first, as I had only done radio and television as an interviewee, but was persuaded to do it. I did about ten of these programs. Some were for occasions, such as May Day or Victory Day, which tended to be steeped in platitudes. I tried to get away from the usual clichés to approach the core realities in a fresh way. Others had to do with my image of the USSR growing up in the Cold War United States and how it had changed, particularly since coming to the USSR. These were all for international broadcast. When I returned home, people told me they had heard them. Although I would have done this work simply because I was asked, I was surprised to be paid lavishly for every broadcast.

This then led to a series of interviews with *Moscow News*, which likewise focused on my impressions of the USSR, and on the contrast between my experiences of capitalism and socialism. In both sets of interviews, I was asked about what problems I discerned and what criticisms I might have. I spoke honestly. I spoke of the scarcity of goods and the atmosphere this produced. I noted the rough and sometimes rude behavior in shops and on the metro, which I contrasted with the warmth and consideration of people in other situations. I expressed my surprise at finding traditionalist notions of masculinity and femininity so prevalent in everyday discourse, in the domestic division of labor, and in labor education in schools, despite the impressive advances made by women in employment and education. I also discussed underdeveloped areas of Marxist theory and unsolved problems in socialist construction, particularly on issues of socialist democracy. I firmly believed that most citizens of the USSR believed in socialism, whether actively or passively, and accepted the superiority of socialism to capitalism. I said so to the world at this time. I felt free to say whatever I thought. I suited their purposes perfectly, because I spoke honestly and freely, but was perhaps just at the limits of what could then be said in public.

On other occasions, however, I pushed beyond those limits. I was invited to speak about my research in the big hall of the Institute of Philosophy of the Academy of Sciences. I was really honored to be asked to do this, as few foreigners had ever done so, and those who had done, such as J. D. Bernal and Roger Garaudy, were far more eminent than me. I outlined the structure of the book I was writing about Marxism and science, reviewed the state of the existing literature, and the philosophical and historical problems that I was addressing. I was working on my chapter on Soviet philosophical debates of the 1920s and 1930s, probing debates that had flourished and were then suppressed. There was an atmosphere of shock when I mentioned Trotsky and Bukharin and alternative paths for the Soviet Union. It almost didn't matter what I actually said about them. It was the fact that I had mentioned the unmentionable names in public. I was especially interested in Bukharin as a major player in philosophical debates as well as a crucial political figure. Whenever I mentioned him, I was usually told simply that "he has not been rehabilitated." On this occasion, I sensed a positive response, a certain frisson, a sense that a barrier had been breached. Perhaps they couldn't say what I said, but they were glad that I said it. There was a lively discussion and then several evaluations of my report without mentioning those names or any of the more delicate issues. They said that my work was serious and original and that they hoped that my book would be published in Russian translation. I had my doubts about that. It was one thing for me to do this in oral form, but I did not think it would be possible to print what I had said there, let alone what I was going to write.

The difference between what I could say at a Soviet academic gathering and what I could publish there became crushingly clear on another occasion. I was invited to speak at an international conference, sponsored by the Czechoslovak Academy of Sciences and *World Marxist Review*, on dialectical materialism and modern science in Prague in March 1978. The papers from it were to be published as a book in time for the World Congress of Philosophy in August of that year. My passport was returned and I was put on a flight from Moscow to Prague. I was met at the airport and taken first to the offices of the journal and then to a chateau in Liblice, which had been turned into a conference center. Most of the twenty-one speakers were leading philosophers and scientists of the socialist countries. All were male, except for me. Also present were representatives of various communist parties on the editorial board of *WMR* and assorted staff. Most papers, but not all, were of a high standard and discussions were quite intelligent. Although they were all older and eminent, they treated me with curiosity and respect, despite my youth and lack of eminence.

My paper was punchy and polemical, going through various trends within Marxism in terms of their conceptualization of science. It was enthusiastically received by the academics present. Most of them were critical intellectuals who were trying to get through a very difficult period for critical intellectuals. These were people whose work had come to my attention in my research, and the opportunity to mix with them in this environment was fantastic. During the two days of formal proceedings, interspersed with meals and walks and late-night drinking and talking, there was plenty of time for informal discussion. I formed strong bonds during these days, which would stretch beyond this event. I responded most strongly (and mutually) to Herbert Hörz of the

Institute of Philosophy and Helmut Böhme of the Institute of Genetics, both of the GDR Academy of Sciences; Radovan Richta of the Institute of Philosophy and Sociology of the Czechoslovak Academy of Sciences; József Lukács of the Hungarian Academy of Sciences; and Theodor Oizerman of the Institute of Philosophy of the USSR Academy of Sciences. I would also have a lot to do with Ivan Frolov of the USSR Academy of Sciences, but that was a more problematic association. Richta invited me to come back to Prague as a guest of the Czechoslovak Academy of Sciences, and Hörz invited me to come to Berlin as a guest of the GDR Academy of Sciences. I said yes to both.

While in Liblice, one night there was a chamber music concert and a banquet on the last night. At this there were a number of less formal and much wittier speeches, especially after a certain amount of drink was taken. Oizerman gave a disquisition of the concepts of possibility and necessity. "To make love with your wife is possible, but not necessary. To make love with this beautiful woman is necessary but not possible." I was urged to speak too and I did, but I cannot remember what I said. This more informal philosophizing continued for a few days. We were taken to a chateau in Libechov for an art exhibition and then to the town of Melnik, for a reception hosted by the regional party committee, who also briefed us on the region, followed by a meeting with the mayor in the town hall. Then we were taken to a local wine cellar and let loose in it. There was again much philosophizing of the lighter sort, with much robust laughter. We then returned to Prague, where we were booked at the International Hotel and taken on a tour around the city—so beautiful on the surface, so simmering with disaffection underneath. There was so much hidden from view. Everyone knew in one way or another, but no one quite said it. I was still thinking that perhaps it was necessary, that perhaps socialism with a human face would still somehow be possible. In fact, the person responsible for the phrase "socialism with a human face" was none other than Radovan Richta, who was now in my company. I was quite intrigued by him. A leading reformer during the Prague

Spring, he was now a leading normalizer in the purged era that followed. There was a tortured ambiguity about him, a longing for something higher. Whatever he was, he was no thug. Others were thugs, all through the society, even in academic and party circles—especially in party circles. It was here that I came up against one of them and caught a glimpse of the ugly side of the Soviet presence in Prague.

At the editorial offices of *WMR*, I met with Vladimir Vyunitsky, who was the technical coordinator of the editorial work on the book, although Ivan Frolov was the formal editor. He told me that my paper would have to be edited for the book *Dialectical Materialism and Modern Science*. I accepted that it had to be cut for length, as did the papers of other participants, but he then proceeded to make unreasonable accusations and demands. He said I had made errors that would have to be corrected, that I was guilty of "ideological distortion," that I had made incorrect assessments of several Marxist philosophers. Moreover, it was not my place to make any assessments of philosophers who had ever belonged to other Communist parties. Only Hungarian comrades could evaluate György Lukács. Only French comrades could criticize Louis Althusser. Only Italian comrades could say anything about Lucio Colletti. The combination of ignorance and arrogance was stunning and absurd. Boris Rubalsky, a Soviet interpreter, intervened and told me that the relationship between parties at the journal was very delicate, and it had been agreed that no parties would criticize positions taken by others. I didn't see why this should apply to philosophical discourse. Nevertheless, I reluctantly compromised and agreed to take out all references to Lukács, Korsch, Colletti, and Althusser. I stayed up all night revising the text and cutting it in half. In between, I went out with other philosophers to Laternica Magica, but I was seething with anger and did not enjoy it. Other philosophers discussed my issues and agreed with my arguments. Hörz tried to reason with Vyunitsky. Richta said that he would submit my full, unexpurgated text to the leading philosophical journal in Czechoslovakia. Soviet philosophers later asked me for the text for *Voprosy filosofii*, the leading philosophical journal of the USSR. I returned to Moscow believing that this had been sorted, however unsatisfactorily, but it was far from the end of it.

A month later I received a copy of the text of my chapter in Russian for me to approve. I went over the text with Valery Terin. It was utterly alien to me. Riddled with logical contradictions, historical inaccuracies, tedious clichés, and convoluted jargon, it bore little resemblance to either the original or revised text. Valery agreed with me that the article was irredeemable and that I should refuse consent. I wrote immediately to Frolov rejecting that text. To be cooperative, I wrote yet another version. The school was very accommodating, providing translation and typing services and the speediest channels to communicate with Frolov. He replied a few weeks later, saying that it was too late to do much about the Russian edition. He admitted that the editorial work was problematic, and that my views had been distorted. He hoped the editorial errors could be corrected and that something of my style could be restored in other languages. He said that it was good that the full text would be published in philosophical journals in the USSR and CSSR. I was unhappy with this, but too busy in my last period in Moscow to do much more about it then. The saga would go on for more than a year, and have consequences that I did not foresee then.

Meanwhile, there was a lot going on in Moscow. My research intensified, and patterns took shape in my mind and in the chapter outlines. I still took time walking around on my own, processing my historical research and current experiences, reflecting on this society in its past and present. Although I was more aware of its complexities and tragedies, I still affirmed Soviet society as a monumental striving toward socialism. I loved the revolutionary iconography of public spaces. My favorite metro stations had gorgeous mosaics and gigantic statues of workers and peasants, honoring labor and socialist construction. Shopping outside the privileged enclave of the school was an endurance test, but GUM was an essential experience. It was a bizarre bazaar, with long queues, much pushing, and elaborate and inefficient procedures for buying an item once you got to it. My worst shopping experience came when I went to a local shop to buy a bottle of wine to take to dinner in a philosopher's apartment. There were lots of men already gathered around the shop. When it opened, they stormed in, and I nearly got trampled in the crush. A shop assistant spotted me, pulled me out and brought me around to the back to buy the wine. I became accustomed to seeing people walking along the street with dozens of rolls of toilet paper wrapped around their bodies on a string whenever there was a sudden supply somewhere. When people saw queues, they joined them before even asking what was for sale, and carried shopping bags with them at all times, just in case.

It was not only what I could observe on the street. I learned of the elaborate arrangements people made to obtain various things I had always taken for granted. The queues to get into restaurants seemed interminable. One evening I met Julian Cooper, a lecturer in Soviet studies in Birmingham and member of the CPGB, to have dinner. We queued for hours. The worst of it was that the queue kept getting longer. The custom was that one of a group would come early to queue and then their friends would join them as they moved farther on in it. It was midnight by the time we left. We walked up to Red Square, which was stunning in the dark and snow, with the red star dominating the whole scene. We both felt a surge of emotion, a sense of the power of the idea of socialism and of the complexities of its embodiment. Another night I queued and dined with Theodor Oizerman and Valery Terin, who both had a particular way of combining philosophy and fun, and I enjoyed the queueing as much as the dining.

I was also very involved in the life of the school. I was expected to attend meetings of the heads of all party groups, which included a few of us who were the sole representatives of our parties. I saw many Soviet films there, although there were so many about the war that they all blurred together for me. My favorite film was *The*

First Teacher. I had already read the novel by Chingiz Aitmatov, which had left a strong impression on me. It showed a communist teacher struggling to set up a school in a Kirghiz village in 1923, battling against traditionalist ideas on politics, education, and gender. There were also screenings of television programs; for example, a documentary on the "spiritual crisis of bourgeois society." There were many socials and rituals, some of them organized by particular parties and some by the school. There was a lot of singing. The most memorable for me was the SACP singing "Give a Thought to Africa," along with other revolutionary songs in wonderful harmonies, which haunted me for a long time afterward.

The school celebrated the big holidays in style: International Women's Day, Victory Day, Lenin's birthday, and, of course, May Day. On International Women's Day, I received presents from men at the school. Sometimes I got presents for no reason at all. The most surprising happened one day when I was returning to the school. I got off the metro just as a professor from the school was getting on. He held a bouquet of flowers that was obviously intended for someone else, but he spontaneously presented them to me. On another occasion the whole school was brought to the great hall in the Kremlin. It was the first time I saw Brezhnev in person, although from far away, such was the vastness of the hall. There were lots of ceremonial speeches of the kind I was finding increasingly numbing. However, I felt a buzz just being in this hall, the site of so many historical events. For Lenin's birthday, there was also the *subbotnik*, a day of voluntary labor, organized primarily through workplaces. I got the clear impression that it was not really voluntary. The school organized the day so that we all worked in factories. I was sent, along with Canadian communists, to a fur factory, where we cut fur for one shift. Then we were treated to a lavish meal at the factory with the management and party and trade unions committees. There were many toasts to socialist labor. When I was next at the Academy of Sciences, I asked about the *subbotnik* there. The scholars said that they had come in and washed the windows.

The most exciting of the holidays and rituals was May Day. We had celebrations in the school the day before, which involved a solemn meeting, concert, dinner, and dance. On the day itself, we rose early and went together to Red Square. We were ushered to good positions. We were full of anticipation to witness something we had seen so many times in international newsreels. I didn't find the tanks and the Politburo very inspiring, but the revolutionary songs, the fluttering red flags, the colorful flowers and balloons, the marching people, all made for a festive air and a sense of being part of an immense world-historical movement. Afterward, I met Betty Sinclair and spent the late afternoon and evening with her. We went up to Lenin Hills, where there was a panoramic view of the city, and saw the fireworks, and then went on to the party hotel for drink and talk. We got on well that day, as she had not yet comprehended my offense, although I had informed her, as the party's representative at *WMR*, of my problems with Vyunitsky. Betty had mixed feelings about intellectuals. Mostly she was inclined to proletarian anti-intellectualism, but had to deal with the fact that the Soviet Union took intellectuals seriously. She told me on this day that she was proud that our party could produce someone who could hold her own with them. During this time, I became very interested in the Lenin School during the Comintern period. I knew it had been affected by the purges and I asked Betty about that, as she had been there during that period, but she was not very forthcoming. As the night went on, our discussion grew more and more inebriated and full of uncritical praise of the great USSR. In the elevator, she was singing a communist drinking song to the tune of "99 Bottles of Beer on the Wall," which I often heard sung in Ireland as well. The most memorable lines to me were "5 for the years of the 5-year plan and 4 for the 4 years taken." All questions were smothered in proclamations of victory and loyalty and denunciations of treachery.

Far more forthcoming was Jan Vogeler, a professor of philosophy at Moscow State University, who had been at the Comintern School when it relocated to the Kazak region during the war, along with Markus Wolf and Wolfgang Leonhard. He told me that Leonhard had written a book about it. I got my hands on *Child of the Revolution* as soon as I could after I left the USSR. It wasn't exactly the sort of book that would be in the library of the Lenin School or any library in the USSR, except the closed access collections for approved specialists. Leonhard vividly described the repressive atmosphere of the period. There were rigid rules: no sex, no drink, no leaving the premises without permission. His friend, who was the son of Tito, was expelled for violating the no-sex rule. Although Leonhard, Vogeler, Wolf, and others had grown up together, they were forbidden to use their real names or to refer to their previous lives. Worst were the criticism/self-criticism sessions, where the most minor offhand remarks were blown up into major ideological deviations. I later learned of how classes at the school were suspended in the heat of the third period of the Comintern, which brought the ascendancy of Stalin and the purging of the Trotskyist and Bukharinist "deviations." Weeks were devoted to writing political autobiographies and confronting each other in criticism/self-criticism sessions. Jim Larkin Jr. was removed as head of the English-speaking section and pressured to renounce "Larkinism." Patrick Breslin was expelled for expressing doubts about dialectical materialism. He had married a Soviet woman and become a Soviet citizen. He stayed in the USSR and worked as a translator and journalist, until he became a victim of the paranoid atmosphere surrounding foreigners, especially those of a critical disposition. He was arrested for espionage and transported to labor camp, and died en route. Most party members knew nothing of this and those who did, such as Betty Sinclair, kept quiet.

The Lenin School was obviously very different in the post-Comintern period. We were free to roam around, although most did not venture very far into non-party enclaves of Soviet life. There was lots of sex and drink. Not quite enough for some, however. One day I was in the lift with an Iraqi comrade, whom I didn't really know, and he started kissing me. Although we didn't have a word of a common language, I made it clear I wanted him to stop. He stopped the lift between floors and kept putting his hands on me. One night I was at a gathering, talking and drinking with a dozen or so comrades. A game started where everyone had to tell of their first sexual experience. There was one exotic tale after another. When pressed, I said that I had been twenty-three and it was on my wedding night. "Come on now," they said, as if that was the most exotic tale of all.

I went on a number of excursions, either organized by the school or with comrades from the school, or with other friends. I spent a relaxing weekend at a dacha with the South Africans. I went to the theater, opera, and ballet on many occasions. The school arranged tickets, if we asked. Many of us were keen to see the play *Kremlin Chimes*. I went to visit a secondary school with some Italians. We were surprised to find a rigid gender division in labor education with more domestic skills for females and industrial skills for males. The principal tried to defend it, but she only made it worse with dubious references to masculinity and femininity. We all waded in with arguments against the traditional division of labor and such conservative notions of gender traits. She wasn't accustomed to such arguments. Finally, she backed into a position that there were too many urgent problems in Soviet society for it to be a priority. I said that even during the civil war, when the very existence of the Soviet state was at stake, the Bolsheviks thought it was a priority. She had nowhere to go then.

I often went to Moscow State University and got to know a number of professors there. One of them brought me to his dacha along with his wife, and I only learned afterward that I had breached a condition of my visa by going that far outside the Moscow city limits without permission. Another MGU professor of philosophy, the logician Alexander Zinoviev, was causing a stir at the time. He had published abroad a satirical novel called *The Yawning Heights*, and although the book was not then available in the USSR except on the most restricted access, it was amazing how many of the philosophers seemed to know all about it. Characters in the story were philosophers I knew, I was told, so I got that book as soon as I got back home. Some of my visits to Lenin Hills were to see Jan Vogeler. My sessions with him were really informative. As I was heading for the GDR, he filled me in on the history of philosophy in the GDR, which was filled with interesting philosophical debates, which often had extra-philosophical consequences, such as the imprisonment of Wolfgang Harich and the house arrest of Robert Havemann. Mick O'Riordan appeared in Moscow during my time there. He gave a talk at the school about the situation in Ireland. He had come for laser surgery on his eyes. I visited him at the party hotel and then in hospital during his stay, reporting on my activities. He was happy the party had someone who could interact on a high level with the Soviet intelligentsia, although he didn't want to hear that much about my actual research or reflections on it.

As my four months drew to a close, I scurried around tying up all my loose ends, taking a flurry of notes in libraries, saying my goodbyes, and spending much of the money I had accumulated. This last issue was odd. I was accustomed to not having much money, and lots of things I wanted to buy. Here it was the opposite. I had so much money, but not a lot I could buy. The monthly stipend of the school was 180 rubles, the average industrial wage, which was easily adequate for my expenses, but once I started receiving money for broadcasting, I had more than I needed. I bought many presents to bring home for my children, took comrades out to eat in restaurants, where we had champagne and caviar, and gave what was left to comrades at the school.

Leaving was really difficult. I was invited to extend my stay yet again, especially to go on an excursion to Leningrad. But I had been away long enough, considering that I had young children. I had to tear myself away from a whole network of strong relationships. The South Africans made a tape of their songs that I loved hearing them sing. I had a big going-away party at the school on my last night. Expectations of keeping in touch went unfulfilled. Every letter or parcel I sent seemed to disappear into a black hole, making me wonder if there was an unstated policy about severing ties upon leaving. It was great to be reunited with Cathal and Clíodna, who had more presents to open than on Christmas. I filled the house in Bayside with Soviet art. I found it hard to adjust to being back home, missing the intensity of discovery and interaction. I resumed my party work, my academic research, and writing. My brain was buzzing.

When I returned to Trinity, I asked if anyone was going to the World Congress of Philosophy. Every philosopher I met in Moscow and Prague was talking about it, but I had never heard it mentioned in Dublin. It was not on their radar. The world of philosophy for them encompassed Britain and America. I mentioned that the theme of the congress was science and philosophy, and there would be many presentations and debates relevant for my thesis. They encouraged me to go, and indicated that the college might contribute to the costs of my registration and trip to Düsseldorf in August 1978.

I was moving between different academic subcultures. Eastern European academics had by this time become integrated into international academic structures, in fact more so than Irish ones. They were involved in organizing, chairing, presenting. There was a high degree of coordination among socialist countries about it. Sometimes it seemed as if they were planning for it in a way that was parallel to staging Warsaw Pact maneuvers. They often asked me what Western philosophers were planning. I tried to explain that they were not really planning anything in the way that they meant. Western philosophers were relating to the congress as individuals, writing their papers and booking their flights, but they didn't see themselves as representing the UK or USA in the way that Soviet philosophers were centrally selected and would be representing the USSR.

At the congress itself, I was one of the few who moved between both sides. I found this quite stimulating, and entered into all of the polemical possibilities and bonding interactions that the situation offered. There were a few others who moved between Eastern and Western subcultures. Some were members of Western communist parties, such as Frank Cunningham and Dan Goldstick from University of Toronto, or non-party Marxists, such as Robert Cohen and Marx Wartofsky of Boston University. There was a reception hosted by the DKP, the (West) German Communist Party, for communist philosophers, east and west. There Erwin Marquit, a member of the CPUSA and a physicist with philosophical inclinations, toasted the CPSU, thanking them for our being there, although the logic of that escaped me. In informal conversation, Adam Schaff of Poland remarked on the poor quality of the theoretical publications of the CPUSA. Marquit went into overdrive against Schaff, firing off a letter to the CPUSA accusing Schaff of interfering with the internal affairs of another party and ranting the rest of the week about Schaff's inciting foreign communists against their parties and demanding that he be expelled from his own party. Marquit had a notion of 100 percent orthodoxy, of everyone being for or against us. He went into loud diatribes against revisionism on crowded trams, which I found embarrassing. I got into fierce arguments with him, not only about Schaff, but about Cohen and Wartofsky, all of whom I respected, while I was finding it hard to respect Marquit.

A Cold War atmosphere pervaded the congress. The West Germans hosting it created a nasty atmosphere from the start. At an opening plenary, one speaker provocatively referred to Marx as "too smart a German to be left to the Marxists." At most sessions, Marxists, phenomenologists and neo-positivists of many varieties all read papers past each other. Some of the Soviet philosophers found it difficult to address arguments coming from other philosophical traditions, but then so did some analytical philosophers. At one session, there was a head-on attack on "diamat." The Soviet philosophers sat there stunned, while I leapt up to speak in defense of dialectical materialism, which left the attacker stunned, as he was expecting a response from an old Soviet male and not from a young Irish female.

Not that my relations with Soviet males were always harmonious. The book *Dialectical Materialism and Natural Science* was

launched and distributed at the congress, and the chapter with
my name on it was utterly alien to me. When I saw Ivan Frolov, I
breathed fire, and a crowd of other Soviet philosophers gathered,
astonished that I would speak that way to someone so eminent. I
found it ironic, when he later emerged as a prominent exponent of
glasnost, to remember the lack of glasnost he inflicted upon me.
Other problems also arose in conversations with Eastern European
philosophers. I sensed that Radovan Richta wanted to speak with
me, but was nervous whenever we did so. I wondered how much
this had to do with the minders that were said to be part of del-
egations to conferences abroad, who monitored and reported on
relations with foreigners. I found the philosophers from socialist
countries quite diverse, not only as individuals, but in terms of
their national cultures. Soviet academics seemed the most sheltered, most inclined to answer questions with slippery evasions or
canned formulations. At the other end of the spectrum were those
from the GDR and Yugoslavia, who, though in many ways thought
opposite of each other, not least in their relation to the USSR, I
found to be the most sophisticated, the most familiar with other
philosophical trends, and the best able to defend Marxism with flu-
idity, sincerity, and rigor. Throughout the ten days in Düsseldorf, I
was on a high. Every day was full of consequential conversations. I
met so many philosophers from all over the world. I was part of a
global process of articulating and debating alternative worldviews,
rooted in geopolitical forces, where so much seemed at stake. I
formed relationships that would persist for decades.

   After the congress, I traveled with philosophers from the
GDR by train to Berlin on an invitation from the Institute of
Philosophy of the GDR Academy of Sciences. When we arrived
at Friedrichstrasse, we had to separate, as I went through the
section of passport control for foreigners. Nowhere have I experienced a heavier border crossing. Never have I had a passport or
visa so closely scrutinized or had guns pointed at me while doing
so. Nevertheless, all was in order and Herbert Hörz and Ulrich
Röseberg were waiting for me. They took me to a nearby flat on

Chausseestrasse, next door to where Bertholt Brecht had lived, where I stayed with Kati and Rudi Grabs. Kati was a secretary at the Academy of Sciences and oversaw the logistics of my program. She spoke only German, which forced me to plunge from my textbook study of the language to everyday use. Rudi was editor of a trade union publication and spoke good English, so he came to my rescue when he was around and I got stuck. He was also very politically articulate and answered many of my questions about the GDR long into the night. It was an old building with many stairs to climb and a communal bathroom on another floor with antiquated plumbing. I stayed in a room that had been vacated by their grown-up daughters. Only steps from this flat was Dorotheenstadt cemetery where I walked among the graves of Brecht, Hegel, and so many other luminaries of philosophical and cultural history.

Walking the streets, I felt that same buzz of being somewhere where my worldview was in power as I did in Moscow, which was such a contrast from its marginalization at home. The image of East Berlin abroad was of a cold, gray, shabby, sinister place. I had grown up with this Cold War mentality about Berlin, especially since my father was stationed in the American sector of the city after the war. Although many buildings had seen better days, and it did seem gloomy in the rain and there were labyrinthine procedures for everything, I found it captivating, even full of color and significance. Especially attractive were the television tower and world clock in Alexanderplatz, museum island, Humboldt University, and the statues of Marx and Engels in Marx-Engels-Forum. I took to the boulevardesque grandeur of Unter den Linden and the monumental buildings of Mitte. As I walked up Karl-Liebnecht-Strasse or through Rosa-Luxemburg-Platz, I sang in my head the stirring and combative song written by Brecht that I knew in both German and English: "For Karl Liebnecht, we have a score to settle. For Rosa Luxemburg, murdered by our foe." It was a strange city, unlike any I had ever visited. It was so obviously half a city. The wall was such a dominating presence. It had only been there for seventeen years, a very short time in the life of this world-historical city. East Berliners, even the most committed communists, were acutely conscious of the western part of it and felt severed from it, no matter how resolutely they defended the wall. Indeed, this was the first time I heard credible arguments for the wall: how the GDR was being bled of subsidized goods and how those educated by a socialist society had a duty to stay and work in it. The availability of Western television made the GDR very different from the USSR, in that its citizens were always aware of Western consumer products and terms of discourse.

During the day, I met with philosophers, sometimes indoors, but more often walking around Berlin, where they showed me different neighborhoods, while we engaged in searching and honest discussions. In the evenings, others took me home for dinner. I also attended philosophical seminars. Discussions ranged from everyday life in the GDR and the problems of socialist democracy to the relation of philosophy to the natural sciences. One of those I got to know was Klaus Fuchs-Kittowski. He was a nephew of Klaus Fuchs, a famous atomic spy whose name I knew from my Cold War youth. Klaus was quite close to his uncle, who had returned to the GDR after his release from prison in Britain and he was at that time a member of the Academy of Sciences and of the central committee of the SED. Klaus told me much about the tragic history of his family. During the Nazi period, his father, a communist, was arrested and his mother committed suicide by throwing herself under a train. Not long after my visit, the BBC broadcast a drama about Klaus Fuchs and I wrote to Klaus about it. I viewed it in a much-enhanced way, because I knew so much more about his life before and after this episode in his story.

I probed the various "affairs," especially the philosophical ones, such as the cases of Wolfgang Harich, Robert Havemann, and Ernst Bloch, but also those of Rudolf Bahro and Wolf Biermann. All had their troubles with GDR orthodoxy, whether denounced, exiled, imprisoned, or house-arrested. Everyone I asked faced these questions forthrightly, spoke more freely if we were talking one-to-one, especially in the open air, but along a spectrum of responses. Those with whom I had the greatest rapport generally replied with a nuanced philosophical or political critique, but no defense of the party's repressive measures. These high-profile cases, behind which there were many low- or no-profile cases, exposed the dark underside of the GDR—what was unseen when you gazed at the hammer and compass framed by stands of wheat and the glittering surfaces of the Palast der Republik, what was unheard when you sang their great stirring songs of class struggle and international solidarity.

One of my best colleagues and comrades, an eminent scientist, said to me one day, "We need socialist democracy, but we have no idea what it is or how to achieve it." Others told me that there was wide support for socialism in the society, but that those who were presiding over it would never be elected. Czechoslovakia 1968, including the GDR's fraternal assistance in the crushing of the Prague Spring, had a chilling effect on those who felt in common cause with what had been crushed. They were trying to find a way to work with integrity, academically and politically, pushing at the limits, but without being labelled as dissidents. They were genuinely loyal to the GDR, but wanted an alternative version of the GDR, facing constant frustration, but living within its limits. This was the dominant view among those with whom I had the greatest rapport and the longest conversations, but I also engaged with others who defended the GDR as it was and took a hard line toward those who questioned it. Some might have been the sort of conformists to be found anywhere, but most of those I met were intelligent and sincere in their convictions. Even within the group hosting me, the section for research on the philosophical problems of the natural sciences, Nina Hager was loyal to the GDR as it was and inclined to see danger in alternative approaches, even Marxist ones. "The party values theoretical unity," she said. That might be laudable on one level, I thought, but the problem was what the party did to enforce that theoretical unity. She was seen as very much her father's daughter, for her father was Kurt Hager, also a philosopher, a member of the Politburo, and the ideological supremo of the GDR. However, if anyone thought she was an opportunist merely coat-tailing her powerful father, they were wrong. She was a true believer, as time would tell. I also saw Erwin Marquit again in Berlin, and so got another barrage of anti-revisionism.

I was asked to speak on the state of Marxist philosophy in Ireland at the Institute of Philosophy. I thought this was too small a topic, given how little Marxist philosophy there was in Ireland, so I began with such Marxism as there was in Irish universities and left parties, and moved outward to the state of Marxist theory across Europe. In this country full of people working in the philosophy of science from a Marxist point of view, many of whom were packed into the room, I had to explain that I was the only one in my country doing so. It was lonely and this, of course, was a large part of my attraction to the GDR. I outlined debates within Western communist parties on a whole range of issues, emphasizing the philosophical controversies. I was quite critical of a retreat from materialist philosophy and from class analysis, but sympathetic to the new emphasis on socialist democracy, on new social movements and to the attention to undeveloped areas of Marxist theory. I also spoke of the difficulty in the communist movement of being honest about our own history, about its complex and often tragic dynamics, including who was arrested and why. I also remarked on the poor quality of some of the philosophical discourse from some of the academic elite of the socialist countries at the recent congress and asked how much of this was due to lack of conviction as well as the sheltered nature of academic life there. Discussion was lively and free-flowing. I felt no pressure to back away from this way of speaking; quite the opposite.

While there, I was asked to write an article on my impressions of the GDR, which I did willingly, and it was published in a trade union magazine. I was also interviewed by philosopher Franz Loeser for a profile in *Die Weltbühne* (The World Stage), which focused on my life story, taking up the "nun who became a communist" angle. I packed a lot into this visit, but left feeling I had much more to explore. I would get the opportunity to do so, as I had an open invitation from the Institute of Philosophy to come back whenever I could, for as long as I wanted. I was developing serious, honest, collegial, and comradely relationships there, ones that I needed to adequately pursue my philosophical and political questions.

When I returned home, I wrote like mad. I had been researching and outlining and discussing, and now it was time for writing. The dining room table in the open-plan house in Bayside was strewn with books and papers that had to be cleared every time we had dinner. The party paper was also laid out there, and much of it written there, too. The television was on nearby and the phone was constantly ringing and children were playing. Somehow I did it.

I focused on deep philosophical questions and debates within the frame of a historical narrative, although there was constant tension between thematic and chronological considerations in making structural decisions. I wanted to capture the real drama of this convergence of science, philosophy, and politics, and the interactions of all these forces in motion. I was happy later when Mario Bunge said the book read like a novel. I tried to imagine the milieu and the characters as vividly as sources allowed, and to ground ideas in the full flow of history. I began with Marx and Engels, moved to the next generation of the Second International, especially in Germany and Russia, then to the October Revolution and Marxism in power in the USSR, and then to the Comintern, as parallel debates played out in the rest of the world. I narrated a story of fierce intellectual debate, analyzed the philosophical issues involved, and explored their sociohistorical contexts. In scrutinizing these controversies, I examined the multiplicity of factors in play, including the impact of new scientific discoveries, new philosophical trends, and new political developments. For example, in the "Lysenko affair" the science of the time had not yet synthesized the emerging discoveries of genetics and evolution and this intersected with longer-running debates about heredity versus environment as well as with the exigencies of the five-year plan and the increasing repression of intellectual life in the USSR. The overall conclusion I reached was that this was a rich and significant history, rooted in the impulse to work out a weltanschauung grounded in the most advanced science of its time and integrally connected to the struggle to create a new social order. I found it to be an audacious enterprise, which generated, not only impressive achievements, but also tragic disasters.

It was a story with a dark side as well as a bright one, and I made every effort to see both in proper perspective, something the historiography of Marxism glaringly lacked. For far too long, it had been polarized in terms of simple and one-sided extremes. On the one side, there was a Marxist history of Marxism, which told only of the bright side, and which was distorted by empty jargon, hollow self-praise, coy evasion, or outright deceit. On the other side, there was an anti-Marxist history of Marxism, which told only of the dark side, which was equally distorted by divorcing events, ideas, and people from their proper context. There were some exceptions, but this was the pattern. Working my way through this history in writing this book forced me to come to terms with various issues in a sharper way than I would have otherwise. At times, I was quite shaken by what I realized I had to write. I mentioned the unmentionable names and delved into matters that others wanted to let lie. I did so regretfully, even sorrowfully, for I could take no joy in the self-inflicted tragedies of the communist movement, as did anti-communist writers, who were, for the most part, the only ones to write about such things. Writing about the transition from the 1920s to the 1930s, when vibrant debate closed down and one correct answer to every question was administratively imposed, and when academic institutions, in line with the rest of society, were purged, often in a way that was not only unjust, but irrational, shook me deeply. There were many crudities, but also complexities, and I took great care to unravel the layers of Lysenkoism and Stalinism, which could not be reduced to clichés about Lysenko being a charlatan and Stalin being a megalomaniac.

In a way, I was living through this history as I was writing it. This was heightened by the fact that I was a member of a communist party and coming to terms with the communist movement for real. My views on many matters evolved, reached points of crisis and then resolution. My relationship to Marxism became more and more complicated, and my connection to the communist movement more and more problematic. My exploration of the story told in my book opened out into another story that carried it into experiences that were not long ago and far away. I was haunted by other people's life stories, often told to me in confidence, and by questions they put to me about my own. At times, I felt as if my painfully evolved intellectual and moral standards were again under assault, this time by certain tendencies within the communist movement, past and present. I disagreed totally with the premises underlying the tradition of sacrificing truth to partisanship, in the name of which so many crimes against science and humanity had been committed. What sometimes began in relative innocence, posed as the sacrifice of some perhaps laudable principle for some supposedly necessary gain in the class struggle, led inevitably to the erosion of all standards of rationality and morality, entrenchment of the habit of lying (even when it had nothing to do with the class struggle), destruction of trust, and sheer human degradation, which outweighed any gains made by such methods. The use of the categories of Marxist philosophy to override the demands of rationality and morality could not but have a corrosive effect on the development of Marxist philosophy. Thus, the catechetical and stale textbooks of dialectical and historical materialism, which gave the impression that all philosophical thinking had reached its finished form in the past and was authoritatively embodied in the interpretations and decisions of the party leadership (primarily the Soviet one). Thus, too, the heresy-hunting preoccupation with revisionism used against those who wished to carry on the process of philosophical thinking in the present and the fear of what conclusions might be reached by proceeding in accordance with considerations of rationality and morality.

All this made my relationship with the CPI more and more fraught. Even at home, Eoin and I had terrible arguments. He was typing my manuscript and often came to a halt and said he wouldn't type another word. I was especially disturbed by the betrayal of honest and intelligent communists by opportunists and thugs as the purges progressed. I was shocked by the secret protocol of the Nazi-Soviet Pact, which involved the NKVD handing over German, Austrian, and Hungarian communists and anti-fascists who had sought asylum from fascism in the land of socialism, to the Gestapo. Eoin and I had a particularly bitter row over that. Even if it was true, he said, I was doing the work of the enemy by writing about it. I was becoming a revisionist, as he saw it. Although it was a far cry from the purges, I felt I was being heresy-hunted. There were many other issues and incidents, but in early 1979, they came to a head around the party congress in Belfast and the fallout from the publication in Prague.

Leading up to the party congress that February, there was intensive discussion in party branches, particularly in mine. Even though the congress had been postponed for a whole year and congress preparation was the major party activity, the quality of the documents was poor. They reflected the state of the party, which was basically ticking along and maintaining the "correct," that is, anti-anti-Soviet, line. There was a smug satisfaction based on having correct answers to questions they had never asked or even understood. In our branch, we discussed whether the documents were even of a standard amenable to amendment. We submitted a resolution critical of the documents overall, making the case that the political and organizational resolutions in particular failed to address the political forces of our time and the organizational problems of our party. They showed a low theoretical level, a lack of structure and proportion, and a dishonest evaluation of the state of the party. Our branch then came under pressure from the national executive to withdraw the motion. After a bitter discussion, to my disappointment, the majority caved and agreed to do so. At a preparatory meeting in Dublin, I went head-to-head with Mick O'Riordan on the stagnation in the party and the suppression of dissent coming up to the congress.

The congress was not only for ourselves to discuss and decide our political position and organizational tasks, but it was a show-case of the party to those outside it, particularly fraternal parties, who would have delegates present. At the congress itself, I felt that the whole thing was a show for the fraternal delegates, and I refused to follow the script. I gave a sharply critical speech on the state of the party, from its low level of theoretical development, exacerbated by indulgence of anti-intellectualism, to its political inactivity to the chaotic state of party premises. I spoke in hope that telling the truth would have some effect on those who, like me, wanted the party to play the progressive role it could play. By the end of this congress, I lost that hope. They came down on me like a ton of bricks. Sean Nolan, whom I had only recently been visiting in hospital every day, turned his back on me. Others didn't speak to me. Betty Sinclair gave a speech that was supposed to be about foreign policy, but turned into a vicious denunciation of me. "Our party doesn't need such people," she said. In her dia-ries, she recounted how pleased she was to use the opportunity "to slap her down." Her self-righteousness was especially hard to take, because she had spent much of the time between one congress and the next in a state of inebriation and had no idea what was going on around her much of the time. She demanded that the party be purged of "Sheehanism," a deviation of intellectuals who thought they knew better than the party. The elections for the national executive elected the recommended list put forward by the outgo-ing national executive. No one who was nominated but not on the list, including me, was elected. No one who was on it, no matter how poor their party work, failed to be elected.

I was devastated by all this and spent much of the rest of the congress with my head held up but on the verge of tears. Some com-rades agreed with me, even if they didn't do so from the podium. A number of the fraternal delegates from abroad came to speak to me with curiosity and muted sympathy. Perhaps I should have left the party then. I didn't, because my ties to the international communist movement, especially my own network within it, were so strong. I had even volunteered to replace Betty Sinclair on the editorial board of *World Marxist Review*, when it became clear that she was to be withdrawn, thinking that I could play a positive role in bringing it out of its malaise. Of course, there was no chance whatsoever of either being sent or being allowed to work effectively if sent. Betty insisted that I would be the last person who would be welcome there. They decided to send Tommy O'Flaherty, a young unemployed graduate, who was affable and considered reliable.

Not long after the congress, on International Women's Day, I was called in by Mick O'Riordan and read the riot act. After the publication of a chapter under my name in *Dialectical Materialism and Modern Science*, despite my explicit refusal of consent, I wrote a letter of protest to the editorial board in Prague. I also spoke about it to Gordon McLennon, general secretary of the CPGB, who insisted that I speak to Bert Ramelson, the CPGB representative on the editorial board, when I was in London. They both agreed that this way of doing things had to stop, as did the whole production of jargon-ridden material that no one wanted to read. Bert had mentioned it to Mick, who was outraged that I spoke to Bert about it.

Moreover, a response to my protest had come to the party from Prague. It was a transcript of an interview that Tommy O'Flaherty did with Vladimir Vyunitsky, full of overt lies, covert distortion, and heresy-hunting accusations of errors. Mick didn't want to hear my side of the story at all. For him, if a Soviet person and an Irish person disagreed about something, the Soviet person was right. He was untroubled when the original article, which a Soviet person now said was full of ideological errors, was published in *Irish Socialist Review*. He was not interested in the substantive issues. He referred the matter to the national executive with the recommendation that I be reprimanded for protesting to Prague and for talking to Ramelson. This was hotly debated, according to Eoin, who was on the national executive and defended me. I received a letter of reprimand from O'Riordan, which also asked me to withdraw allegations made against himself, that is, that he was indifferent to the substantive issues and expected absolute servility to the USSR. As a compromise with those who felt I had a case, the party also decided to inform *WMR* that they regretted the publication of a chapter that distorted my views and "inadequately represented the philosophical level of our party." I refused to withdraw anything I had alleged, and I received a further letter saying that the party noted my refusal. While I was going through all this, I was writing about the purges in the USSR in the 1930s, specifically their impact on academic debates and institutions, and how they permeated every workplace, every community, during that time. It was all the more vivid to me, because I could see so clearly how it all worked. I could imagine the parts played by people very like Frolov, Vyunitsky, O'Riordan, Sinclair, and others, and I could see where I would be in it all too. People far more compliant than I were sent to a gulag or shot in the back.

Tommy O'Flaherty turned out not to be as compliant as the party had intended. He hit the ground running, because he had to deal with my situation and believed they had a case to answer. Unlike Betty, he paid attention to the debates that were going on at *WMR*, even if they weren't reflected in its pages. There were vigorous discussions of the issues raised by Eurocommunism. Tommy was increasingly convinced by Bert Ramelson's arguments. A bear of a man and a robust debater, Ramelson was a left Eurocommunist, in that he still held to the centrality of class analysis, but advocated for socialist democracy. Tommy also began to learn Czech and to talk to Czechs, who spoke honestly about their lives, which cast an unflattering light on the party line. He later told me that, because he had been a young hardliner, he realized that in another time and place he could have been a mass murderer. After he was withdrawn, he became less active in politics and regarded himself as someone who should leave a light imprint on the world.

That was not my path. As my relations with the party became more and more problematic, I plunged into it all the more, first to understand it and then to bring my understanding of it to bear upon the world. I was in a turbulent state and felt buffeted by tempestuous cross-currents. In Ireland, I felt quite isolated. There were those who agreed with me about the state of the party, but no one was so caught up in coming to terms with the whole past and present of the international communist movement. A postal strike, lasting over four months, intensified my isolation. I needed desperately to talk it through with others who knew and cared about the movement in that way. At the top of my list was Adam Schaff. I set out for Vienna, chessboard of spies and statesmen, locus of Cold War plots and counterplots. There was heavy security at the airport, because it so happened that Carter and Brezhnev also arrived on that day in June 1979. I walked around the city, seeing the traces of many eras of history and thinking how different forces came to ascendancy, from the Austro-Hungarian empire to Austro-Marxism. Austro-Marxism interested me, because of the way it tried to forge a path between the Second and Third Internationals, sometimes called the Second-and-a-Half International.

Schaff moved between Warsaw, where he was a professor at the University of Warsaw and a member of the Polish Academy of Sciences, and Vienna, where he was president of the European Center of Comparative Social Research, a UNESCO institute. Unlike many who declared themselves Marxists only when Marxism was in power, he was a Marxist before and after it was in power. He was a member of the Polish Communist Party since 1931 and on its central committee until 1968. Though often identified as "the chief ideologue of the Polish United Workers Party" (as the Communist Party was called after 1948), by 1979 he no longer was. For several days, we met and talked for hours about the state of Marxist philosophy and the communist movement.

Schaff was devastatingly direct in answering all the most difficult questions. He took me through his experience of all the upheavals in the Polish party over the decades and his own developing position in relation to them. He now believed that Eurocommunism was the way. It was necessary to win wide support before taking power. There had to be multiparty elections, with real parties that could take power. Otherwise, it was rule by terror. Life in countries of "really existing socialism" was surreal. People were afraid to speak freely in their homes and workplaces. They could only talk with those they trusted in the open air. Philosophers spoke sense, but then wrote nonsense. Moreover, he argued, socialism could only be built in advanced societies. There had been an attempt to impose socialism on countries not ready for it, which brought incompetence, compulsion, deceit, corruption. He had written a book called *The Communist Movement at the Crossroads*, but thought it would be suicide to publish it. Marxist philosophy, he thought, would have to be developed outside countries where Marxism was the orthodoxy of those in power. It had to flow freely and to be grounded in concrete knowledge. It should pay more attention to the discoveries of the natural and social sciences than to interpreting past texts, including Hegel and Marx. It should deal with other philosophies, such as neo-positivism and existentialism, by learning from them and taking up the problematic they raised from a Marxist perspective, rather than just rejecting them as bourgeois philosophies. It should develop the underdeveloped areas of Marxism. There were lacunae everywhere, especially in psychology and morality. This was an area he had addressed himself. I had read his books such as *Marxism and the Human Individual* and *Alienation as a Social Phenomenon.* I also reviewed his *Structuralism and Marxism,* which was a critique of Althusserianism and theoretical anti-humanism. He was scathing about playing fast and loose with formal logic in the name of dialectics. His was a version of Marxism that was both more scientific and more humanistic than either the Communist Party catechetical orthodoxy or the more fashionable revisionisms. He saw the category of totality as central. All problems were profoundly interconnected.

I thought that he was honest, rigorous, erudite, wise. Some of what he was saying was what I already passionately believed, but other arguments came to conclusions that I was approaching but still resisting. I argued back that communist parties were right to take power in whatever way was possible and to use this to win people to communism, and that we needed to stand by such socialist countries as existed, imperfect as they were. He replied that the method of taking power was linked to how power was exercised. He was still a communist and believed that communism was the future, but it was necessary to be honest about where the movement was at present. He asked about my problems with the CPI. I outlined them. He asked how many members it had, and what forms of activity it undertook. When I replied honestly and not in the evasive way that party leaders did, he laughed scornfully. "That's not a party," he said. "That's a small and insignificant sect."

We also discussed my dispute with Prague, which he thought was ridiculous. He advised me in the strongest terms not to compromise, not to let them break me. My duty, he advised, was to keep Marxism alive, to stand by real knowledge and higher values. He had seen many people broken. In all these hours, he also told me many stories from the hidden history of the communist movement. Whenever I left him, I was in a heightened and turbulent state, struggling to come to terms with all that we had discussed, which corresponded exactly to all that was already troubling me. So much that had been whirling around in my mind crystallized during these days. I had been thinking that there was some piece of the puzzle I was missing, some factor I would discover that would explain all that I found inexplicable. Now I felt that I knew, that I was finally facing the worst, and I felt the cold comfort of clarity.

During one of my walks around Vienna, I came upon a park, where an Austrian band was playing the Soviet national anthem and then the US one. There stood Brezhnev and Carter at some ceremony, possibly laying wreaths, and I walked up quite close, as there were not many people there. Brezhnev looked like a corpse. The scene struck me with unexpected force. I thought of the great divide symbolized by these two men, these two nations, these two blocs. I felt my whole life pass before me. I was on one side, and then I was on the other, but where was I now? Tears flowed. On other occasions, I went to the natural history and art history museums. I didn't take in much detail, but had a heightened sense of the whole of history flowing through me, from the most primitive forms of matter to the most complex art and thought, and challenging me to carry it on.

I had yet another intense series of encounters while in Vienna. I had read that Wolfgang Harich, a philosopher who had been imprisoned in the GDR, was in Vienna. When I asked Adam about him, he said he had known him as a bright young philosopher, when he taught at Humboldt University and edited *Deutsch Zeitschrift fur Philosophie*, but he was broken now. I spoke with Harich for many hours over several days, much of it spent walking in the open air. We had to stop at regular intervals for him to rest, because he had recently had cardiac bypass surgery. He was fifty-five, but seemed older. He told me the story of his life, in much detail. He was still a convinced communist, despite serving eight years of a ten-year sentence, seven of them in solitary confinement, for "forming a conspiratorial and counterrevolutionary group" in 1956. At that time, he was advocating a third way, between Stalinism and capitalism, a democratic and humanistic socialism. To my surprise, he defended his imprisonment to me. Such ideas were dangerous, he contended, especially in light of Hungarian events in 1956. He put the problem quite starkly. In countries of existing socialism, communists were only a tiny minority of the population and could only maintain power through ruthless suppression of opposition. It was what Schaff had also been saying, but drawing the exact opposite conclusions. Harich had no sympathy for Eurocommunism or any interest in problems of alienation or socialist democracy. He said he felt no common cause with dissidents under socialism, and refused any connection with Havemann, Bahro, or Biermann. The ecological crisis added another dimension to this, he argued, because it necessitated centralized and compulsory action to be solved. We also discussed problems of philosophy. He had played an important role in the debate on dialectical logic, defending formal logic, although not in a positivist way, on the same side as Schaff. On the state of philosophy in socialist countries, he claimed that it was second-rate, that small men excluded better ones. He had been excluded, not only when in prison, but also on his release. He was told by the Stasi that his career in philosophy was finished, but he could work as a philologist. He wistfully reflected: "Politics killed the philosopher I wanted to be." His relationship with the communist movement, was no longer like a new marriage, he said, so he expected less and was disappointed less.

He asked me about my own life, my politics, my philosophy. When I told him of my recent problems in Dublin, Belfast, and Prague, he was sympathetic and said he identified with me, although what was happening to me seemed so tame compared to what he had endured. He then came out with a sentence that haunted me for many years: "The communist movement is like a dragon. It eats enthusiastic young communists and it expels cynics, careerists, broken personalities." I walked away grieving for all who had been broken, and for all who had been annihilated, whose lives had been ripped from them, especially the honest communists who were executed in the name of communism. How did Hessen, Uranovsky, and Bukharin feel as they walked along the corridor to be shot? I was filled with sorrow and rage.

On the way to and from Vienna, I spent time in London, pursuing my research and having similar talks with communists in other parties. I spent many hours talking to Klaus Schmautz, a GDR journalist for *Neues Deutschland*, who covered Britain and Ireland. He asked me many questions about Ireland, such as the strength of the CPI vis-à-vis SFWP, which I answered more honestly than party members usually did. In turn, I asked him many questions about the GDR, which I felt he answered honestly. He told me he didn't approve the house arrest of Havemann or the imprisonment of Bahro. I also met many British communists. On the terrible things I felt I had to write, Maurice Cornforth advised me to do so truthfully, not to compromise. Another night, when I was staying at his house and reading the manuscript of a book he was writing, I responded to a very engaging autobiographical introduction by asking him if he ever felt shaken or disillusioned. Yes, he said. Why, then, did he carry on? He replied: "Communism is the great movement of our time. It must be reformed." He was recovering from a recent stroke and his speech began faltering late at night, but this he said unfalteringly. I also spent more time with Gordon McLennon, both in King Street and over dinner at his home. He tried to pull me back from the negativity of my view of the CPI, urging me not to leave, but to stay and persuade others.

I returned home to Dublin feeling I had been away a long time, because so much had happened and I had had such intense interactions. Now it was back to the same old problems, the low-intensity interactions, the small scale of everything, the self-satisfaction amid stagnation. At an area committee meeting, I attacked the complacency of it all and admitted that I was finding it hard to argue for change in the party as if there were anything at stake anymore. I returned to my writing with total concentration. I was calling up many dusty tomes from the library stacks as I plunged into prewar British Marxism, finding much to impress me about Bernal, Haldane, Caudwell, and many others.

I took time out from my writing to attend a high court case involving a philosopher at Maynooth. P. J. McGrath had been a priest, one who had become increasingly critical of Catholic teaching and ecclesiastical authority. When he became laicized, he was asked to resign his chair. He refused, but was dismissed. He did not win his case to be reinstated, which I regretted. I came to know him and admire his intellectual rigor and wry humor. This was a very difficult interval for him. He was forty-four, unemployed for several years, and living with no fixed abode. I also got on well during this time with David Berman in the philosophy department at Trinity. We talked about working on an anthology of atheism. During these years, I had gone from being an agnostic to an atheist.

In August, I was away again. I was presenting a paper at the International Congress of Logic, Methodology, and Philosophy of Science in Hannover. The DKP again arranged my accommodation, as they had also done in Düsseldorf. It was interesting that they did so this second time, as the person responsible had witnessed my speech and the repudiation of it at the party congress. I thought the DKP was prone to a certain rigidity of conception, but they were far more rigorous and vigorous than the CPI. My paper, on the history and historiography of philosophy of science, was a polemic against the canonical story that told of a progression from positivism to neo-positivism to post-positivism, and made a case for the parallel and superior line of development that was Marxist tradition. Papers were published in advance, and mine received a lot of attention even before I presented it, mostly in the way of a surprised but affirmative responses from non-Marxists. In fact, people were seeking me out, saying it was very striking, but wondering if Marxism was really worthy of such a strong defense. These inquiries tended to be sincere rather than sarcastic and I had many rich conversations with those who were willing to reconsider their evaluation of Marxism.

This was not the response to many of the papers from Eastern Europe. The dominant response from others was: where's the Marxism? I had come to realize that many philosophers in Eastern Europe, who professed Marxism when necessary and joined communist parties for career purposes, were not Marxists or communists at all. Despite the fact that there had been many ideological debates about logic, science, and philosophy of science in the past (my research area), it was evident that these disciplines had become refuges for those who wanted to pursue academic life with minimal ideological involvement. At the opposite end of the spectrum was Erwin Marquit. He wanted to bludgeon all into submission to the "correct" ideological position on all things. I was again plagued by him throughout this congress. He was constantly butting into my conversations with others, with all kinds of in-talk about revisionists and renegades, which was especially inappropriate when I was in the company of non-Marxists. Indeed, he hammered non-Marxists over the head with Marxism, preaching the superiority of dialectical materialism, deriding them over their failure to have read the classical texts, and complaining how he was being persecuted, demanding support for his battle for tenure at the University of Minnesota.

At one point, Marquit was involved in a vociferous argument with someone who was an ex-Marxist, and I was drawn into it. I asked him why he was no longer a Marxist, while Marquit kept interrupting his reply with simplistic assertions and sectarian denunciations. After a while, Marquit left, and I was able to hear his story. He was Imre Toth, a mathematician originally from Transylvania. An atheist and communist from a young age, he was active in the resistance and spent the war in a concentration camp. After that, he was teaching philosophy and history of mathematics at the University of Bucharest and was a member of the Communist Party of Romania. He began having trouble over publications, particularly one on ethics and scientific research. He attacked the notion of partisanship, arguing that mistakes might be inevitable but lies were not. Against the idea that truth had to be subordinated to the interests of the working class, he asserted that what was in the interests of the working class was truth. He was denounced as anti-Marxist and moves were made to expel him from the party and dismiss him from the university. There was a meeting to denounce him that he called a "macabre burial." This was connected to a power struggle between Khrushchev and Molotov. The party in Romania took the side of Molotov, leading to a purge of others, whose stories he also told me. In 1969, Toth went to West Germany on an academic invitation and never returned. Time went on, and many of my communist colleagues passed by and asked if I was coming to the Soviet reception. Yes, I was coming, I said, but still I stayed talking with a "defector." Eventually I went to the reception, but all my conversations seemed so shallow compared with the intensity of the encounter from which I had just come. When I saw him the next day, he said he felt as if he had known me for years. He said he had wanted to meet me from the time he read my paper and remarked on its purity and courage. He told me the story of Sodom and Gomorrah and said that I was one of the people for whom the world deserved to be saved.

In these days, I often thought of what Ignazio Silone said to Palmiro Togliatti: "The last fight will be between the communists and ex-communists." I still intended to be on the side of the communists. Yet I was finding it hard to be on the same side as people like Marquit, Vynitsky, or O'Riordan, especially if it was against people like Harich or Toth. Of course, the question of who was a communist was far from simple. Among people I met, including academics at this congress, there were some who were members of communist parties, but clearly not communists. I had a number of encounters with Karel Berka, a Czech logician. We engaged in genial banter, but it brought home a number of things to me. In one conversation, he taunted me with an assertion about science being incompatible with femininity, because women would neglect either work or home, and about men finding clever women unattractive. When I protested, he was both amused and argumentative, finally throwing up his hands and saying he was just an old-fashioned man and a simple logician. I asked if he was a member of the Communist Party. He was. Then he had no business holding such backward views, I countered. He was not the only example. Even Marquit, who constantly claimed the superiority of the socialist countries in all things, had to admit they left a lot to be desired on the debates opened by feminism. On another occasion, on seeing an outline of my book, Berka laid down the law to me about the Prague Spring. If I wrote about it, he insisted, I would not be welcome in Prague. I probed further. I asked about the role played by philosophers, such as Radovan Richta and Karel Kosik, who had been leading thinkers of the Prague Spring, but took opposite paths after it was suppressed. Berka believed that it all came down to the fact that there were two kinds of people: sceptics and believers. He was a skeptic, whereas Richta, Kosik, and I were believers.

I expanded my sense of the philosophical landscape, east and west, during this congress, talking with many philosophers I had read but not yet met. One was Mihailo Marković of the Praxis school in Yugoslavia. He taught for one semester every

year at University of Pennsylvania, and we agreed to meet soon
in Philadelphia. I also saw philosophers I knew from Moscow,
who were more ironic and less orthodox the more I got to know
them. I was invited to a late-night session in the hotel room of
Igor Akchurin, where I interacted with Soviet philosophers in a
more relaxed way than in the Soviet Union. I didn't spend all my
time with Marxists, however. Unlike Marquit, I didn't believe that
non-Marxists were to be either converted or condemned. I had
meaningful interactions with them, even when our worldviews
clashed. I hit it off particularly well with Ernan McMullin, a professor at Notre Dame and much respected philosopher of science.
He was also a Catholic priest from Donegal. I had heard him give
a public lecture when I was a student and was deeply impressed.
He wondered not only how I could make such a strong case for
Marxism, as I had in my paper, but how I could possibly write
a whole book about it. I asked him how he could be a priest as
well as a philosopher of science. He took the question as a sincere
query and not a sarcastic quip, and gave an explanation of his
belief in the existence of God that wove together Thomistic and
Teilhardian strands in a way that was intelligent and impressive.
When he asked me about my own life, his tone was collegial, but
also somewhat pastoral. Also from Ireland were Desmond Clarke
and Dolores Dooley, a couple who were both in the philosophy
department at University College Cork. Des was an ex-priest and
Dolores an ex-nun, so we had a lot in common from our pasts,
even if we were coming to different philosophical conclusions in
the present.

So much happened between the first day and the last that
it seemed as if the congress lasted a month rather than a week.
Afterward, I took a train from Hannover to Berlin in the company
of a Finnish philosopher, who told me that life in Scandinavia was
not so bad, therefore there was no push to change anything, and
thus life was very boring. Academic life centered on work done
elsewhere. He was very lighthearted about it, but remarked on
how unsuited to it I would be. I was even longer getting through

the border at Friedrichstrasse this time, although my visa and letter of invitation were all in order. I met with philosophers and scientists that I had encountered the previous year, along with some new ones. As well as meeting in offices, homes, and cafes, we walked around the streets and parks and even the zoo in Berlin and Potsdam. I also went to Dresden to meet Herman Ley, a wiry and intelligent man with sharp, alert movements and a robust humor. He had been a communist since 1930 and active in the political and intellectual life of the Soviet zone and subsequently the GDR. He claimed that the quality of the intellectual life of the GDR was higher and freer than that of the USSR. This had become obvious to me.

This time my discussions were far more intense and sharp-edged, reflecting what I realized through my research. I pushed further at all the difficult areas. I aired all the dilemmas tearing at me. I groped toward terrible conclusions about all the self-inflicted tragedies of the communist movement that engulfed the science, philosophy, politics, and everyday lives that were welling up in my pages. One person after another told me that this was a book that had to be written, but could not be written in the GDR. They said they thought that it was in the right hands. I spoke about this not only in one-to-one encounters, but also in my presentation to the Institute of Philosophy. Nina Hager sometimes seemed agitated, making comments like "Bloch wasn't a Marxist" and "Trends in Czechoslovakia were counterrevolutionary." Others took a more open attitude. One asked another for a dictionary, because he wanted to find the word for *Mut* (courage). At another meeting of the section, there were reports of various conferences and research projects. I contributed to the discussion of the Hannover congress. I brought my manuscript and several of them read it while I was there. I was keen for Helmut Böhme to read the section on biology, so I would have the expertise of a geneticist for my treatment of Lysenkoism. The existing literature was dominated by glib references to it as a cautionary tale against ideological interference in science. It was far more complex, however, and needed to be understood in terms of intricate scientific debates as well as complex sociohistorical forces. Helmut had strong feelings on the subject, having played an important role in moving the GDR away from a Lysenkoist position. He praised me for my precision in dealing with both scientific and political issues. Uli Röseberg was also especially emphatic about the manuscript, having read the whole of what I had so far written and telling me that it read like a thriller in places and that he learned a lot that he didn't know. He was in intellectual agreement with it, but knew it was on the edge politically, and might be denounced in the USSR.

Where was the Stasi in all this? What I guessed at the time was later confirmed. Uli, with whom I had great respect and rapport, later told me that everyone who spoke to me wrote routine reports. However, they were blandified, stressing that we discussed prospects for world peace and leaving out our talk of purges and prisons. He said that Kurt Hager would have known about our discussions at the Institute of Philosophy, but a member of the Politburo knowing was less of a problem than the local Stasi knowing. I asked Helmut once about his opinion of Kurt Hager. He couldn't give me one opinion, he said, because he was two persons, so he had to give me two opinions. There was the serious philosopher and there was the ideological enforcer.

Not only was I presented with books at the institute, but Uli took me to bookshops and bought all the books in which I indicated any interest, as gifts from the institute. While I was often accompanied, I was also able to make my way around on my own when I had no appointments. On one occasion, I ran into Erich Albrecht, who had represented the SED at the CPI Congress. Despite knowing I was persona non grata at the congress, he was unreservedly warm and made me promise to call him when I was next in Berlin. On another occasion, I went shopping and arrived back with lots of children's clothes. Kati informed that it was illegal to export them, as they were heavily subsidized. Asked what I should do, she and Rudi suggested I take them to my children and plead honest ignorance if I was searched. Once again, Cathal and Clíodna were delighted with all the new clothes and toys, and were reinforced in their belief that my trips away were to buy presents for them. As to what they made of the adult conversations they heard arising from my trips, I sometimes wondered. One day I overheard an altercation between them. Clíodna shouted to Cathal, "I'm going to tell Adam Schaff on you."

The house was full of political activity and discourse. The party branch met at our house on Sunday mornings. There was a constant flow of political visitors, many of them from foreign communist parties, often as overnight guests, with drinking and talking long into the night. Chilean refugees stayed for many months. Not all were communists. My family arrived at intervals, one time with a clatter of crazy charismatics. My brother Mark came and stayed for a year, solving our babysitting problems for a while. My brother Joe, although a US Marine, had not yet solidified into the ideologically right-wing position he would eventually adopt, and once minded all the children in a communist crèche during a weekend school that I organized. Others from different periods of my past arrived, too. Tom Hayden came with his son Troy, and we walked the hills of Howth. Fran Malinowski, Jack's brother, still a priest, came, as did my two cousins, Anna Gorman and Kathleen Sheehan, who were still nuns.

In the autumn of 1979, I was away again to the United States, combining academic lectures and conferences with research interviews, political meetings, and family visits. It was my first time back in six years. At the University of Bridgeport, in a lecture on philosophy of science, in response to a question, I addressed the effect of the purges on philosophy of science, and a New York CPUSA member declared that I was doing the CIA's work for them. He continued to pursue me, tracking me down from city to city, twisting from cajoling to threatening me, slandering Marxist philosophers who were not party members, and demanding that I cancel engagements and take up others he wanted to organize. In Boston, I spoke at Harvard and at the Boston Colloquium for the Philosophy of Science. Boston and Cambridge held such a rich intellectual culture. There were so many people with expertise in my area, or parts of it, that I was running from one stimulating conversation to another, trying to fit in as many meetings as possible in such a short time. There were dates for breakfast, lunch, and dinner and parties in the evenings, as well as intervals in between. I had breakfast with Loren Graham of MIT, who wrote a masterful book, *Science and Philosophy in the Soviet Union*. I was thrilled when he later used the word "masterful" for my book. We had a great talk, because we were so much on the same wavelength on matters of philosophical and historiographical interpretation, if not political orientation. Unusually, he was more interested in Marxism as a philosophy of nature than of politics and economics.

The parties were dazzling intellectual soirees. I also had occasion to air my issues about the communist movement with others with experience of it. Dirk Struik, a Dutch Marxist, was a professor of mathematics at MIT and a founder of the journal *Science and Society*. He had been hauled before HUAC during the McCarthy era, accused of being a Soviet spy, and was suspended from MIT for five years. I asked him if he ever felt shaken as a communist. Yes, he said, but history moved forward, even with very poor human material. He kept his distance from the CPUSA for various reasons, including their uncritical attitude to the USSR. Mark Wartofsky was once in the CPUSA. I sat in on one of his lectures at BU before going to lunch with him. He had an earthy and ebullient presence, making him a fine teacher, a compelling writer, and a very attractive person. We had the Sturm und Drang conversation about being at the crossroads with the international communist movement, then changed key, as he told a series of jokes about communists and communist parties that brought me cathartic laughter.

My next port of call was Philadelphia. I sought out many of my graduate school colleagues and New Left comrades. As well as meeting many of them one on one, many of us gathered together at a meeting of Philadelphia activists with Tom Hayden and Jane

Fonda. The seriously committed ones were still there, along with new faces and groups. What most struck me was how modest and scaled-down it all seemed, compared to the soaring imaginations and grandiose aims that characterized our meetings earlier in the decade. It was a sign of the times. I had many state-of-the-movement talks in subsequent days over dinner in communes, attended a concert of labor songs, visited the law offices of Kairys and Rudovsky, walked the parkway with Dave Gracie on Super Sunday, and took a train journey with Muhammed Kenyatta. David Kairys informed me of my appearances in his FBI file.

I scurried around the various campuses to meet my former teachers and colleagues. It was strange being back at Temple, even physically. The philosophy and religion departments had both moved to a high-rise with tight security. It was impossible even to use a lavatory without getting a key from a secretary. I got a great welcome and a barrage of questions. Paul van Buren was now head of the religion department. He told me that he had run out of steam in philosophy of religion and gone back to theology. I had gone in the opposite direction. Our conversation was cordial, but we were so far apart intellectually. Bill Wisdom was now chair of the philosophy department. He was deeply interested in Marxism and philosophy of science, and was delighted that I was putting them together. I spent most time at Penn, where I saw a lot of Mihalio Marković. It was strange walking around Penn and downtown Philadelphia with him and talking about Eastern European life and various Marxist philosophers, bringing my different milieux together on this old ground. We formed a strong bond during these weeks, going to dinner, attending lectures and films, and reading and commenting on each other's work.

I came and went from Philadelphia to New York several times. I spoke at a conference on Marxism and science sponsored by the New York Marxist School and the NYU Center for Marxist Studies. The CPUSA member stalking me warned that I was not to attend it, that I was not to engage with Trotskyists, and then that I should be careful about giving comfort to the enemy by criticizing

the USSR in any way. Nevertheless, George Novack, a prominent Trotskyist, asked me to lunch, and I accepted. I found him
serious and sincere, and we had a good talk about philosophy of
science. He also spoke of his wife, Evelyn Reed, who had recently
died, whom he was missing very much. I had read her writings
on Marxism and feminism and respected her. There were fine
presentations by Richard Levins, Richard Lewontin, and others.
I gave a lecture at Queens College, where I was pushed hard on
the question of what distinguished Marxist philosophy from other
positions based on a non-reductionist and processive materialism.
I also lectured at the University of Toronto, where the chairman
expressed great surprise that Marxism had within itself so much
diversity and controversy.

Pope John Paul II was also traveling the world, going from
Dublin to Boston to Philadelphia. I left Dublin and Boston just
before he arrived, but he caught up with me in Philadelphia. He
was a master of spectacle. I found it distasteful to behold the
crowds. I saw it as an intellectually lazy affirmation of the combination of religion and celebrity culture.

After a month in America, I came back to Ireland. Eoin wasn't
pleased to hear how badly I had got on with the CPUSA and said
that he didn't want his children's minds poisoned by my revisionist
ideas. In the next few weeks, I decided not to attend party meetings, only partly because I was busy finishing my book/thesis. I
was at odds not only at home and in the party, but at the university
as well. Michael Slote was making trouble for me over the PhD.
He vetoed every external examiner that was nominated, arguing
that my examiner did not need to know anything about Marxism
or even philosophy of science. The thesis should be judged purely
on the rigor of its philosophical argument. He worried that it
was "too historical," although he had not read it. I built a strong
polemic against this into my introduction, which I was revising
at the time. I gave a paper at our colloquium that was a Marxist
critique of analytical philosophy that was far more rigorous in
philosophical argument than most of what I heard presented at

previous sessions. I responded to a talk Slote gave on metaphysics to the Metaphysical Society. It started with a potted and ahistorical history of philosophy and moved to an outline of his substantive position that was really woolly and lacking in precision or depth. After a few genteel students with posh accents asked their sycophantic questions, I argued my historical and philosophical critique of his position. He came back on all my points with arguments from authority. His response to my taking issue with his assertion that philosophy of language was the core of contemporary philosophy was that it was what the "best people in the best universities" were doing. His reply to my charge that he had caricatured the realism–anti-realism debate was that Dummett was more influential than Shapere, McMullin, Bunge, or Wartofsky, whether I liked it or not. Of course, I was defying him just when he could do me most harm. I knew that the point was not the balance of historical or philosophical considerations, but that he wanted to punish me and to find an external examiner who would be hostile to my thesis and fail me. I plowed on, completed and submitted the thesis and hoped that the examiner he chose would somehow be fair and see the value of my work.

As 1979 ended, I felt buffeted by strong crosscurrents and it took all my strength not to be shattered on the rocks. I was under conflicting pressures. Academic career considerations pulled one way and party activism pulled another, but I had developed a position that did not augur well for either. In academe, I had declared myself, and decisions about doctorate and employment were now in the hands of others. In the party, I had also declared myself, and there was now a decision I had to make myself. I decided to leave the CPI. I was still a communist, but it would have to be without the party card, the everyday camaraderie, the marching bands, the embassy invitations, the subsidized trips, or the clear sense of belonging to an international movement. I still felt I was part of this history, this movement, but I could not let certain forces within it break me. Without my integrity, I had nothing to offer. I still wanted to clench my fist and to sing

"The Internationale," but I didn't know where or when I could do that now. I felt cast adrift. Once again, I had to navigate new and turbulent waters.

7

So Strong

Feeling cast adrift, I tried not to drown. Although Labi Siffre's song "So Strong" would not be released until 1987, I needed it in 1980. I had barriers to scale and refusals to resist. I needed to be so strong. After years of being so busy with thesis writing and party activity, those dimensions disappeared. I had no job and no party. I still had a home, although only just, because that wasn't right anymore either. The year 1980 was much like 1965. I was struggling to find a place for myself in a world that didn't seem to have a place for me. The difference was that I had laid the foundations of my worldview in the intervening years, so I faced no crisis about my basic beliefs and values. I had intellectual and moral clarity, and that was my "something inside so strong." I wasn't always so sure that I was going to make it, however.

The good news was that I got my PhD. My thesis had been sent to Nicholas Rescher, a professor of philosophy of science at the University of Pittsburgh, an analytic philosopher, who had no association with Marxism. In his report as external examiner, he noted that he recognized himself as the sort of philosopher who was being polemically attacked in my introduction. Nevertheless, he said, he could recognize good scholarship when he saw it. He characterized it as a work of intelligence and passion, a massive and significant production. He thought it was even too ambitious for a doctoral thesis, more like a life's work that should be done at the further, rather than the nearer side of a PhD, and that it would be a monumental publication. I was delighted. I was keen for the viva. Then I was informed that there would be no viva, because the external report was so affirmative and unambiguous. Perhaps Slote didn't want an eminent philosopher coming and praising my work. His strategy had backfired, which made the result all the sweeter for me. Donning the red robe, I received my doctorate in June 1980. It was tainted, however, by what I considered to be the intellectually dishonest and anachronistic nature of the ceremony, in which I was conferred in the name of a deity in which I did not believe, surrounded by iconography honoring a class against which I struggled.

So I was now a PhD, but basically an unemployed one. I applied for jobs in Ireland and abroad. There were not many positions teaching philosophy in Ireland, and those there went to others, much to my resentment. My applications abroad yielded several interviews, but no offers. Perhaps it was because I was a Marxist. I didn't know, but I didn't believe it was because I wasn't good enough. Every rejection hit me like a ton of bricks. I did get bits of work: invigilating and grading exams, copy editing, guest lecturing, feature writing, book reviewing. I got my first book manuscripts and journal articles to peer review for international publications. I was offered a postdoctoral fellowship at Harvard in the history of science. My book covered a period of a hundred years, from the origins of Marxism to 1945, and this fellowship was to allow me to write a second volume, from 1945 to the present. I really wanted to take this opportunity, but there were multiple obstacles, including a transatlantic tug of war over the children, so I had to turn down this enticing offer.

I was tied to a home where I didn't want to be. Eoin and I got on with practical matters, but we related primarily as parents of the same children. I was on my own with them a lot during 1980 and 1981, while Eoin went on trips to the USSR and GDR. He was also ill with pneumonia, and all domestic tasks fell to me during his hospitalization and convalescence. This was the least I could do, after all he had done to help me with logistics of my research. Our relationship, already strained, was put under further pressure by my leaving the party. I still lived where party meetings took place and where the party paper was produced. I hosted overnight international guests of the party. I answered calls and took messages about party business. One day, I received word that a meeting was cancelled because a comrade had committed suicide. I was still on good terms with many comrades, but had a feeling of being both connected and disconnected at the same time. I received invitations to Mick O'Riordan's seventieth birthday party and Sean Nolan's eightieth.

Cathal and Clíodna started school. There was no separation of church and state in the school system. There was no secular option. I had no objections to world religions being taught in national schools, but thought it inappropriate for schools to teach religion, mostly Catholicism, as truth, and to integrate preparation for sacraments into their schooling. First communion was a huge rite of passage. Girls dressed as little brides and children made the rounds of friends, neighbors, and relations, receiving money. Cathal and Clíodna went to Scoil Neasáin, a school that taught through Irish as the first language. When Cathal's class came for first communion, he declared that he didn't believe in it, and the school allowed him to absent himself from the preparations and ritual. When Clíodna's time came, she didn't want to be excluded. What did she want? I asked. Did she want a new dress, a special day, and all that, or did she believe that the bread was the body of a dead god and she should eat it? She admitted that she only wanted the perks and the pomp. I said that I would buy her a new fancy dress, although not a little bridal outfit, that we would have a big day out and asked if that would make her happy. She said yes, but then came back and asked if she could go to church on the day and watch. So I took her to church on the day and she saw her classmates make their communion. When the teacher asked if she could be in the photo with the class, I said yes to that, too. When Cathal's class went to spend a period of study in the *gaeltacht*, he lived on a farm in Donegal with an older couple. He wrote charming letters to me about how harsh the weather was on the boggy

land, how he got up early to take the cows to graze, how lessons
were going in the local school, how he had made both friends and
enemies. He had enemies, he explained, because he didn't believe
in God.

I found the persistent and inappropriate presence of the Church
even more difficult to negotiate at funerals. I was appalled at the
funerals of communists-atheists that were no more than off-the-
shelf requiem masses, with no acknowledgment of their actual
lives and beliefs. That was the case with Paddy Carmody. At the
funeral of Eamonn Dillon, the priest even went on the offensive
and declared that there were no true atheists, even though the
church that day was full of them. From Prague, I received notice
that Radovan Richta had died. I wondered how that funeral
would be. It would tell more of the truth about the man and his
beliefs, but not all of it, I thought. There was no funeral for Marian
Jeffares, in the sense that there was no body, which had been given
for medical research, but there was a memorial, a secular event
in her own home. Sam was asked to give the oration, but not to
mention that she was a communist, because it might offend the
neighbors. I believed in the importance of rites of passage, which
made me more concerned that we evolve ways of marking birth
and death and turning points in ways that were appropriate and
honest. People still turned to the Church for such rites long after
they fell away from the beliefs on which the rituals were based.
There was still a default presumption of Catholicism that showed
in the angelus on RTE and in the dropping of collection envelopes
from each local parish through all the doors in their area. One day
I returned them personally to the priest and gave him an angry
lecture on Catholic triumphalism.

Through it all, the children survived the battles between conflicting worldviews at school and at home, even the ideological
differences between their parents. Perhaps it even prepared them
better for a world in which they would have to make their way as
adults. Cathal was much more interested in the ideas at stake than
Clíodna was. One day Eoin and I were arguing about the one-party

state. He was defending and I was opposing. Cathal kept coming in and asking questions, such as what we meant by "de facto" and "de jure," while Clíodna just rolled her eyes and wondered how she landed in the middle of this. I'm sure they were disturbed to some extent by the growing distance between their parents as our lives became more and more separate.

It wasn't just my domestic situation that felt so constraining. It was Ireland itself. It seemed like a backwater, given my interests and longings, and I felt trapped. I wrote and received many long letters, keeping in touch with my network abroad, which buoyed me up with a constant flow of philosophical interaction and personal encouragement. It seemed that everyone who understood me was abroad. I lived with a certain intensity when abroad, intellectually and emotionally, and felt starved for that life when I was home. I felt constantly on the verge of a wave of depression that would overwhelm me. I went for long walks along the sea, weighing everything up and trying to find a way forward. I kept going. I often lacked confidence, not so much in myself, but in the world. I felt I had much to offer as a teacher, a colleague, an author, an activist, but there didn't seem a place for me to do that. I still got up early and worked every day with the same discipline that had driven me this far. During this period, I regularly received phone calls in the middle of the night. I dragged myself out of bed and downstairs to answer and heard only heavy breathing and clicking. I had no idea who or why. The world seemed hostile and menacing much of the time. I paid more attention to my health than I had in some years. I joined a gym and worked out with similar discipline. I became fit, taut and trim. Physical fitness helped me to the psychological well-being that I needed to work effectively.

My big project was to publish my thesis as a book and to write my projected second volume. I had assumed it would be published by Lawrence and Wishart, a Marxist publishing house in Britain. I had been dealing with Maurice Cornforth, the managing editor, but his health was failing, and in 1980, he died. His successors strung me along, then declined to publish my book for reasons they never explained. Harvester Press then expressed interest, and their reviewer gave it enthusiastic endorsement, but the editors decided that at some 500 pages and 250,000 words, its length made it commercially unviable. I had the same problem with a few other publishers. I had some interest from editors of series in history and philosophy of science, academic volumes so expensive as to be affordable only by libraries, but I didn't want to go that route. Princeton University Press had two peer reviews, one affirmative and one negative, but did not reject it. Each publisher took months over it and kept me hanging in the air. After a while, I withdrew it from Princeton and submitted it to Humanities Press International, where I got an enthusiastic acceptance. Once it was accepted, however, I had an incompetent copy editor, which created further difficulties and stretched the process out for several years, as the technology of the time required mailing typed and tippexed [liquid paper] pages back and forth across the Atlantic.

In 1985, *Marxism and the Philosophy of Science: A Critical History* was published. There followed reviews, highly positive, in academic and political journals, a Choice Book Award, as well as many letters over many years, first arriving in the mail and later by email. It has had a long shelf life, with continuous citations and subsequent editions.

I also decided to write a shorter book in the interim, an intellectual biography of Christopher Caudwell. He had loomed much larger than I had expected in my previous book, and I thought that he was much more important in the history of Marxism than had been recognized. A British writer who had become a Marxist on his own, then joined the CPGB in the East End of London, and volunteered to drive an ambulance to Spain, where he joined the international brigades and died in the Spanish Civil War. He wrote a number of book-length theoretical manuscripts of breathtaking brilliance, which were only published after his death. He was like a shooting star that burst through the sky, burned with fierce intensity, and then collided to destruction. He wrote with a driving vision, in an interaction with the world that was wider, deeper, warmer than anyone else I was reading. His rationality and emotion seemed to fuse, in such a way that the sharpness of an argument brought the heightening of passion, which in turn made the argument sharper still. He so embodied my striving for synthesis, my passion for purposeful connection to the world.

I became caught up in a search for whatever could be known about him. I became like a detective on his trail, turning over every trace that was left of him forty-three years after his death. With the help of those who had previously been on his trail and his executor, Rosemary Sprigg, I spoke to his friends, comrades, and colleagues, many of whom were still alive at that time. I walked the streets of London, tracing his steps. I pored over his unpublished manuscripts and letters, which arrived from an archive in Texas, and which I read using the microfilm reader in the library of Trinity. I had a strong sense of him then, a feeling of intellectual exhilaration as well as excruciating grief. There was a strange intimacy to it. I mourned him as if he had just died. I felt so deprived of all he might have written, all he might have done and been, had his blood not drained into the earth of Spain, had his brain not stopped processing the world on that day in Jarama in 1937. There were some moments of this research that gave me a real buzz. One day, searching the archives of the *Daily Worker*, I found a photo of a group setting off for Spain, and realized that one of them was Caudwell. Previously there had only been one known photo of him. On another occasion, I was speaking to Elizabeth Beard, a friend of his, who told me that she thought I knew him better than anyone did when he was alive. I hit it off really well with his sister Rosemary, who was production editor of Routledge and keen to publish a biography of him—but others decided it wouldn't be commercially viable, and so did not commission it or provide an advance. I still wanted to do it, but the exigencies of my life, particularly the struggle to earn a living, stood in the way.

I was back and forth to Britain on the boat every few weeks, pursuing this research and attending conferences and interviews. I no

longer stayed at Maurice Cornforth's house in Highgate, but visited him in hospital instead, until he died. Ralph Miliband invited
me to stay at his home in Primrose Hill. His wife, Marion Kozak,
a sociological researcher and political activist, was warm and welcoming. Their sons, David and Ed, were accustomed to people
coming and going, and being surrounded by an atmosphere of
intense political discussion in this house, which was a salon of the
international left intelligentsia. They seemed precociously engaged
in it all, giving no indication of how far from it they would go in
staking out their own prominent political lives as adults. One night
Ralph and Marion took me to the home of Tamara Deutscher, who
was friendly and hospitable. This felt like a big step, comparable
to my lunch the year before with George Novak. This had been
the home of Isaac Deutscher, world-renowned Trotskyist. I had
read, admired, and quoted him when writing my book. My friend
Monty Johnstone, a member of the CPGB, was there, which gave
me some comfort, having someone else there from the CP tradition too. The whole atmosphere of the evening was stimulating
and comradely. During these trips to Britain, I attended many
conferences and seminars, both mainstream academic ones and
left ones.

In Ireland, too, I was attending mainstream conferences in
philosophy as well as those in other disciplines such as history,
politics, sociology, and science studies, under such auspices as
the Royal Irish Academy and the Irish Philosophical Society, as
well as left initiatives under the umbrellas of the Irish Labour
History Society and the Society of Socialist Social Scientists.
The ILHS had a longer life than the SSSS. The former was dominated by economists, although there were some sociologists and
historians. I gave a paper arguing that there was an epistemological crisis at the core of every academic discipline. It was in a
very different register from the others, and they responded with
indulgent but temporary interest, and returned in subsequent
sessions to more concrete matters, such as alternative tax policies and investment strategies.

I also attended conferences and pursued research in the United States, Canada, France, Yugoslavia, and Romania in the early 1980s. All of these involved an intense effort to feel the pulse of the times and to sense shifting intellectual trends. I listened to many presentations and entered into polemical exchanges. Traveling abroad and moving around international conferences as a young woman on my own was rarely a problem. Usually I was treated with respect and consideration. I was invited to dinners and smaller gatherings, and found the informal interactions even more fruitful than the formal sessions. Sometimes there was a flirtatious edge to these professional relationships, which was grand when welcome, but otherwise not. There were a few occasions when I was unduly pressured, and even a few times when I was stalked, but it was mostly more irritating than menacing.

Another difficulty for me arose in situations where wives accompanied their husbands to these conferences. When I first started attending conferences, there was often a "ladies program" with touristy excursions. This was dying out, but wives wanted attention and it was often assumed that I should be the one to talk with them, woman-to-woman, when I wanted to be talking to the men as colleagues. I never thought it appropriate to take a spouse to work and disliked the idea of people who traded on the status of their spouses, especially first ladies. I also found the attitude of wives at trade union socials irritating. They thought that talk of wages, conditions, class politics was so very boring, and they just wanted to consume food, drink, and travel on union expenses. One woman totaled a union car she was not entitled to drive. There was a certain kind of woman emerging in these years who wanted all that she could get by both sets of rules, old and new. Such women wanted men to pay for them in restaurants and to go to work and give them the option of not working, but they also wanted all that feminism had achieved, without the effort of achieving it. I found it hard to respect women who didn't work. In public, I argued that labor was essential to liberation. I resisted the "wages for housework" bandwagon. I dissented from a version of feminism that defended women, almost no matter what. This was a very controversial position, and I came under attack from many who agreed with me about other matters.

Conferences also brought me back to Eastern Europe and gave me the opportunity to explore other dimensions of the region. I really took to Yugoslavia. Dubrovnik seemed an idyllic setting for my interactions with Yugoslav philosophers, especially Mihailo Marković, Svetozar Stojanović, both of the Praxis school, and Srdan Lelas, as well as others from abroad. There was healthy interaction both between Marxists and non-Marxists, and between different schools of Marxism. Not that there were no problems, not so much in Dubrovnik, but in Belgrade, where the Praxis philosophers had lost their university positions. Much of the agenda in Dubrovnik was dedicated to mobilizing international support for them. I attended two conferences at the Inter-University Center, one in social sciences and one in philosophy of science. I was also impressed with Yugoslav ideas of self-managing socialism and its freedom from a Moscow line. I came back to Yugoslavia on other occasions through the decade for holidays as well as for work.

Romania was something else. I went there in 1981 for an International History of Science Congress in Bucharest. I was often in the company of British academics, with whom I shared flight and hotel arrangements. One was Joseph Needham, whom I was delighted to meet, because I had written about him in my book. The rest had no particular sympathy with Marxism or socialism, but neither were they hostile. I found myself constantly on the defensive, embarrassed even, because of the face presented by Romania. Elena Ceaușescu was put forward as a great scientist to give a plenary address. Her scientific achievements were highly suspect, and this address was considered farcical by an educated international audience. As if that weren't bad enough, the local organizing committee had accepted a disproportionate number of papers from Romania. Many of these asserted that many scientific and technological advances attributed to others had in fact been made by Romanians, which was even more absurd.

Then there was Poland. Or not. I was to be the guest of the Polish Academy of Sciences and was ready to go in December 1981. However, martial law was declared in response to a period of ferment spearheaded by Solidarity, a trade union intent on breaking free of the standard role of trade unions under communist rule. Wladyslaw Krajewski, who had invited me, was a philosopher and a communist, but also a supporter of Solidarity. He was interned, and thus my trip was cancelled. I tried my best to find out what was happening to him and others I knew, but it was difficult. I managed to contact Adam Schaff, who was in Vienna, and he confirmed that various academics I knew were interned, but assured me that their conditions were not too bad, and he believed that they would be released soon. He was quite disturbed by martial law, but argued that there were other possibilities on the horizon that would have been worse. In time, they were released and resumed their academic lives. I felt ambivalent about Solidarity. Thatcher, Reagan, and others who devoted themselves to crushing the power of unions in their own countries were enthralled by Solidarity, the more so as it became more explicitly anti-communist. Conversely, many communists were scathing about Solidarity. Knowing Krajewski and other critical communists in Poland made me think about it more carefully.

From 1980, I felt the ground shifting in a way that radically and profoundly reshaped not only academe, but the entire economy and society. The ascendancy of Thatcherism in Britain and Reaganism in America symbolized a massive worldwide shift to the right. A tidal wave of reaction overtook the progressive advances of previous decades in a blatant backlash against socialism, feminism, secularism, and virtually every cause ever championed by the left. The New Right displaced the New Left. So thoroughgoing was this onslaught that neoliberalism became the common sense of the era. Even those with most to lose accepted its masking of the structural inequality of class with the illusory equality of equivalent exchange on the marketplace and its identification of strident selfishness and blatant greed with the public good. This sense of world-historical defeat intensified my sense of personal reversal.

The 1980s were hard times for the left. We sometimes felt washed out, and left high and dry on abandoned shores by the receding tide. For my generation, who moved to the left in a time of upsurge and felt the world was ours to reshape, it was a shock to be dismissed as dinosaurs in this new decade for which we seemed ill-adapted. We had to learn to live with the pathos of the world moving on in a direction so disdainful of our desires. The same world that had once seemed so malleable in our hands became so recalcitrant and so resistant to our touch. Not only had history turned on us, but we had to acknowledge that we helped to put it on a course that led to consequences that were the opposite of what we intended. The postwar consensus of liberal rationalism and social reform, underpinning the edifice of the welfare state and public enterprise, which we attacked from the left, now came under far fiercer attack from the right. The New Left played a major part in undermining it and creating the vacuum into which stepped the New Right, which turned it to very different ends.

Postwar capitalism had represented a compromise with socialism, resulting both from the pressure of progressive forces and the interests of enlightened capitalist development. It provided the stability it needed to hold its ground and to advance, but it also made inroads into the rate of profitability and gave scope to new destabilizing forces. In response, there came an attempt to reorganize the system and to restore a more acceptable rate of profitability, through a new cycle of capital accumulation made possible by the increasing internationalization of the world economy, deregulation of market forces, and the use of new technology, all bringing new patterns of production, distribution, and exchange, and new forms of labor and social relations. Unprecedented centralization at the top was masked by a great flurry of decentralization at the bottom, squeezing out the middle level of forces, which heretofore had been at the center of power. Simultaneous globalization and localization displaced nationalization.

Thus, the dismantling of nationalized industry and the privatization of the public sector, the erosion of the power base of the trade union movement, indeed the growing powerlessness of the nation-state itself in the face of stateless money. With the forces at work becoming ever more faceless and distant and with the overall process seeming so impenetrable and out of reach, the attempt to understand the world and to get a grip on it gave way to various ideological strategies, from pre-modernism to postmodernism, that served either to evade or to justify this sense of impenetrability and dislocation. Some took refuge in old certainties and appeals to supernatural intervention to take external control of a world with no apparent means of internal control. While satellites whirled in orbit overhead, much of Ireland retreated into its peasant past and fixed its gaze upon a dark world where plaster statues moved and muttered messages for mankind.

In the summer of 1985, there were numerous news reports of statues moving spontaneously. In Ballinspittle in County Cork, crowds gathered and prayed and sang hymns. Many talk shows discussed it. I was on one RTE television program debating the topic with poet Nuala Ní Dhomhaill, who hailed it as a reassertion of the "female principle" and drowned it in obscurantist New Age nonsense. I spoke of the power of suggestion, mass hallucination, and psychosocial displacement. On such occasions when I expressed an atheist position in the media, I received many letters. Most were reaching out to save my soul. Some threatened me with hellfire. Interestingly, some of these letters came from priests, even one from a bishop. These were very respectful, but they basically saw me as a seeker after truth that they didn't want to get away. One, a professor of theology at Maynooth, said I spoke with dignity, reflection, honesty, and lucidity, whereas she on the other hand was intellectually absurd and unspeakably vulgar. On another occasion, I was on the popular *Gay Byrne Show*. For an hour, Gay Byrne probed me on the story of my life, focusing on my loss of faith and on my search for meaning without God. The following day he talked to a Jesuit priest responding to my interview.

These two segments were mentioned on the show every day for the next few weeks, referencing viewers' responses. Everywhere I went, at meetings, in classrooms, in pubs, in shops, people talked to me about it. I received invitations to speak to religious groups. Many of the letters that RTE and I received were full of biblical quotations and exhortations for me to submit myself to the Lord, whether in threatening or inviting tones.

Flights from Knock to Medjugorje symbolized Ireland's ironic mixture of apparitions and airplanes. Ireland was not alone in manifesting confused and contradictory ways of combining old and new, of welding anachronistic traditions to advanced technologies. The United States spawned a plethora of fundamentalist evangelists preaching born-again Christianity, creationist biology, and reactionary politics, all via satellite broadcasting. My mother was captivated by the televangelists. A society that mastered silicon chips, laser surgery, supersonic transport, satellites, and space shuttles fantasized itself as Rambo. The most sophisticated cinematography produced the silly supernaturalism of *E.T.* The most complex technology was enlisted in the headlong flight from complexity into simple images, which were infantile but by no means ideologically innocent. It was a society whose technological capacity had far outstripped its wisdom.

Anyone looking to academe for wisdom would be sadly disappointed. Anyone attending academic conferences was confronted with a babel of incommensurable discourses, for virtually every academic discipline was in crisis. From philosophy to physics, from literary criticism to economics, every discipline was rent by extreme polarization, not only on specific issues, but reaching to the theoretical foundations of the discipline. In fact, the closer to questions of theoretical foundations, the deeper the crisis and the more extreme the polarization. The natural sciences, once thought to be the rock bottom of our knowledge, were declared to be only a discontinuous succession of incommensurable paradigms, in respect to which questions of truth or falsity, rationality or irrationality, could not meaningfully be raised. This left no criteria for judging between one theory and another. Meanwhile, experiments proceeded and empirical data accumulated, but it became more difficult to know how it all added up, what the overall shape of it was. The natural sciences were in the grip of an escalating specialization, which made it almost impossible for scientists to understand what was being said by scientists within the subdivisions of their own discipline, let alone other disciplines.

The social sciences were in worse chaos. Discussions on matters of some substance and importance inevitably swung between extremes of voluntarism and determinism, nativism and environmentalism, realism and conventionalism. One encountered everything from the airiest, anti-empirical, rootless theoreticism to the most pedestrian, simple-minded, fact-gathering empiricism. Every sort of false dichotomy proliferated. Never before in human history had there been so much empirical research. Never before had there been so many contradictory ideas and contending theories in the air. Never before had there been such confusion, such despair, such intellectual and moral chaos.

There was no point in turning to the philosophers. There was so much to know, and it had become so complicated to know what it meant to know, that philosophers despaired of knowing at all, and urged us to renounce the notion of philosophy as a foundational discipline, much less a constructive one. Philosophy was in the worst state of all. There was no consensus regarding its nature, its scope, its aims, its methods, its subject matter, its relation to other disciplines or to anything else, indeed its very right to exist. There was no agreement on how to interpret its past history, how to analyze its present situation, how to conceive of its future prospects. As philosophy departments were being closed, philosophers themselves put the defense of the discipline on very shaky ground. While some built careers announcing the death of philosophy, others proceeded as if there was no problem, retreating into one of the sub-trends of the sub-divisions of the discipline, existing professionally within a reassuring and self-enclosed network of self-validating texts, which never needed to be justified in terms

of anything outside itself. Some contented themselves with anti-
quarian scholarship and wrote one more book on Plato, Berkeley,
or Hegel. Others aimed for facile relevance in service courses on
the philosophy of sport, of business ethics, of sexual desire, and so
on. Still others wallowed in the obscurantism of Derrida and *dif-
férence* or whatever nouveau melange was sweeping the Parisian
lecture halls at the time.

Never had such a torrent of words, so many reams of paper,
yielded so little illumination. Beneath all the tedium posing as
rigor, all the paraphernalia of rationality covering the most grotesque irrationalism, there was a massive failure of nerve on the
part of the era's intellectuals. I was passionately and polemically
preoccupied with these ideas, and I spoke at many conferences and
seminars along such lines. I was in demand as a public speaker,
both in Ireland and abroad. I also appeared as a talking head on
radio and television, on current affairs and book review programs.
I was offered work in university teaching, too, although full-time
and secure employment continued to elude me.

In 1981, I was teaching political philosophy and sociology
of knowledge in the politics department at University College
Dublin. It was a two-bus journey from Bayside to Belfield. I found
the atmosphere at UCD very different from TCD, each alienating
in its own way. When politics was discussed in the senior common
room at Trinity, it tended to be detached observation from
Olympian heights. In contrast, the political discourse in the staff
common room at UCD was colored by an oligarchic intimacy with
political power. It was routine to refer to cabinet ministers and
politicians by their first names, often recounting recent conversations. Ireland was then under a Fine Gael–Labour Party coalition
government, and I too was having conversations with ministers
and politicians, but Labour ones. This was my first time to mix
with people in and around Fine Gael. I got on well with colleagues
and students, athough obviously found more affinity with some
than others. I prepared my lectures and assessed student work
with great care, putting in many hours for rather poor pay. It was a

huge institution, where most traditional academic disciplines were represented, and full of many people I never met. There were three philosophy departments: metaphysics, philosophical psychology, and ethics and politics. This had its origins in three influential priest-professors, each carving out their own empires. At Queens University in Belfast, there were two philosophy departments, corresponding to the Catholic/Protestant, republican/unionist divide. One was called the Department of Philosophy, which was in practice analytical philosophy. The other was called the Department of Scholastic Philosophy, which embraced not only Thomism, but Marxism and all varieties of continental philosophy.

In November 1982, I began teaching at the National Institute for Higher Education in Dublin. The government had created two NIHEs in Limerick and Dublin, to provide university education along nontraditional lines, emphasizing new and practical disciplines such as biotechnology, computing, and communications. They were formally constituted as universities by 1989, becoming University of Limerick and Dublin City University. I received a call from the president of this institution, who asked me to teach a course called technology and society. My field was philosophy of science, not sociology of technology, but that seemed near enough. It was already supposed to have started, and they hadn't found anyone to teach it, so I scrambled to learn about the subject in order to teach it. I put in many hours, as if it were a full-time job. The students, who were in electronic engineering, had not had a female lecturer until then. After that I taught another technology and society course to industrial design students at the National College of Art and Design, and in January 1983, I was asked to teach political economy of the media to communications students at NIHE. This was a year-long course that had begun in the autumn of 1982, but the lecturer had fallen out with the head of school and didn't return for the second term. This class was even more of a challenge. Not only did I have to learn the subject in order to teach it, but to do so with students who had already been studying it for three months longer than I had. Nevertheless, I did it, putting in many more hours than anyone ever could have asked of me. The next year I was asked to teach communication theory, which was much closer to philosophy, although I still had to make a major effort to master an unfamiliar body of literature.

NIHE was a new institution. It was making itself up as it went along. There was constant chopping and changing of the curriculum, sometimes for better, sometimes for worse. It was also a small institution. The staff common room could not have been more different from either TCD or UCD. Professors and porters mixed together there and at staff socials, and all were in the same trade union. I threw myself into the life of the place, hoping I could help to shape it. I also hoped that my part-time precarious employment might lead to full-time secure employment. However, others who were less qualified and committed were given such positions in preference to me. For example, I had a PhD and was author of two major books, as well as being a very conscientious teacher, but was passed over in favor of someone who had no PhD, no significant publications, and thought teaching meant turning out the lights, showing videos, and then asking students what they thought.

I found the students different from any others I had so far taught. Many were brash and blatantly ambitious, much more skilled at self-promotion than interested in philosophical reflection. They were by no means all this way, but those who were dominated the distinctive atmosphere of the place. This was more the case in communications than in other schools. Students called lecturers by first names from their first conversation, and even cited authors by their first names. They had an attitude of extreme entitlement, especially when it came to grades. They could be quite crass in demanding what they wanted, without bothering to make a persuasive intellectual case. They graduated with degrees in communication, but had nothing meaningful to communicate. I got on well with most students, but stood up to this self-promoting shallowness, which stunned me at first but became ever more pervasive as time went on, with the increasing commercialization of academe, where students became customers and teachers became service providers. It wasn't so much the place itself as a sign of the times. NIHE was merely ahead of the curve in this global trend.

My colleagues in the school of communications included psychologists, linguists, journalists, broadcasters, and graphic designers. This multidisciplinarity could have been a stimulus for creative interaction, and it was at times, but it wasn't on the whole. Even after much turnover of staff, it never quite gelled into anything coherent, and there was never much in the way of esprit de corps. Yet working at NIHE was good for me. Being forced into new disciplinary areas broadened my horizons and deepened my philosophical thinking. I was finding the atmosphere in philosophy departments too stifling, too myopic, too much about esoteric debates between philosophers who lacked grounding in experience. I came to think that the best philosophy was being done elsewhere, among those who were grappling with questions at the theoretical foundations of their disciplines. In preparing my lectures, I encountered authors and debates that were new to me, but also familiar, in that they confirmed my sense that the same tensions were playing out in diverse fields. I also thought that academic disciplines were becoming too hermetical. Most questions I asked involved me in history, sociology, politics, even sometimes economics and science, as well as philosophy. Moreover, the new disciplines, such as communication studies, cultural studies, media studies, science studies, in which I was becoming immersed, were by definition multidisciplinary.

I became involved in forming professional structures for media studies. I was on the executive board of the Media Association of Ireland, which brought media academics together with media professionals. Radio Telefis Eireann and Irish Film Institute played a role in promoting media studies, sponsoring scholarships, publications, seminars, and an annual summer school. I presented at the seminars and summer school. Michael D. Higgins asked me to write a paper on broadcasting, which he delivered at a conference in Athens. I attended international television studies conferences in London in 1984 and 1988. Also in 1988, I presented a paper on images of the 1960s in the 1980s in television drama. The debates at these conferences were more about the theoretical basis for media studies than about analysis of particular programs. I threw myself into this, often drinking and debating into the night. The basic tension was about the "cultural turn," about whether culture and cultural studies were autonomous fields or grounded in political economy. I was actively on the side of the latter.

My teaching in media studies led me to research and publication in this area, too, specifically on television drama. I started to write a social history of television drama, although I later split the original plan for one book into a plan for several books, as seemed to have become my way. In 1984, I approached RTE with a proposal that involved giving me a stipend, full access to archives, offices and productions in progress. They agreed. I scoured files, watched old and new dramas, and interviewed writers, directors, producers, and executives. Informally, I talked to actors, cameramen, floor managers, journalists, presenters, archivists, and secretaries. I observed drama being made, both in studio and on location. I was even in two episodes of *Glenroe* as an extra.

I had the run of RTE and learned a lot. It was fascinating to see television from the other side of the screen. People spoke to me in much detail, but rarely did they see any pattern in it. I began to see patterns that eluded those who were within the process. Storylines reflected the changes and tensions in Irish social history on such matters as class, gender, religion, politics, and economics. Some got the impression that I was writing a glossy coffee-table book and wanted to include their names and pet productions. Actors regaled me with theatrical anecdotes. One bombarded me with every scrap of knowledge he could muster, as well as tales of how he was so famous that he was recognized wherever he went. He tried so hard to impress me, but the harder he tried the less he impressed me. I was always polite, but reserved. After some weeks of failing to achieve the adulation he craved, he turned on me and called me a "bluestocking intellectual bitch." In fact, I was wearing blue stockings that day.

At the time, the culture of public service broadcasting was still strong, but the international climate was bearing down on its economic base from without, while its ethos was eroding from within. Many producers were setting up their own production companies. Those doing conscientious work in the public sector were often criticized for their reluctance to venture into the private sector.

In 1987, my book *Irish Television Drama: A Society and Its Stories* was published. It was a history of Irish television drama within the larger panorama of social history. It got a big launch and a lot of attention. It was positively reviewed, not only in academic journals, but in mass media. All the published reviews were positive, though some were more astute than others. There was a lengthy one in the *Irish Times*, where Fintan O'Toole concluded that no one could write of Irish social history in the future without referring to this book. I then started writing a history of US television drama. I wrote my way through the 1950s to the 1980s. I intended to continue the story into the 2000s in due course, but the project fell by the wayside under the pressure of other projects.

Also in 1987, I acquired my first computer, an Amstrad 8256. The whole operating system was on one floppy disk with room for some files. After writing two big books by hand and already six chapters into a third one, I found the ability to produce typescript myself liberating, and never looked back. I thought the transition might be difficult after so many years, but it was amazingly effortless. As time went on, I leapt at each new advance that computers made possible.

Although I wasn't in a political party in 1980, I continued to be politically active. I marched on May Day. I picketed against apartheid. I demonstrated for tax equity, even though I earned too little to pay much tax myself. The Dublin Council of Trade Unions organized massive tax marches in 1979 and 1980. Sam Nolan gave rousing speeches from the GPO to huge crowds. At these events, most members of the CPI still treated me as a comrade.

In 1981, I joined the Labour Party, primarily because others who had left the CPI for similar reasons as mine had previously done so. It was a small country and we didn't have many options. We thought we could join with those already in the party pulling it to the left. I became active at the branch, constituency, and national level. I was often asked by party members if I had considered "going into politics." This at first puzzled and then enraged me. Invariably I answered, "I am in politics." The question was very revealing. Their conception of politics was so impoverished, so narrowly electoral, that they were inquiring about whether I intended to put myself forward for election. I did not. I did canvass for the party during elections, but was never willing to reduce myself to canvassing fodder. There were some in the party who saw all members as either candidates or canvassing fodder for candidates. I was still committed to politics as the "long march through the institutions" of society. Electoral politics and parliamentary institutions only constituted part of that. I considered work in universities, where I hoped I had a more meaningful contribution to make, as just as important. So was work in trade unions, mass media, schools, and elsewhere. I was constantly arguing for this broader conception of politics.

The dominant debate within the Labour Party in Ireland paralleled that in Britain and many other such parties throughout the world during this period. There was the social democratic view, which was talking of not clinging to socialist dogmas of the past and instead adopting a new realism, adapting to new times to justify what was essentially a retreat from the Keynesian postwar consensus to varieties of neoliberalism with a human face. Then there was the democratic socialist view, which proposed a more systematic analysis of the capitalist mode of production and the social order generated by it and a more radical vision of socialism as a systemic alternative, bridged by attempts to work out a strategy for moving from the one to the other. Although we could find some common ground on short- and even medium-term demands, the social democrats could see no further. They perceived neither capitalism nor socialism in systemic terms. They accepted the terms of the dominant discourse with respect to the national debt and the need

for drastic cuts in public spending, only engaging in special pleading on behalf of the poor and vulnerable and arguing that they
could manage the system better. It was a discourse about the needs
of consumers rather than about the rights of producers. It was a
discourse oblivious to concepts such as class (never mind class
struggle), the division of labor, and the mode of production. It had
no strong inner core. Everything was ad hoc, all bits and pieces,
particularistic problems matched with particularistic solutions, in
ever more threadbare proposals for piecemeal social engineering.
In practice, they settled for even less, justifying Labour's participation in coalition government through much of the decade simply
in terms of protecting what they called the "weaker sections" of
the community (not the working class) against the worst that Fine
Gael might do otherwise.

In discussion with Labour students at UCD, we decided to
explore forming a network of those in the party sharing more
radical views. I agreed to talk with the ex-CPI group about it. A
key person to convince was Sam Nolan. I arranged a meeting with
him, where we discussed this thoroughly and affirmatively, but
also emptied an entire bottle of brandy and began an affair. He
was on the Labour administrative council and was secretary of the
Dublin Council of Trade Unions. He had worked most of his life as
a carpenter, but was now a full-time trade union official in the construction industry. He left school at fourteen, but was educated in
the movement and read eagerly, and was much respected among
older and younger activists alike. He was also attractive in many
ways.

We formed a group called Labour Left. Other ex-CPI comrades
joined, as did those who had been in Left Liaison, as well as some
public representatives, such as Frank Buckley and Emmet Stagg.
There were others we didn't expect to join, such as Tony Browne,
the international secretary, and Brendan Halligan, a former general
secretary of the party. We opposed coalition throughout the 1980s.
I was keen that it be more than an anti-coalition lobby group, but
a force bringing a broader left intellectual culture into Labour. We

organized many educational events that sought to raise the level
of debate in the party beyond immediate policy issues to another
level, dealing with the history of the left and alternative political
philosophies. We published a journal called *Labour Left*.

In the course of this, I also formed a strong relationship with
Michael D. Higgins, who was a TD and chair of the LP. He was
against coalition and for intellectual activity. He had been a lecturer in sociology in Galway. In the course of 1981–82, we had
three general elections. During these, I went down to Galway
whenever I could, stayed in his house and worked on his election
campaigns. I saw sides of him that didn't show in public. I especially liked his scathing humor, finding him most eloquent when
he was most negative. Canvassing in Salthill in winter was freez-
ing, but I liked working for a candidate in whom I believed and
enjoyed the camaraderie of the Galway LP. I also wrote notes and
speeches for him. He proposed that we co-author a book making
the case for socialism. We had intensive discussions, and even created an outline and plan of work, but other tasks pulled at each
of us, especially him. At one stage, while he was also mayor of
Galway, he decided to award freedom of the city to E. P. Thompson.
He asked me to write the speech for this, focusing on Thompson's
work as a Marxist historian and not only on his nuclear disar-
mament activism, which was the immediate justification for the
award. I brought this speech into him in Dail Eireann. He said that
there was crucial vote in the Dail and he couldn't go to Galway, and
asked me if I could run for the train and give it in his place. Some
of the councilors seemed bewildered by who I was and why I was
talking about Marxism and "history from below." Thompson was
pleased, although disappointed not to meet Michael D. I did other
work for him and was often in Leinster House.

I got to know other members of the parliamentary party. Some
were so caught up in the relentless demands of clientelism that
they could barely raise their minds to national legislation, let
alone a higher vision. Others tried to cope with it while keeping a sense of proportion. At this time, many of them served on

the local councils as well as in the national parliament, until the dual mandate was abolished. Michael D. spoke acidly to me of his schedule of "pancakes today, wheelchairs tomorrow." One day we were on the train from Galway to Dublin, trying to discuss philosophical and sociological matters, but it was impossible to get through a single sentence uninterrupted, as one constituent after another came up to him with opinions, issues, jokes, banalities, all demanding his attention, some of them addressing him as if they owned him. When I was staying in his house, there were constant phone calls from constituents, colleagues, and journalists. He did not find it easy to be torn in so many directions all at once. He was often stressed, even frazzled, but when the lights went on and the microphone went live, you would never guess. He never did finish his PhD on clientelism, which he was trying to do at the time. He once showed me an anonymous letter written to him, telling him that he was doing the work of the devil, that he was trying to change, not only the constitution, but the Ten Commandments.

I organized political education at branch, constituency, and national levels, although I didn't always find acceptance and appreciation for my efforts. My constituency had asked me to devise a program, and I came back with one to which I had given careful thought. One comrade, a gasbag whom I had to rule out of order constantly when chairing branch meetings, responded with a top-of-the-head counterproposal based on the idea that reading and rereading James Connolly was all that was needed. To my astonishment, he won. However, he didn't back it up with any organizational effort and it never happened. Our lectures, seminars, and weekend schools attracted a lot of interest. We usually had attendances of fifty to a hundred, sometimes many more. Most successful were ones set up as debates. One was organized around the question: "Is Marxism relevant to the 1980s?" I decorated the head office with my photo-collages posing the question in different visual contexts, combining photos I took myself with images cut from magazines and mounted on large boards. Ex-CPIs spearheaded the case for the affirmative, while Tony Browne articulated a thoughtful social-democratic position and critique of Marxism, although it was by no means hostile to Marxism. I found that many LP members had an interested and respectful attitude to Marxism, even if they were not Marxists.

I spoke up during party discussions at every level, introducing controversial motions and fighting hard for them. One, which I got submitted to a national conference in the name of my constituency, concerned left cooperation and a more constructive attitude to the Workers Party, which was advancing its electoral position. Another, which I drafted and got submitted in the name of the international affairs committee, was a really radical position on restructuring the United Nations and challenging the power of the US over the UN. I introduced it and defended it. Although sharply contested, it passed, much to my surprise. It was a hollow victory, however. At that time, our party leader, Dick Spring, was *tánaiste* and minister of foreign affairs. He didn't agree with it and totally ignored it. Many good motions passed at the conference suffered the same fate: nothing was ever heard of them again.

Some motions did have consequences, however, especially those having to do with coalition. The party had been in coalition with Fine Gael from 1973 to 1977. When the issue came up again after the election of 1981, there was a highly contentious special conference at which the decision to go into coalition was passed, despite formidable opposition, and the party went back into coalition government. When another election was called in 1982, the issue came up again. After a heated debate into the night, the vote in a joint meeting of the parliamentary party and administrative council was tied. Michael D as chair used his casting vote against coalition. Fianna Fail formed a minority government with the support of Tony Gregory, who cut a deal involving investment in Dublin Central. This government was unstable and fell within months.

In the interim, Michael O'Leary, the party leader, wanted to roll back the procedure whereby a special delegate conference would have ultimate power to decide if the party went into coalition. He lost the vote on this in conference in autumn 1982. O'Leary was furious, and went incommunicado during the final day of the conference. The next day he resigned and crossed the floor to Fine Gael, which was shocking, even considering his erratic personality. During the interval when he was party leader and *tánaiste*, O'Leary invited me to lunch. He wanted to set up some kind of think tank and wanted to sound me out about it. However, the conversation was all over the place and the result was inconclusive. From this and his modus operandi at meetings, I formed the impression of a person with a shockingly short attention span and not much of an inner core. In the 1960s, he had been on the left of the party and against coalition, but when he had the chance to become a cabinet minister in the 1970s, he changed his mind. At party conferences, he sat on the platform and often rolled his eyes in ridicule and yawned in boredom as others spoke. Photographers invariably captured these poses and published them in the press. Although we had won the vote on procedure for deciding on coalition, we lost the substantive vote of the special conference on going into coalition, so the party was back in government in 1982. Not all of these votes represented active members of the party, but were people who could be bussed in and whipped to a vote when numbers were tight.

The next party leader was Dick Spring. He was young and good-looking, as was O'Leary. A lawyer, a former rugby player, and son of a Labour TD from Kerry, he had no real connection to the intellectual and cultural traditions of the left. I could imagine him just as easily in Fine Gael. All my conversations with him were polite, but quite spiky. The battle lines had been drawn, and I was on the other side. He couldn't have cared less about our seminars on left history and theory, but he was hostile to our ability to harness opposition to policies and strategies that he wanted to be decided between himself and his closest confidants.

Labour Left was the strongest force on the other side, but the party left also included the Trotskyist Militant tendency, as well as other members who shared some of our views. We mounted strong opposition to coalition, even if we often failed to carry the day. We did win strong representation on the administrative council and other bodies in elections that were hotly contested. Unlike Militant, which was a tight entryist organization, Labour Left was a loose and open formation. Our meetings, although not all our conversations, were open to any member of the party, or to anyone off the street, for that matter. Our relations with Militant were not close, but we did find ourselves on the same side on many matters and we stood up against their expulsion. We connected our position to an international wave, looking to the Socialist Party in France then coming to power under Mitterrand and the Panhellenic Socialist Movement (PASOK) in Greece under Papandreou, as well as trends in the British Labour Party struggling for power around Tony Benn. The younger members of our group were especially fired up by these currents, whereas those of us who were older tended to support them while seeing them within a longer history, with an undercurrent of skepticism toward social democratic parties.

One of our battles was for direct election of party leader by all members of the party. We put it forward as a motion for conference. I held up my card and continued chatting with Mary Robinson, expecting that the vote would yield a respectable defeat. I was astonished that it won. We weren't the only ones to be surprised. Our opponents screamed for a recount, and Michael D succumbed to pressure and granted it. Thereupon all the delegates who spent most of the time in the bar were rounded up and whipped in to defeat the motion. Eventually we did win this battle. It wasn't all high-minded political debate. The major confrontations were procedural, especially about eliminating or expanding democratic discussion and decision. There were underhanded tactics generating considerable personal bitterness. Motions were deliberately mislaid, lies were told, branches were packed. Ray Kavanagh, who became general secretary of the party in 1986, gleefully admitted to these tactics, which he thought were justified to defeat the left, in his book *Spring, Summer and Fall: The Rise and*

Fall of the Labour Party. Occasionally blows were struck. Numbers were so tight, especially at the administrative council, that people were afraid to go to the lavatory in case a vote would be lost to the other side. The media reveled in it, and thought the Labour Party made great color copy. It tended to be reduced to a Spring versus Stagg battle between two male superegos, in which the rest of us and our ideas were obliterated. We were far more principled than our opponents, but there were Kildare buses to match the Kerry buses at crucial conferences. Emmet Stagg, who was previously in the CPI and now active in Labour Left, was elected to the Dáil in the 1987 general election from Kildare and began to emerge as an alternative leader of the party.

Contestation for positions was often fierce. There was much lobbying, horse-trading, and complex calculation involved in elections of party officers and administrative council. Counts using proportional representation went on long into the night. As the results of each count were announced, there was more and more drink consumed and fury if the numbers indicated that pacts had not been honored. Crucial to this process was control of membership credentials. In Michael D. Higgins as chair and Colm Ó Briain as general secretary, we had officers who were sympathetic to us, whom we trusted. In 1986, when Michael D's term finished and Colm resigned after finding it difficult to work with Spring, we were anxious about succession. The panel selected Bernard Browne for general secretary, a trade union official, who was ex-CPI and part of Labour Left. However, he scored an own goal by giving an interview as if he had the job before it had been formally ratified. So it went to Ray Kavanagh. When Emmet Stagg was elected vice-chair and went to the head office to access membership files, he was blocked by Ray Kavanagh. Dick Spring and his advisor, Fergus Finlay, arrived, and a difficult confrontation ensued.

Selection of candidates for the Dáil and councils involved much maneuvering. In Dublin Central, where I was based from 1984, it was quite fraught, especially since several of the contending candidates were in Labour Left. I was quite friendly with Pat Carroll and

Joan Burton, who both shared my strong interest in Africa and were strongly opposed to coalition with a right party that was on the left on many issues. Pat was our preferred candidate. He had stood before and had been elected to council and nearly elected to the Dáil. Joe Costello was also vying for nomination. When Joan came forward as a candidate, Pat stood aside, but Joe didn't. This wreaked havoc in our branch and constituency, because of her ambition and the tactics she was willing to use to advance it. She went far, eventually becoming party leader and *tánaiste*. During elections, when I was less than inspired by candidates in my own constituency, first in Dublin North East and then Dublin Central, I made time to go to Galway West and Kildare North to lend support to those for whom I had higher regard and ideological affinity.

Although such tactics are banned now, in those days every polling place had people from all parties canvassing voters on their way in to vote. During a by-election in Dublin West, I found myself at one such place with Garrett Fitzgerald, who was taoiseach at the time. When he heard that I was a philosopher, he was keen to discuss philosophy. I was moved by his sincerity, if not by his clarity. I couldn't imagine the alternative taoiseach, Charles Haughey, having such a conversation. He might bluff it and scatter some random knowledge to make an impression, but not speak as an honest seeker in the way Fitzgerald did. I would never vote for his party, Fine Gael, but I respected him as a person. As to my canvassing, I don't know if I ever convinced anyone, but I know I learned a lot in doing it. I never knew who would answer the door or what they might say, and it brought me in touch with many ways of life and points of view that were outside my normal circles of experience. The tally and the count were uniquely Irish rituals around which there was great buzz. I tallied in both Galway and Dublin and beheld the calculations, the transfers, the hopes raised and dashed, and all the intricacies of our complex voting system of proportional representation.

My former party, Sinn Féin, had now become the Workers Party, and they were also players in these elections. Labour members had a range of reactions to this electoral challenge from the left. Many were hostile and saw them as usurpers of territory that was rightfully theirs. Spring didn't reply to letters from the WP seeking discussion on left cooperation. I was on good terms with them, however, and spoke at their events and wrote for their publications. I introduced a conference motion promoting left unity, but it would take much more than motions to make it happen. Sometimes we were all together on the streets.

The visit of Ronald Reagan to Ireland in 1984 brought massive numbers into the streets, and the whole of Ireland was divided for and against Reagan, with particular attention to his foreign policy. All forces on the left mobilized, but so did priests, nuns, and bishops. Lots of other people, including many who never protested before, came out, too. Over 20,000 came out on the streets of Dublin to march to Leinster House, where Reagan was addressing the joint houses of the Oireachtas, and make a massive din outside as he spoke. Some TDs and senators boycotted it. Others spoke up during his speech and walked out when they were ruled out of order. Academics objecting to the honorary doctorate conferred on Reagan by University College Galway organized a "de-conferring" ceremony, where they wore their academic gowns. Peadar O'Donnell, the venerable author and activist in the republican socialist tradition, who had recently been awarded an honorary doctorate by UCG, presided, and Michael D spoke at it. Recipients of honorary doctorates handed over their degrees and disrobed. Graduates burnt their doctorates in protest. Everywhere Reagan went, there were protesters, even in Ballyporeen, his ancestral village, though they were kept well away by the massive security operation. Of those who came to welcome him, the expected 50,000 turned out to be less than 5,000. There was also a women's peace camp in Phoenix Park.

I met Peadar O'Donnell around this time, after he summoned me to come see him. He was not so much interested in me as interested in my being interested in him. He seemed to expect that I would ask him questions and he would answer, so I did so. He was keen to leave his mark on younger activists and intellectuals. Although he was a much-revered figure on the Irish left, I remembered that Jim Gralton remarked that O'Donnell wanted to be "the bridegroom at every funeral and the corpse at every wake." In 1986, I attended the funeral where he was indeed the corpse. It was in Glasnevin, where I also attended funerals of such iconic left figures as Liam O'Flaherty and Luke Kelly, who also died in this decade.

The aforementioned Jim Gralton was an Irish communist who was deported from Ireland in the 1930s. He built Pearse-Connolly Hall on his family's land in Leitrim, where the local community gathered to read, think, talk, box, sing, and dance, which brought hostility from those who could not allow such activities outside the hegemony of church and state. Later Ken Loach made a film based on the Gralton story called *Jimmy's Hall*. By the early 1980s, he was a legendary figure, and a group of Irish left activists started a magazine called *Gralton*. They also organized the Gralton Forum, which met in Parnell Square, to bring together different sections of the left to focus more on where we agreed than disagreed. The organizers included Brian Trench, Des Derwin, and others, who were from the Trotskyist tradition but were trying to reach out to other groups. Some of the bigger players, the Labour Party and the Workers Party, took little notice, although some of their members were more open to such initiatives. I certainly was.

Even with all that was going for me in the universities, the media, and the streets, still none of it added up to a full-time, decently paid job. There were intervals where I had no paying work at all. In 1985, I signed on at the labor exchange for the first time. I found this excruciating on several levels. When the gates opened at Navan Road, there was an aggressive scramble to be first in the queue, especially among those with black economy activities to pursue. There were many manifestations of rudeness and roughness to civil servants and other claimants. There was a protection racket for cars and bikes. What was most infuriating was seeing a society where there was work to be done paying people not to work. This experience, which went off and on for several years, hardened my ideas about the importance of a work ethic for a healthy social order and my disdain for the lumpen subculture created by capitalism and for a tendency on the left to romanticize it. I recognized that social welfare was an important achievement, brought into being through pressure from the left, but I could see close up the corrosive effect of generations of social welfare dependency on those forced into it. I was determined to work. I tried to be ever more flexible about job applications. I applied for jobs outside of academe, such as in editing, journalism, and radio and television production.

I considered various forms of writing. I attended writer's workshops. I got accepted into a very competitive one co-sponsored by the Arts Council and Trinity College. It was presided over by John McGahern, a fine writer and a gracious man. He was a better writer than teacher of writing, although I'm not sure who really knows how to teach writing. Others were inclined to treat him as a guru and ask him philosophical questions about life and literature. He was a very modest man and not inclined to bluff, but he also didn't want to let people down, and sometimes overreached himself on these matters. At least, I thought so, and sometimes argued with him, which he didn't mind so much as others did. He often asked me to stay behind to talk further. He offered me a lift home one day, and we had a long talk about our lives and discovered that we had both been dismissed as teachers in 1965 at the hands of Catholic forces. In the workshop, we each had to write a short story and read it. I wrote one called "May Day," about political activism and the night that one activist died. The characters were the sort of people I knew, and the incident bore a rough resemblance to something that had happened. It was not well received by the group. McGahern was gently positive, but others were hostile, primarily, I believe, due to their aversion to political writing, all of which was by definition agitprop, as far as they were concerned. A priest in the group was particularly scathing. Liz McManus, a left politician, wasn't too sympathetic either. Her story steered clear of politics. The priest wrote one about a marriage encounter group. I resisted the temptation to be spiteful and to find fault. I thought his story was sharp and insightful, so I said so. A civil servant wrote a witty story about civil service bureaucracy. A housewife from Kildare, wearing expensive clothes and always chattering about horses and land prices, with a Fine Gael/Mills and Boon view of the world, wrote a dreadful story full of clichés like "she knew he was the right one for her" and "he knew how to satisfy a woman." Everyone tiptoed around her, even though they took off their gloves with me. I attended a playwriting course, too. I wrote an outline of a television mini-series called *Rites of Passage* that began with the death of a Labour TD and reconstructed his life from the points of view of three different women: his mother, his wife, and his lover. I also wrote an outline for a long-running series (a soap opera) called *Dublin Central*, with settings in parliament, trade unions, universities, and media.

I was involved in the formation of the Irish Writers Union, and got to know many writers. I had already met some in doing research for my television drama book. Eugene McCabe, who, like John McGahern, was also a working farmer, was really encouraging to me in my experiments with fiction writing. However, I didn't go any further in this direction. McGahern said that life was too "thin" for fiction, but I found the opposite. For me anyway, life was too thick for fiction. Both McCabe and McGahern urged me to write a semi-fictional autobiographical novel. They said my writing was energetic and muscular and bristling with ideas, but I needed to be more attentive to images and details. I had a go, but came back to factual autobiography, although it had to be put on a back burner, due to other demands. I continued my involvement with IWU, however, and argued that factual writing could be as creative and artistic as fictional writing. I also continued to argue that political fiction could be as complex and nuanced as any other fiction, maybe even more so. I attended a Celtic Film and Television Festival in Newcastle, where I saw a student film called *Passing Glory*, about the funeral of a Scottish female communist, that was funny and nuanced and true, that embodied the sort of thing I was going for in *Rites of Passage*.

In 1984, I left the house in Bayside and went to live with Sam Nolan. He was fifty-four and I was forty. We were both living in the ruins of relationships that had burned out and decided to move on with one that was alive. Each of us had separated in a way that was relatively amicable, if not financially favorable, especially in his case. In my case, I did not believe that I had a claim to the house in Bayside, because Eoin had paid the mortgage, and I was the one who wanted to separate. This was not the norm at the time. Sam left his house in Finglas, although he had paid the mortgage and it was basically all he had. My work continued to be precarious labor. So we didn't have much money. We rented a tiny box of a flat on Infirmary Road, consisting basically of one room that served as living room, kitchen, dining room, and office, plus a bedroom and bathroom. It was not as claustrophobic as it might have been, because I made good use of mirrors to enhance the sense of space. I had my desk by a window overlooking Phoenix Park, near the zoo. Once a peacock appeared behind our building. I called the zoo, expecting that someone would come for it within the hour. Surprisingly, it was there for nearly a year.

I often walked in Phoenix Park. Sometimes I took my work out there, often my reading and sometimes even my writing. Usually I could do this undisturbed by anything more than wind blowing my pages away or sudden rain soaking them. Occasionally, someone would break into my work to talk to me, either a man trying to chat me up or someone so bored that anybody would do. One day it was neither. I was reading a book with accumulating disappointment and reflecting on the discrepancy between the book it was and the one I wanted it to be. A young man demanded my attention as if it was his right, quizzing me on the book and my literary criteria for judging books, but only as a launching pad for declaring his own. What is the most important thing for a writer? he asked. To have something to say that is worth saying, I replied. No, that was nonsense, he argued, building up a steam of aggression.

Poetry was about voice, not meaning. He pronounced that he was a postmodernist poet and had written one of the six most important poems of the last century. No, he had not yet been published, but wouldn't consider publishing with anyone other than Faber and Faber. Moreover, he was saving the original manuscript, because it would be valuable someday. Googling his name all these years later, there is no sign of him or his great poetry.

I mixed with all sorts. Our social life revolved around left and trade union events. I learned a lot about the trade union movement from this and from Sam's everyday account of his job, which brought me into contact with life on construction sites, branch meetings, labor courts, appeals tribunals. There were also "posses" where organizers of unions for carpenters, bricklayers, painters, plasterers, plumbers, and electricians would team up and go to building sites to check for union cards. Sam had had a hard time in his own union, UCATT, in the years when it was hard to hold even a branch office because he was a communist. While the situation seemed to have improved, there were still underhanded tactics used against him when he went for the job of regional secretary and someone less qualified got the job instead.

After 1981, I didn't enter the United States for another decade. I didn't intend it, but I couldn't afford to travel, and I was busy in Ireland and elsewhere in Europe. I did see my family when they visited Ireland. My parents had more time to travel once my father retired and the nest thinned out a bit. My brother Joe signed up for another tour in the Marines and traveled the world on NATO maneuvers. He arrived in Ireland talking like a character out of *M*A*S*H*. He had a vocabulary full of unfamiliar technical terms and acronyms and I was constantly asking for explanations. He was highly opinionated, but was still open to other perspectives, and we could still talk, before hardening into a stance where that would no longer be possible. As the decade moved on, all my brothers and sisters had found their niches as a factory manager, a teacher, a scientist, a nurse, a soldier, a truck driver, and a chef.